EMERGENCY POWERS AND THE PARLIAMENTARY WATCHDOG: PARLIAMENT AND THE EXECUTIVE IN GREAT BRITAIN, 1939-1951

by

John Eaves, Jr.

THE HANSARD SOCIETY
FOR PARLIAMENTARY GOVERNMENT

39 MILLBANK, LONDON, S.W.1

First published in 1957

PRINTED IN GREAT BRITAIN AT THE CHISWICK PRESS, LONDON, N.11

CONTENTS

A*

CONTENTS

FOREWORD

ALTHOUGH the British Parliament is one of the most ancient and respected of all British institutions and has exerted an immense influence, direct and indirect, in all parts of the world, there are still many people who misapprehend its true purpose or perhaps I should write that they are unaware of its most important purpose the fulfilment of which was more than any cause the reason for the creation and the evolution of Parliament at Westminster.

I often hear people, including members of Parliament, say in effect that it is the business of Parliament to make laws.

So far as any generalization about Parliament can be accepted it would be more correct to say that it is the business of Parliament to prevent laws being made.

For the prime purpose of Parliament is the preservation of the liberty of the individual and it carries out the function or should do so by insisting that the Executive or Cabinet produces adequate reasons proving that it cannot carry out its duties unless it is given further legal powers.

I am disposed to believe that the first instructive thought of any elected representative of the people on hearing that "The Government" intends to introduce legislation should be: "Why?" This rather simple and primitive conception of the duty of Parliament has become lost to sight in the complexities of modern civilization; nor does the extent to which the power of the party machines has increased do anything to bring it to the forefront of men's minds.

The duty of Parliament to *control* legislation should be considered as one of the most important aspects of Parliament's duty and sovereign right to exercise a general control over the Executive, a control extending to the limits of life and death. The Executive is the creature of Parliament and what Parliament has created it may properly destroy even if by the destruction of the Government it returns its own life to its begetter the sovereign electors who create the creators of Government!

In time of war the fundamental task of Parliament becomes exceedingly difficult and as war has become more total and more complex its direction has created serious problems in the sphere of Parliamentary control. The Executive faced with the enormous task of mobilizing all the resources of the nation in the struggle for existence is not on technical grounds likely to welcome the interference of a grand committee of some 500 persons—excluding the 100 M.P.s who are in one way or another members of the Executive. Indeed, the magnitude of the task is so great that experience has shown that even at the highest executive level, i.e., the Cabinet, it has been found necessary in the great Wars of the twentieth century to establish an inner Cabinet which can make quick decisions. In addition to this difficulty there is the further point that in time of war much action and proposed action must be kept secret from the enemy.

On the other hand the perils of war tend to overshadow party political issues so that the members of the House of Commons who are not in the Government tend to become more united—irrespective of party—in an atmosphere of being members of a Council of State. This development reaches its final stage if and when a national Government is formed and all members are then in support of the Government. But this happy event from the point of view of the Executive is tempered by the reflection that since all members are supporters of the Government so all members are potential critics of the Government.

Another consideration which has to be borne in mind in assessing the relationship between Parliament and the Executive in time of major war is that it was deemed to be technically impossible to hold a general election whilst hostilities were in being. This meant that Parliament could get rid of the Government, but the Government was bereft of one of its powerful weapons—the power of dissolution.

I think it to be true to maintain that during the period 1939-45 Parliament never lost effective control over the Government although in the opinion of the present writer who sat as an Independent member of Parliament in that Parliament, it came close to the point of no return when it accepted that the Home Secretary's powers to detain without trial included the persons of members of Parliament.

Mr. John Eaves in the notable study to which these words are an introduction has produced an invaluable account of the relations between Parliament and the Executive during the years 1939-51. We must hope that this detailed and scholarly analysis of events will never have to be used as a guide to conduct in a third World War. But as a record for the historian and student of a series of delicate relationships which were so conducted that they did honour to both parties and illustrated in a singular degree the flexibility and common sense of the British parliamentary system, Mr. Eaves's book will remain a classic.

STEPHEN KING-HALL,

Chairman of the Council
of the Hansard Society for
July 1957   Parliamentary Government.

CHAPTER I

THE CONTEMPORARY PROBLEM OF EMERGENCY POWERS IN BRITAIN

"IF HARD cases make bad law, emergencies may make worse."[1] With these words, Sir Cecil Carr introduced his Columbia University audience in the fall of 1940 to a consideration of the fate of constitutional government in war-time Britain, which at that time had been living for more than a year under a Government vested with broad emergency powers. Sir Cecil was suggesting that crisis legislation may break through the established constitutional pattern, may take long steps towards dictatorship, and that liberties temporarily surrendered may end up irretrievably lost. But he reassured his audience that constitutionalism remained intact in war-time Britain: Parliament had not lost control of the executive.

The transfer by Parliament to the executive of wide legislative powers is not a new phenomenon in Britain, and the need to meet emergencies has contributed significantly to the development of the practice. Executive legislation flourished under the Tudors, and Henry VIII's Statute of Proclamations of 1539, which gave to the King in Council the power to issue proclamations having the same force as Acts of Parliament, is sometimes cited as the high point of non-parliamentary legislation in Britain. The preamble to the Statute of Proclamations reveals the influence of emergencies upon executive power:

> Considering that sudden causes and occasions fortune many times which do require speedy remedies and that, by abiding for a Parliament, in the meantime might happen great prejudice to ensue to the Realm. . . . It is therefore thought in manner more than necessary that the King's Highness of this Realm for the time being, with the advice of His Honourable Council, should make and set forth proclamations for the good and politic order and the governance of this His

---

[1] Sir Cecil T. Carr, *Concerning English Administrative Law* (New York: Columbia University Press, 1941), 65.

Realm . . . for the defence of His Regal Dignity and the advancement of His Commonwealth and good quiet of His People as the cases of necessity shall require.[1]

Threats of war, war, and economic dislocations have required all states to concentrate power in order to organize and harness effectively and expeditiously the total resources of the nation.[2] The problem for a constitutional state is to keep the power from being exercised arbitrarily and to minimize the violence done to the basic liberties of individuals. In response to war and economic crisis, the British Parliament, in the twentieth century, has conferred extensive emergency powers upon the executive.

The constitutional problem involved in the contemporary conferral and exercise of emergency powers in Britain is, in a sense, the culmination of the more long-standing constitutional problem which has resulted from the practice of delegated legislation. After 1832, greater demands began to be made upon Parliament, and lack of time, lack of specialized technical knowledge, and the need for flexibility in administration resulted in Parliament's resorting to the practice of delegating some legislative power over details to the departments.

Initially, the practice seemed to embody no constitutional difficulties and did not seem inconsistent with the rule of law which Dicey formulated for nineteenth century Englishmen. Indeed, Dicey himself welcomed the practice, saying that "the substance no less than the form of the law would, it is probable, be a good deal improved if the executive government of England could, like that of France, by means of decrees, ordinances, or proclamations having the force of law, work out the detailed application of the general principles embodied in the Acts of the legislature".[3] Parliament was supreme and the practice did not derogate from its sovereignty. It relieved Parliament of some of

---

[1] Cited by Sir Cecil T. Carr, "Delegated Legislation," in Sir Gilbert Campion *et al.*, *Parliament* (London: George Allen & Unwin Ltd., 1952), 241.

[2] In former times, parliamentary grants of emergency powers were often made in response to epidemics and sudden economic crises. For example, in the face of a plague in the Baltic, the Queen in Council was empowered, by an Act of 1710, to make quarantine rules and orders. When contagious distemper overtook the cattle of England in 1745, Parliament authorized the King to make regulations in order to prevent its extension. In 1776, in the face of acute danger of famine, the King placed an embargo on wheat and wheat-flour. (For a more extensive treatment of emergency powers and delegated legislation prior to the nineteenth century, see Marguerite A. Sieghart, *Government by Decree* (London: Stevens & Sons Ltd., 1950), 9-81.

[3] A. V. Dicey, *Introduction to the Study of the Law of the Constitution* (9th edition revised by E. C. S. Wade; London: Macmillan & Co. Ltd., 1950), 52-53.

the burden which new demands were putting upon it, and left it free to concentrate on more important issues. The ordinary courts stood ready to protect the individual from arbitrary executive action by applying the principle of *ultra vires*. England was, Dicey thought, meeting the new demands of a new civilization without adopting a *droit administratif* which made officialdom judge in its own case, and which violated the sacred English principle that there was only one law for all, and that all were equal before it. Thus, "a trusted watchman chanted reassuringly that all was well".[1]

Parliament itself generally approved of the practice. An observer has told us that, during the nineteenth century, delegated legislation had not become "an active habit". Parliament still had confidence in its supremacy, and "the investment of important rule-making powers in the hands of the Ministers and the Civil Servants was thus made without serious question".[2] By the middle of the century, Parliament had stopped apologizing for delegating its legislative powers,[3] and "many of the bills passed between 1832 and 1906 delegating legislative powers were enthusiastically received by Parliament".[4]

The experts joined Dicey and Parliament at the door to extend a welcome to delegated legislation. In 1877, Lord Thring, First Parliamentary Counsel, wrote in his book, *Practical Legislation*, that "the adoption of the system of confining the attention of Parliament to material provisions only, and leaving details to be settled departmentally, is probably the only mode in which Parliamentary government can, as respects its legislative functions, be satisfactorily carried on".[5] His successor, Sir Henry Jenkyns, gave his blessing to delegated legislation in 1893, saying that it was "of great public advantage" in that it "mitigate[d] the inelasticity which would often otherwise make an Act unworkable".[6]

The advent to power in 1906 of a Liberal Government bent

---

[1] Carr, *Concerning English Administrative Law*, 21.

[2] Chih-Mai Chen, *Parliamentary Opinion of Delegated Legislation* (New York: Columbia University Press, 1933), 65.

[3] Carr, *Delegated Legislation* (Cambridge: Cambridge University Press, 1921), 24.

[4] Chen, *op. cit.*, 43.

[5] Cited by Chen, *op. cit.*, 24.

[6] Cited by Carr, *Concerning English Administrative Law*, 34.

upon effectuating an extensive programme of social and political reform caused the practice of delegated legislation to grow apace. The average annual number of Statutory Rules and Orders of general application registered from 1895 to 1905 had been 177. Pursuant to Parliament's granting to the departments powers to carry out the Government's reform programmes, the annual number of Statutory Rules and Orders registered increased significantly. In 1912, the number reached 342, and in the following year, 414. This increase in delegated legislation did not go unnoted. Parliament "was beginning to realize . . . the necessity as well as the dangers and risks of the delegation of legislative powers".[1]

The powers of the executive government increased so rapidly that Parliament began to lose faith in itself. It began to shy at the menace of ministerial and bureaucratic encroachments. As more and more legislative powers slipped from its hands, Parliament sought to tighten its grip. Criticisms of delegated legislation were profuse and amendments providing for better safeguards and for more control became abundant.[2]

The courts, too, regarded the rapid growth of the practice of delegated legislation uneasily. In a decision in 1911, Farwell, L. J., called attention to the practice of excluding the jurisdiction of the courts. "If ministerial responsibility were more than the mere shadow of a name," he said, "the matter would be less important, but as it is, the Courts are the only defence of the liberty of the subject against departmental aggression."[3] The same year, Sir H. H. Cozens-Hardy, Master of the Rolls, noted that the real legislation was not to be found on the statute book alone and added that he regarded administrative law-making "as a very bad system and one attended by very great danger."[4]

The outbreak of World War I put an end to the Liberal Government's reform programme, but resulted in an even greater extension of the practice of delegated legislation. The original

[1] Chen, *op. cit.*, 53.

[2] *Ibid.*, 66.

[3] *Dyson v. Attorney-General* (1911), 1 K.B., 410, cited by C. K. Allen, *Law and Orders*. London: Stevens & Sons, 1945), 35.

[4] Cited by Allen, *Law and Orders*, 35.

Defence of the Realm Act, passed in August, 1914, without any parliamentary debate, gave the Government power to make regulations for securing the public safety and the defence of the realm. "From this grain of mustard seed," it has been said, "sprang a goodly forest of regulations."[1] The regulations made pursuant to DORA came to affect an extremely wide area of the nation's life. Controls were imposed on large areas of the economy, and basic individual liberties were restricted. DORA was not popular, but was accepted as a necessity of war. Occasionally, the far-reaching regulations made under DORA were challenged in the courts, but, for the most part, Englishmen put up with DORA in the same way that they might put up with a meddle-some, over-bearing nurse whose presence, although distasteful, was necessary to the patient's surviving his illness. Parliament made few attempts to control or influence the exercise by the executive of its powers, and the courts tended to permit the executive a broad leeway.

DORA and her unpopular brood of regulations had succeeded in drawing public and parliamentary attention to the greatly-increased legislative activities of the departments. After the con-clusion of hostilities in 1918, courts, Parliament, and people tended to look less tolerantly upon these activities, and the immediate post-war years saw a great deal of litigation which challenged executive action taken pursuant to delegated legisla-tion. In bulk, subordinate legislation outweighed Acts of Parliament. In 1920, for example, eighty-two Acts of Parliament were passed, while more than ten times as many Statutory Rules and Orders were registered.[2] Parliament attempted to shake off memories of its war-time status, and tried to reassert its control over the executive. Jealous of executive usurpation of legislative powers, members of Parliament sought to resist further encroach-ments. The Emergency Powers Act, 1920, designed to give the Government power to forestall the community's being deprived of the essentials of life because of widespread strikes, "was greeted with endless protests from all parts of the Houses of Parliament."[3] During the 1920's, almost every delegating statute "went through

[1] Carr, *Delegated Legislation*, 18.
[2] *Ibid.*, 2.
[3] Chen, *op. cit.*, 58.

a very trying parliamentary ordeal."[1] On the Local Government Act, 1929, Parliament attempted "to make a last and desperate stand," and "every provision delegating rule-making powers to the Ministry of Health or to local authorities was hotly debated and bitterly contested."[2] Despite these parliamentary protests, British Governments of the 1920's continued to employ, and to extend the employment of, delegated legislation. New departments, such as the Ministry of Health and the Ministry of Transport were created, and important rule-making powers were granted to them. Parliament frequently balked at the executive's requests for legislative power, but the whips were put on, and the Government proposals almost always prevailed.

Although the volume of subordinate legislation declined considerably in the post-war years from the peak it had reached in war-time, it remained, nevertheless, approximately double that of the immediate pre-war years.[3] Many practices had developed in connection with delegated legislation that were thought disturbing. There were, for example, four different methods of laying subordinate legislation before Parliament. Regulations, rules, and orders might (1) be simply laid, without provision for any parliamentary action; (2) be laid with the proviso that they were not to come into effect until the expiration of a specified period; (3) be laid, subject to a prayer for annulment; or (4) be laid with the proviso that they would lapse, after a specified period, unless expressly approved by Parliament. No consistent method governing the choice of a laying procedure had, however, been developed. Other practices also caused concern, especially to the bench and bar. Orders were given statutory effect by virtue of Parliament's use of "as if enacted in this statute" clauses, and, hence, thought to be removed from the jurisdiction of the courts. "Henry VIII" clauses gave the departments power to modify the parent statute or other existing statutes in order to bring the parent Act into "full operation." "Conclusive evidence" clauses, under which the Minister's approval of a piece of subordinate legislation served as evidence that the instrument was,

[1] *Ibid.*, 64.

[2] *Ibid.*, 61.

[3] Statutory rules and orders of the general class averaged 210 a yearf rom 1894 to 1913. From 1922-1931, the annual average was about 400. Sir Cecil Carr, "Delegated Legislation" in Campion *et al.*, *Parliament*, 241.

ipso facto, a legitimate exercise of his powers, were frequently employed by Parliament in passing delegating statutes. It appeared to many that these practices did much to undermine the sovereignty of Parliament and the competence of the courts.

Delegated legislation became the subject of several books which appeared in the 1920's. Among students of law and politics there was, as one writer has put it, "a general realization that our constitution was passing through an awkward phase and that it was necessary to take stock."[1] In 1921, Mr. Cecil T. Carr wrote the first book devoted entirely to the subject of delegated legislation. He pointed out the usefulness of the practice, and concluded that "if it [delegated legislation] did not exist, it would be necessary to invent it." Carr injected a *caveat*, however—"In so far as delegated legislation contains the germ of arbitrary administration, every possible safeguard must be devised.'[2]' Some of the writers tended to stress the constitutional difficulties of the practice,[3] while others suggested a reconsideration of the place of administrative law in Great Britain.[4]

The uneasiness of legal, judicial, and parliamentary observers over the increasing practice of delegated legislation reached a climax in 1929 when the Lord Chief Justice of England took the unusual step of aligning himself publicly with those who feared the worst. Lord Hewart of Bury (who, not many years before, as Sir Gordon Hewart, Attorney General, had defended the Government's requests for legislative powers before the House of Commons) in his intemperate but seductive book, *The New Despotism*, charged the Civil Service with conspiring to undermine both Parliament and the courts.[5] The charge was a serious one, and coming, as it did, while Parliament was bitterly attacking delegated legislation in its debates on the Local Government Act, 1929, it was clear that an investigation of the allegation was in order. Accordingly, in October, 1929, the Lord Chancellor, Lord

[1] Allen, *Law and Orders*, 42.

[2] Carr, *Delegated Legislation*, 26.

[3] See, for example, C. K. Allen, *Bureaucracy Triumphant* (London: Oxford University Press, 1931); Sir John Marriott, *Mechanism of the Modern State* (2 vols.; Oxford: Clarendon Press, 1927).

[4] See, for example, W. A. Robson, *Justice and Administrative Law* (London: The Macmillan Company, 1928); F. J. Port, *Administrative Law* (London: Longmans, Green & Co. Ltd., 1929).

[5] Lord Hewart of Bury, *The New Despotism* (London: Ernest Benn Ltd., 1929).

Sankey, appointed the Committee on Ministers' Powers to deter-mine, in Sir Cecil Carr's words, "whether Britain had gone off the Dicey standard and, if so, what was the quickest way back."[1] The committee, under the chairmanship, first, of the Earl of Donoughmore, and then of Sir Leslie Scott, was a distinguished one, made up of civil servants, members of Parliament, practising lawyers, and university scholars. It held fifty-four meetings, heard several witnesses, and reported in April, 1932.

The committee's report served to allay most of the anxieties which had developed. The conspiracy charge against the Civil Service was dismissed, and delegated legislation was found to be necessary, valuable, and inevitable. Lord Hewart's book was commended "as a warning against possible dangers of great gravity," but the committee added that there was "no ground for public fear if the right precautions are taken." Potential danger lay in the absence of a system, the lack of direction, and the failure of Parliament to devise any effective machinery of control. The Donoughmore Committee called attention to four excep-tional instances of delegated legislation to which special vigilance ought to be devoted:

(*a*) Instances of powers to legislate on matters of principle, and even to impose taxation;

(*b*) Instances of powers to amend Acts of Parliament, either the Act by which the powers are delegated, or other Acts;

(*c*) Instances of powers conferring so wide a discretion on a Minister, that it is almost impossible to know what limit Parliament did intend to impose; and

(*d*) Instances where Parliament, without formally aban-doning its normal practice of limiting delegated powers, has in effect done so by forbidding control by the courts.[2]

In addition to stressing the avoidance, whenever possible, of these exceptional types of delegated legislation, the committee made several specific recommendations, including the standard-ization of nomenclature and laying procedure, the repeal of the Rules Publication Act, 1893, the extension of the departmental

[1] Carr, *Concerning English Administrative Law*, 26.

[2] *Report of the Committee on Ministers' Powers*, Cmd. 4060 (London: His Majesty's Stationery Office, 1932), 31.

practice of consulting affected interests, and the establishment by each House of Parliament of a standing committee to scrutinize every bill containing any proposal for conferring legislative powers upon the executive and every regulation required to be laid before Parliament.

The Donoughmore Committee's report reassured those who had been alarmed, and the country breathed a sigh of relief. During the remainder of the 1930's neither Parliament nor Government pressed for the adoption of any of the major recommendations of the committee. Delegated legislation continued to flourish. In 1932, the number of general Statutory Rules and Orders registered approached 600; in 1938, the volume topped 800.[1] Yet Parliament did not seem to be unduly concerned. On 27th January, 1937, Mr. Dingle Foot moved in the House of Commons that "the power of the Executive has grown, is growing and ought to be diminished." He deplored the continual granting of legislative powers to the departments, and contended that Parliament had no real control over the exercise of those powers. During Mr. Foot's speech, however, notice was taken that forty members were not present, and the House was counted out. It seems possible, therefore, that Parliament and country might have remained in what has been called "that soporific state of re-assurance"[2] had not World War II opened the flood gates of executive legislation.

We began by noting Sir Cecil Carr's concern that emergencies may make worse law than that reputed to result from hard cases. Arbitrary power is the antithesis of constitutionalism, and Dicey believed that even wide discretionary power was incompatible with the rule of law. Yet, since 1939, in response, first, to war, and, later, to economic crisis, Parliament has conferred upon the executive the broadest discretionary powers and has indulged in all the practices termed "exceptional" by the Donoughmore Committee. Sir Ivor Jennings has suggested, however, that

> . . . the key to the operation of the rule of law is to be found . . . in the word "arbitrary." The exercise of governmental powers must not be capricious or unrestricted. . . . Above all, the exercise of the power must be subject to control. . . . It

---

[1] Carr, "Delegated Legislation" in Sir Gilbert Campion *et al.*, *Parliament*, 241.
[2] *Ibid.*, 233.

is . . . the lesson of history that the only effective control is that in the hands of a free people. Dicey's fundamental error lay not in the nature of the analysis . . . but in the material which he analyzed. He omitted the most fundamental element in the British system of control—the control of the Government by the House of Commons and the control of the House of Commons by the people.[1]

The House of Commons has attempted to exercise control over the executive by acting as watchdog. With the virtual disappearance of the judicial safeguard, and the continuation of circumstances which have demanded the prolongation of emergency powers, the ability of Parliament to act as watchdog has assumed great significance. The problem before us, therefore, is to evaluate the effectiveness of Parliament in pursuing its role as watchdog and to shed some light on the extent to which the legislature of a constitutional state may act as a restraint upon the executive in time of emergency—a condition which in Great Britain, since 1939, has been the rule rather than the exception.

---

[1] Sir W. Ivor Jennings, "The Rule of Law in Total War", *Yale Law Journal*, L (January, 1941), 371-372.

CHAPTER II

PARLIAMENT'S ATTEMPTS TO GUARD ITS INDEPENDENCE

IT IS an indication of the sense of realism and responsibility of the British Parliament that it did not wait until war had actually begun before arming the executive with the powers necessary to mobilize the resources of the country for such an ordeal. From the spring of 1939 it became increasingly apparent to the Chamberlain Government that involvement in war with Germany was likely. As the summer wore on, Hitler's overtures to Poland were reflected in Great Britain by increasing awareness of the imminence of war. The Government, having decided to arm itself with sufficient powers to meet such a contingency, recalled Parliament from its summer recess in the last week of August, specifically for the purpose of enacting legislation which would grant the Government the wide powers it believed it needed to deal with the existing emergency. On 24th August, Sir Samuel Hoare, the Home Secretary, introduced the Emergency Powers (Defence) Bill, which within a few hours proceeded through three readings in the House of Commons, and was approved by 457 votes to 4. On the same day the bill was approved by the House of Lords, and before Parliament adjourned that evening, it had received the Royal Assent and had become the Emergency Powers (Defence) Act, 1939.[1]

Under the Act, the King in Council was empowered to make, by Order in Council, "such regulations . . . as appear to him to be necessary or expedient" for the five following purposes: (1) the public safety, (2) the defence of the realm, (3) the maintenance of public order, (4) the efficient prosecution of any war in which His Majesty might be engaged, and (5) the maintenance of supplies and services essential to the life of the community. In addition, and without prejudice to the foregoing general purposes, the Crown was authorized to make regulations for the following more specific purposes: (1) the apprehension,

[1] 2 and 3 Geo. 6, c. 62.

trial, and punishment of persons offending against the regulations, (2) the detention of persons whose detention appeared to the Secretary of State to be expedient in the interests of the public safety or the defence of the realm, (3) the taking of possession or control of any property or undertaking, (4) the acquisition of any property other than land, (5) the entering and searching of any premises, and (6) amending or suspending any enactment and applying an enactment with or without modification.

In a decision arising from the application of the Defence of the Realm Act (DORA), the House of Lords had not allowed the Treasury to impose charges under that act.[1] In order to avoid a possible repetition of a similar judicial limitation of executive powers, the Emergency Powers (Defence) Act authorized the Treasury to impose charges in connection with any scheme of control under the defence regulations.   Any such Treasury regulation would, however, require an affirmative resolution of the House of Commons within twenty-eight days. The Act specifically prohibited the introduction by defence regulation of compulsory military service, industrial conscription, or the trial of civilians by courts martial. Provision was further made for the sub-delegation of all powers to such authorities as might be named in the regulations.

Each of the specific prohibitions was subsequently overcome. Compulsory military service was imposed by separate National Service Acts. In May, 1940, Parliament enacted the Emergency Powers (Defence) Act, 1940,[2] which provided that, by defence regulation, the Crown could require persons "to place themselves, their services, and their property at the disposal of His Majesty," as appeared to him necessary for the same general purposes stated in the 1939 Act. In August of the same year, by the terms of the Emergency Powers (Defence) (No. 2) Act, 1940,[3] the Crown was authorized to establish special courts, in areas which, because of present or imminent enemy action, might be called "war zones", for the trial of civilians without jury. In addition, by the Treachery Act of May, 1940,[4] Parliament authorized the trial by

---

[1] *Attorney-General v. Wilts United Dairies, Ltd.* (1922), 38 Times Law Reports, 781.

[2] 3 and 4 Geo. 6, c. 20.

[3] 3 and 4 Geo. 6, c. 45.

[4] 3 and 4 Geo. 6, c. 21.

court martial of enemy aliens accused of sabotage and espionage.

It can be seen from a mere recital of the provisions of these statutes that the Government was equipped by Parliament to deal by regulation with almost every conceivable aspect of human activity in order to insure national survival. The Crown could apparently still not levy taxes or borrow money by Order in Council, but otherwise its powers were of the broadest possible nature, seemingly sufficiently wide and discretionary to enable the Government to meet any contingency.

With the granting of such broad powers to the executive, Parliament had virtually abdicated its legislative function. From the beginning, Parliament demonstrated that it was sensitive to any encroachments upon its powers. "We have, even in times of emergency and crisis", said Mr. Arthur Greenwood during the debate on the first Emergency Powers Bill, "to watch and see that the powers and rights of Parliament are not whittled away."[1] Lord Strabolgi, speaking in the House of Lords on the same day, urged that "Parliamentary control should be maintained as far as possible."[2] Members realized that the problem confronting Parliament was the same difficulty which every constitutional state must face in a similar situation: the necessity of maintaining restraints effective enough to prevent the Government from becoming arbitrary and from unduly suppressing the liberties of individuals, yet not so strong as to hinder the Government from taking effective action when necessary. While Parliament did not wish to embarrass or impede the executive, some sense of its appraisal of its own functions may be seen in the following statement made on 22nd May, 1940, by Sir Percy Harris:

> When the occasion arises, Parliament must be vigilant to see that these powers are not unfairly used [Hon. Members: "Agreed."] The House of Commons has its function to perform. It does not help the Government if members do not express their views. These are drastic powers. I reiterate that members will have the responsibility of examining the use of these powers in practice and protecting individuals.[3]

---

[1] 351 House of Commons Debates, 5th series, 69. (Hereinafter cited as H.C. Deb. 5s.)

[2] 114 House of Lords Debates, 5th Series, 899. (Hereinafter cited as H.L. Deb. 5s.)

[3] 361 H.C. Deb. 5s., 152-153.

While judicial control of executive action had not been expressly excluded by the emergency statutes, it was generally realized that the discretion granted to the Government was so broad that a wide degree of judicial control would probably be precluded.   Under the Defence of the Realm Act, 1914,[1] executive action had been to some extent subject to judicial review.   DORA had given the King in Council "power during the continuance of the present war to issue regulations for securing the public safety and the defence of the realm," thereby allowing the courts some competence to declare regulations *ultra vires* if they exceeded the purposes laid down in the statute.   While the courts had, under DORA, permitted the executive to exercise a substantial discretion,[2] they had, nevertheless, on occasion, called the Government to account for overstepping its statutory powers.[3] In the Emergency Powers (Defence) Acts, however, His Majesty was empowered to make such regulations "*as appear to him* necessary or expedient"[4] for securing the general purposes of the Act.   The inclusion of these words had the effect of introducing an essentially subjective criterion, one which seemingly excluded the jurisdiction of the courts, so long as the Government could testify that the actions taken appeared necessary or expedient to His Majesty.

Provision was accordingly made in the original Emergency Powers Act for parliamentary control.   Special opportunity for the exercise of parliamentary restraint was provided for in two ways.   First, a twelve-month time limit was placed upon the operation of the Act, and, unless renewed by Parliament, the Act was to expire at the end of that time.   Opportunity for parliamentary criticism would thus exist on the annual renewal debate. Secondly, all defence regulations made pursuant to the Act were to be laid before both Houses of Parliament for a period of twenty-eight sitting days, during which time either House, by resolution, might annul any regulation.   The regulations, however, were to go into effect as soon as made.   Some apprehension had been expressed in the original debate in the House of Commons, on

[1] 4 and 5 Geo. 5, c. 8.

[2] See *Rex v. Halliday, ex parte Zadig* (1917), A.C. 260.

[3] See, for example, *China Mutual Steam Navigation Co. v. Maclay* (1918) 1 K.B. 33; and *Chester v. Bateson* (1920) 1 K.B. 829.

[4] Italics are author's.

24th August, 1939, over the effectiveness of the negative resolution procedure for dealing with the defence regulations, and an amendment had been put forward to substitute an affirmative resolution procedure. The adoption of the latter procedure would have meant that while regulations would come into effect from the time made, they would lapse unless formally approved by Parliament within twenty-eight days. Thus the procedure prescribed in the Emergency Powers (Defence) Act for Treasury regulations which imposed charges would have been applicable to all regulations issued under that statute. The Home Secretary resisted the amendment, saying that the Government had given lengthy consideration to the possibility of affirmative resolution but had concluded that such a procedure would be impracticable, since it would delay executive action and impose too heavy a burden upon Parliament.[1] Most of the debate reflected the concern of members over the width of the powers asked for, and over the ability of Parliament to control their exercise.[2] The Home Secretary recognized that the powers for which the Government was asking were "wide, comprehensive, and flexible," but he assured the House that they would be exercised with "moderation, tolerance, and common sense." Further, he added, the Government had no intention of using the emergency powers for peace time purposes.[3] The House, accordingly, accepted the two special safeguards and gave its assent to the bill. Sir Dennis Herbert, at that time Chairman of Committees of the House of Commons, perhaps best expressed contemporary parliamentary sentiment when he said that the House had "transferred to the Government and Government departments authority and powers which properly belonged to Parliament, and which Parliament ought not to have handed over otherwise than under the exigencies of the time, but which had to be so handed over if they were to be exercised effectively."[4]

The role which Parliament set for itself was that of watchdog over the executive. It had voluntarily surrendered most of its legislative function, and it was soon, after the formation of the

[1] Sir Samuel Hoare, 351 H.C. Deb. 5s., 67, 100.

[2] Mr. Arthur Greenwood, *ibid.*, 69; Mr. Edmund Harvey, *ibid.*, 75; Mr. Benn, *ibid.*, 99-100.

[3] Sir Samuel Hoare, *ibid.*, 63-67.

[4] Lord Hemingford, *Back-Bencher and Chairman* (London: John Murray, 1946), 215.

Coalition Government, to give up its elective function, for any practical purpose. There remained the functions of criticising the Government, presenting grievances, and informing the public. Parliament thus settled down to use the methods at its disposal —Questions, adjournment debates, supply debates, the debates on the Address, and prayers—to bring its critical faculties to bear on the Government's use of the emergency powers.

In order for the House to exercise an effective vigilance over the Government, it seemed necessary that it should possess, first, a sufficient body of critical opinion within it, and, second, sufficient opportunities for this opinion to air itself. From the outbreak of war, in September, 1939, until May, 1940, a formal Opposition existed in the House. When hostilities began, Mr. Chamberlain had broadened the basis of his National Government somewhat by bringing Mr. Churchill and Mr. Eden, representatives of dissident factions of his own party, into the inner circle. But the Labour and Liberal parties remained outside of the Government. In the early months of the war the Parliamentary Labour Party attempted to play the role of "candid friend"[1] to the Chamberlain Government, and refrained from opposing the measures for which the Government asked in order to prosecute the war. It soon became clear, however, that there was no place in the British parliamentary system for "candid friends"; one had either to oppose the Government and stand ready to form an alternative Government, or to support it and share responsibility for it. As dissatisfaction mounted on all sides of the House with Chamberlain's conduct of the war, Labour was forced to choose whether it would continue to support the Government or vote against it, and thus bring it down, for "it is not possible to wage a major war if there is a real Opposition."[2] Asquith had recognized this in 1915 when, although possessing a majority in the House of Commons, he realized that it would be impossible for him to prosecute successfully the war without the support of the Conservatives. Labour made its choice and, on 10th May, 1940,

---

[1] The term is Sir Ivor Jennings's: "The Formation of Great Britain's 'Truly National' Government," *American Political Science Review*, XXXIV (August, 1940), 728.

[2] *Ibid.*, 730. More recently, E. C. S. Wade has made the same point: "For it is no part of His Majesty's Opposition to oppose when the safety and welfare of the whole nation is in peril from abroad, but rather to stimulate, if need be, the formulation and implementation of a common policy." E. C. S. Wade, "The British Constitution in 1950," *Parliamentary Affairs*, IV (Spring, 1951), 213.

voted against Chamberlain. It was on this crucial vote that Mr. Chamberlain also lost the support of several of the most influential members of his own party who were not then holding ministerial positions. Labour made it clear that it would not serve under Chamberlain, and so the Prime Minister immediately resigned. On 12th May, 1940, Mr. Churchill formed a Government with Labour and Liberal support. No formal Opposition remained, since only the three members of the Independent Labour Party and the lone Communist member withheld their support from the Churchill Government.

The disappearance of a formal Opposition was an extremely significant event. To a large extent, the opportunities for parliamentary criticism of the executive are inherent in the normal organization of the House. Jennings has explained that, in normal times, criticism of the Government is almost exclusively the province of the organized Opposition, and he has found in the existence of an organized Opposition which criticises, informs, and stands ready to form an alternative Government the most important institutional safeguard against executive action.[1] The formation of the Coalition Government, then, appeared to have put important difficulties in the way of the House's performing its function of criticism and vigilance, for, as Sir Stafford Cripps said on 13th May, 1940, "the whole of our procedure and practice in the House of Commons is built up on the basis of having an effective organized Opposition."[2] The framework of practice within which parliamentary discussion took place depended so much upon the existence of an Opposition that it was necessary for a Labour member, Mr. Lees-Smith, to assume the procedural functions (although not the salary) of the Leader of the Opposition in order that the business of the House might continue to be carried on.

With all the major parties participating in the Government, it was evident that if there was to be any criticism of the Government it would have to come from private members. The difficulties which the absence of a formal Opposition engendered in the ability of the House to function as a critical agency were

---

[1] Sir W. Ivor Jennings, *The Law and the Constitution* (3rd edition; London: University of London Press, 1943), *passim*.

[2] 360 H.C. Deb. 5s., 1513.

pointed out by Earl Winterton. He informed the Prime Minister that it was extremely difficult to arrange debates through the "usual channels" when all parties were in the Government. "If a sufficient body of gentlemen constituted themselves an Opposition," Mr. Churchill retorted, "they could be definitely recognized as such and we should know who and where they were."[1]   The Prime Minister's challenge was not acted upon.

Soon after the creation of the Coalition Government, however, it became discernible that something in the nature of a "shadow Opposition" had in fact emerged. It has been described as a " 'ginger' group, not connected by party ties or doctrine, but a collection of capable individuals, mainly back-benchers, Labour side," who "sometimes individually, and sometimes in concert . . . constituted themselves into a band of independent thinkers and critics, demanding debates, asking questions, interrupting speeches," and who formed the basis of their campaign "from answers to Questions, from information obtained from the Departments, from the revelations in the Press, from their constituents, from aggrieved persons, [and] from their colleagues on the Select Committee on National Expenditure."[2]   The existence of this group (which consisted of men of such diverse political sympathies as Emanuel Shinwell, Aneurin Bevan, Clement Davies, Earl Winterton, Sir Herbert Williams, James Griffiths, and Leslie Hore-Belisha) insured the Government's exercising its powers "under a running commentary from the House of Commons" and under "constant sniping from the back benches."[3]

The existence of the Select Committee on National Expenditure, which was appointed on 13th December, 1939, to examine expenditure connected with the war, and to report possible economies, provided a means by which members might gain information which could be translated into criticism.[4] It consisted of thirty-two members and was to sit notwithstanding any adjournment of the House. Six sub-committees were appointed to examine expenditures of specified departments, and thus the

[1] 369 H.C. Deb. 5s., 640.

[2] Herman Finer, "The British Cabinet, the House of Commons and the War," *Political Science Quarterly*, LVI (September, 1941), 353-354.

[3] Sir W. Ivor Jennings, "Parliament in Wartime, III," *Political Quarterly*, XI (1940), 353.

[4] "House of Commons: National Expenditures," *Journal of the Society of Clerks-at-the-Table in Empire Parliaments*, IX (1940), 80-88.

committee "developed in its members a specialized knowledge of particular departments' operations—a point worth noting because the normal select committee is less a collection of specialists than a microcosm of the House as a whole."[1] The existence of the committee, which during its five war-time years of operation held nearly 1,700 meetings and examined over 3,500 witnesses,[2] enabled several back-benchers to make fairly intensive studies of the administration of various Government departments. It was reported in the spring of 1941 that the committee's criticisms carried "the weight of an all-party committee with full access to the facts at a time when the party system in the House no longer functions" and that it was "becoming the substitute for an organized Opposition."[3] In October, 1941, it was reported that four members of the Air Services sub-committee had resigned because the Government had suggested that a report should be submitted privately to the Prime Minister rather than being presented publicly to the House. The four members withdrew their resignations upon receiving an assurance from the Government that the House would receive the report and that the criticism of serious maladministration would receive the personal attention of the Prime Minister.[4]

Thus, although there existed after May, 1940, a great three-party Coalition Government which could seemingly override any force which private members might muster, private members attempted, nevertheless, to devise substitute means of carrying on the critical and informative functions of the House of Commons. During the first three years of the war, Parliament directed its attention, in the first instance, to governmental actions which it felt unduly restricted the independence of private members or unnecessarily curtailed the House's opportunities to criticize and publicize the Government's activities. These parliamentary growls, of varying intensities, were heard on almost every occasion when Parliament felt its position threatened beyond what it considered reasonable under the exigencies of the emergency situation. The fear of the watchdog was that it might be first

[1] Sir Courtenay Ilbert and Sir Cecil Carr, *Parliament* (3rd ed. rev.; London: Oxford University Press, 1950), 89.

[2] *Ibid.*

[3] *New Statesman and Nation*, XXI (31st May, 1941), 547.

[4] *Ibid.*, XXII (18th October, 1941), 355.

muzzled and then ignored. Accordingly, Parliament tended to growl at anything resembling either a leash or a muzzle.

Most members appeared to sense that if the House were to fulfil its function of criticism, its members would have to enjoy a considerable measure of freedom from executive control. It was therefore with excitement and apprehension that members heard Mr. Speaker, on 23rd May, 1940, read to them a letter from the Home Secretary announcing the detention under regulation 18B,[1] of Captain Archibald Henry Maule Ramsay, Conservative member for Midlothian and Peebles. On 5th June, the Speaker read a letter which he had received from Captain Ramsay claiming that his arrest was a "grave violation of the privileges and vital rights of members." The following day, the Home Secretary was asked, during Question Time, whether a report on the detention of Captain Ramsay would be made to the House, and the Home Secretary replied that he would consider carefully how far he could inform the House without prejudicing the interests of national security. A week later, on 13th June, the Home Secretary was asked when he would report on Captain Ramsay's appeal to the Advisory Committee, to which he answered that the necessity of considering a large amount of documentary material had delayed the decision of the Advisory Committee. Several further questions concerning Captain Ramsay's detention were put to the Home Secretary during the ensuing weeks, until, on 23rd July, he reported that the Advisory Committee had recommended detention, and that, after careful consideration, he had agreed with the Committee's recommendation. In a supplementary question, the Secretary was queried on whether or not the Advisory Committee's report would be made available to the House, and upon receiving the Home Secretary's statement that it would not, a member retorted that the freedom of all members of Parliament was now at the Home Secretary's personal disposal.[2]

A motion was then placed on the Order Paper urging the referral of the Ramsay detention to the Committee of Privilege,[3]

---

[1] By virtue of Regulation 18B, as amended in November, 1939, the Secretary of State, if he had "reasonable cause to believe any person to be of hostile origin or association or to have been recently concerned in acts prejudicial to the public safety or the defence of the realm or in the preparation or instigation of such acts," was authorized to "make an order against that person directing that he be detained" (S.R. & O., 1939, No. 1681).

[2] 363 H.C. Deb. 5s., 611-612.

[3] Ibid., 1165.

and the Prime Minister announced that the Government was willing to refer the question to the Committee, a select committee appointed at the beginning of each session to inquire into alleged breaches of the privilege of the House and its members. Accordingly, the Committee of Privilege met on 6th August, and subsequently held five other meetings, at which four witnesses, including Captain Ramsay and Sir Gilbert Campion, Clerk of the House, were examined.[1] The detention order made by the Home Secretary against Captain Ramsay was produced,[2] and the Home Secretary stated that he had not detained the member for anything he had said in Parliament. The Committee concluded that the detention of Captain Ramsay was within the Government's power under 18B, and that no breach of privilege was involved. On 11th December, the Lord Privy Seal, Mr. Attlee, moved that the report of the Select Committee be accepted, and the motion was passed.

The report of the Select Committee did not allay the fears of several members of the House. Specific questions with regard to the detention of Captain Ramsay, and more general enquiries concerning safeguards against a possible repetition of such governmental action, were repeatedly raised. It would be tedious to recite each manifestation of parliamentary interest in this question, and it will suffice to recount only a few of the more concerted efforts either to secure the release of Captain Ramsay or to exact safeguards from the Government against possible detention of other members. Later in December, following the report of the Privilege Committee, a motion was placed on the Order Paper asking that the detention of a member under 18B "should be reported immediately to the House and should not continue without the approval of the House after consideration of the charges against the member and his defence against them."[3] The Prime Minister stated that he could not "accept the suggestion that the existing procedure does not provide adequate safeguards."[4] In February, 1941, a further motion occasioned by the

---

[1] The account of the operations of the Committee is drawn from "The Ramsay Case." *Journal of the Society of Clerks-at-the-Table in Empire Parliaments*, IX (1940), 64-79.

[2] For the text of the detention order see *ibid.*, 70.

[3] 367 H.C. Deb. 5s., 1348.

[4] 368 H.C. Deb. 5s., 24.

Ramsay detention was tabled in the House by seven members.[1]
During 1941 Captain Ramsay had instituted a libel suit against
the *New York Times*, and thereby arose an opportunity for judicial
scrutiny of the charges against him. The court dismissed the suit,
and reviewed at some length his hostile associations.[2] Nevertheless, many members continued to press the Government for a re-
examination of his detention. As late as 16th June, 1944, a lively
debate was held on Sir Irving Albery's motion that the operation
of 18B should be reconsidered, "and in particular, that the
detention of an honourable member for over four years without
trial or charge conflicts with the ancient and well-established
right of the House to the service of its members . . . constitutes a
precedent damaging to the prestige of the House, and dangerous
to the Constitution of the country and ought to cease unless
justified to the House, if necessary, in Secret Session."[3]   The
motion was defeated, 135 votes to 31. Captain Ramsay remained
in detention until 26th September, 1944, when, after spending
fifty-two months in Brixton Prison, he was released. He resumed
his seat in the House on the following day.

A further matter of considerable concern to members arose in
February, 1941, when the Government introduced legislation to
modify further the Place Act of 1707, which prohibited the holders
of offices or places created after 1705 from sitting in the House of
Commons. Much confusion surrounded the application of the
Act of 1707, and the Attorney-General, in introducing the House
of Commons Disqualification (Temporary Provisions) Bill, called
the old statute "archaic, obscure, illogical, and in all respects
unsatisfactory."[4]   Becoming an ambassador had not disqualified

---

[1] *The Times* (London), 13th February, 1941.

[2] In August, 1940, the *New York Times* published a series of articles written by Colonel
William J. Donovan and Edgar A. Mowrer on fifth column activities in Europe. On
25th August, 1940, in its Sunday news-of-the-week review section, the *New York Times*,
under the heading "Britain's Fifth Column," discussed Captain Ramsay in the following
words: "Before the war he was strongly anti-Communist, anti-Semitic, and pro-Hitler.
Though no specific charges were made against him on his arrest . . . informed American
sources said that he had sent to the German Legation in Dublin treasonable information
given him by Tyler Kent, clerk in the American Embassy in London." Captain Ramsay
contended that those words alleged that he had committed high treason, and he brought suit
for libel. On 31st July, 1941, the King's Bench court awarded damages of one farthing to
Ramsay and ordered him to pay all his own costs as well as all costs of the *New York Times*.
In his summation, Justice Sir Cyril Atkinson said that Ramsay "was disloyal in heart and
soul to his King, his government and the people," that "his efforts were destructive of that
will to win which is essential for victory," and that "the expression 'fifth columnist' applied to
Captain Ramsay beyond question." (*New York Times*, 1st August, 1941, 5.)

[3] 400 H.C. Deb. 5s., 2317.

[4] 369 H.C. Deb. 5s., 655.

a member from retaining his seat,[1] and the Act had been modified whenever a new ministry was created in order to allow the Minister to continue sitting in the House. But the House continued to resist strongly any attempt by the Government to pack the House with place men. The immediate cause of the Churchill Government's introducing the bill was its desire to permit the Minister of Health, Mr. Malcolm MacDonald, to retain his seat in the House in spite of his appointment as High Commissioner to Canada. The bill, which became known as the "MacDonald Bill," encountered strong parliamentary opposition, and the Labour Party decided to allow a free vote on the measure in its own ranks.[2] Mr. Churchill, however, decided to make the vote a matter of confidence, and there thus developed a double resentment, both at the bill itself and at the Prime Minister's decision to make it a matter of confidence.[3]

Strong antipathy towards the bill was expressed on Second Reading from all corners of the House.[4] It was pointed out that about 200 members were already engaged in some sort of Government service, exclusive of those serving in the armed forces, that twenty-two new Ministers, who carried with them Parliamentary Private Secretaries, had been appointed since the outbreak of war, and that 116 members were on active service.[5] "If the House suffers further decapitation," a member stated, "there is the risk that we shall find ourselves reduced to the 75 Ministers, 75 P.P.S.s (Parliamentary Private Secretaries), and those other members of this House in whom His Majesty's Government can find no usefulness except the inconsequence of their criticism, the

---

[1] Sir Stafford Cripps and Sir Samuel Hoare were at the time serving as Ambassadors to Moscow and Madrid, respectively, without being disqualified from membership in the House.

[2] See Mr. E. Shinwell, 369 H.C. Deb. 5s., 651; *New Statesman and Nation*, XXI (8th March, 1941), 231.

[3] The following exchange is indicative of parliamentary sentiment:
Mr. Churchill: "Those who have no confidence in the Government will have full liberty so to testify in the lobby."
Mr. Shinwell: "May we not repose our confidence in the Government and at the same time be free to express our opinions on a matter of this kind?"
Mr. Churchill: "If this Bill were not acceded to by the House, very great inconvenience would arise to the war effort of the country. [HON. MEMBERS: "No."] That is my opinion. If there is a desire to bring the matter to the test, the House is perfectly free to have every opportunity to express itself."
Sir Percy Harris: "Is it not one thing to have a free discussion, as we shall have today, and quite another thing to vote against the Government?" (369 H.C. Deb., 5s., 641-642.)

[4] Among those who spoke strongly against the Bill were Messrs. Bevan and Barnes (Labour), and Colonel Gretton and Mr. Pickthorn (Conservatives).

[5] Mr. Mander, 369 H.C. Deb. 5s., 707-708.

loose-mouthed loquacity of their questions, and the debate-killing monotony of their vocabulary."[1] The Prime Minister intervened in the debate to term the names of members serving the Government (which had been listed in a recent White Paper) a "roll of honour" and added that "the roll is not by any means necessarily final."[2] The Prime Minister's inference that the ordinary duties of a member were less important than his inclusion on the "roll of honour"[3] was called an "outstanding doctrine."[4] This, coupled with anxiety over the prospect of future increases in the size of the roll, resulted in the continued existence of uneasiness at the end of the Second Reading, and it seems fair to conclude that, if Mr. Churchill had not made the bill's passage a question of confidence, a sizeable opposition might have been revealed on a division.[5] The fears of many members were allayed when, on the committee stage of the bill, the Lord Privy Seal announced two concessions: first, that a select committee of the House should study the entire problem and make recommendations for war-time as well as for after the war; and second, that an opportunity would be given for debate on all further appointments to the "roll of honour."[6]

The freedom of a member to pursue his parliamentary duties without executive interference was the subject of a debate in the House in October, 1941. Mr. McGovern, member for Shettleston, and one of the three Independent Labour Party representatives in Parliament, had requested the Home Secretary's permission to visit Northern Ireland in order to investigate the case of Mr. Cahir Healy, a Nationalist member of the Ulster Parliament, who had been detained under Regulation 18B. Mr. Herbert Morrison, the Home Secretary, had refused the request, and on 14th October, Mr. James Maxton of the Independent Labour Party, at Question Time, asked him why Mr. McGovern had been refused permission

---

[1] Mr. Pickthorn, *ibid.*, 698.

[2] Mr. Churchill, *ibid.*, 734.

[3] Mr. Churchill stated that, in the times of Queen Victoria, great respect had been paid to members of Parliament. "As the franchise became more democratic," he added, "it grew to be the fashion in certain social circles to speak with contempt about Members of Parliament as a class and a type. They were represented as mere spouters and chatterboxes. . . . That period is over. The White Paper is a proof that it is over . . . it is a roll of honour" *Ibid.*, 733-734).

[4] Mr. Aneurin Bevan, *ibid.*, 734.

[5] *Round Table*, XXXI (June, 1941), 563.

[6] Mr. Clement Attlee, 369 H.C. Deb. 5s., 833-834.

to visit Ireland. The Under Secretary for the Home Office had replied that "the reason for the visit must be that it is of national importance or for domestic purpose" and that Mr. McGovern's proposed visit had met neither of these requirements. The same principle was applied, he added, to members of Parliament as to the general public.[1] Dissatisfaction with this answer was shown by Sir Herbert Williams (Conservative), Mr. Maxton (Independent Labour Party), Mr. Hore-Belisha (Liberal National), and Sir Irving Albery (Conservative). The latter announced that he would raise the matter on the Adjournment as early as possible. On 21st October, the question was raised on the Adjournment, and the issue turned on the right of the Home Office to prevent Members of Parliament from travelling in the United Kingdom on parliamentary duties. During the debate, members of such varied political sentiments as Sir Hugh O'Neill, Mr. Mander, Squadron-Leader Donner, Earl Winterton, and Mr. Aneurin Bevan protested against the Government's action, and Mr. Morrison modified the previous position of the Home Office by stating that members of Parliament should not be treated in exactly the same way as ordinary members of the public, but should "have special right of consideration."[2] Even after Mr. Morrison's statement, however, the attack was continued by Earl Winterton (Conservative), Mr. Maxton (ILP), and Sir Archibald Southby (Conservative) until the Prime Minister intervened in the debate, supporting the Home Secretary's action and stressing the Government's desire to remain accountable to the House. The debate was thus brought to a close, but Mr. McGovern was not subsequently given permission to visit Ireland.

In December, 1941, another question concerning the freedom of members to perform their parliamentary duties arose on consideration of the National Service Bill, by which the Government was asking power to compel a large segment of the population to serve in the armed forces, civil defence, or industry. On the Second Reading of the bill on 9th December, the Minister of Labour and National Service was asked if members of Parliament were to be exempt from the provisions of the bill, and he replied

---

[1] Mr. Peake, 374 H.C. Deb. 5s., 1249.

[2] Mr. Herbert Morrison, *ibid.*, 1717, 1721.

that they were not to be.[1] During committee stage the following day, some sentiment was evidenced that the executive possessed too much power over members by being able to order them into National Service. Mr. George Strauss (Labour) and Sir Percy Harris, the Liberal Whip, spoke in this vein, and Mr. Aneurin Bevan (Labour) asked the Minister if he intended to consult the Cabinet about the inclusion of members of Parliament. The Minister replied that he did not.[2] Another member then asked the Minister if he would consent, not to the exemption of members, but "to declare that any duty placed upon them by this bill would not interfere with their Parliamentary duties."[3] The Minister indicated dissent. Mr. Bevan called this a "reasonable request" and another member said that "Parliamentary duties and rights ought not to be defined by the Minister."[4] The Minister, however, remained adamant during the committee stage, but later capitulated to the parliamentary demand after receipt of a memorandum from the Prime Minister which embodied the views that had been put forward in the House.[5]

In addition to attempting to keep its members free from executive control in order that they might fulfil their duties as watchdogs, the House concerned itself with trying to maintain sufficient opportunities for the expression of its criticisms. "In these days when we are governed almost entirely by Orders in Council," Mr. Dingle Foot said, "all that Members of Parliament can do is to exercise such vigilance as they can, and move a prayer when the occasion offers." "In other words," Mr. Foot added, "the main function of this House nowadays is to watch and pray."[6] In order to turn a phrase, Mr. Foot restricted the critical function

---

[1] Mr. Ernest Bevin, 376 H.C. Deb. 5s., 1415.

[2] *Ibid.*, 1625.

[3] Mr. Edmund Harvey, *ibid.*, 1625.

[4] Dr. Russell Thomas, *ibid.*, 1625.

[5] The memorandum, dated 10th December, 1941, follows: "I see it reported that you say Members of Parliament are liable to be called up equally with others. The rule I have made, which was followed in the last war and must be followed in this, was that service in the House of Commons ranks with the highest service in the State. Any Member of Parliament or Peer of Parliament has a right to decide at his discretion whether he will fulfil that service or give some other form. Members of either House are free, if at any time they consider their political duties require it, and reasonable notice is given, to withdraw from the armed forces or any other form of service in order to attend Parliament. I could not possibly agree to any smirching of this principle." Winston S. Churchill, *The Grand Alliance* (Boston: Houghton Mifflin Co., 1950), 840.

[6] 352 H.C. Deb. 5s., 1829.

of the House to formal prayers, but he and other members determined to resist most attempts of the Government to dispense with
the services of the House or to restrain the effective expression of
criticism.   Considerable opposition accordingly developed to
attempts of the Government to recess the House or to move an
early adjournment. In peace time, the House rarely met during
August and September, but it insisted on meeting at intervals
during the summer of 1940. As late as 1944, the Prime Minister
was forced to postpone his war review for two hours because
Mr. Shinwell was opposing the Government's motion that the
summer recess should last seven weeks. This event evoked the
following comment from the editors of *Round Table*:

> If there are still any people overseas who are under the
> delusion that this country has had to go totalitarian in order
> to win the war, they might usefully ponder on the fact that
> the Prime Minister was prevented from starting his review
> until two hours after the intended time, because a small
> minority in the House of Commons insisted first on debating
> and challenging the Government's proposal for the length of
> the Parliamentary recess.[1]

When the Prime Minister announced, in September, 1941,
his intention of adjourning the House for a further recess, he
encountered strong opposition. Mr. Aneurin Bevan informed the
Prime Minister that if the Government was short of subjects for
debate, members could supply them.[2] It was reported that members of both the Liberal and Labour parties had told their leaders
in the Government that they would not condone a further recess
after a short autumn session.[3] Dissatisfaction reached a peak
when the Government proposed to send the House home for a
prolonged Christmas holiday. Mr. Shinwell's alternate proposal
for a substantially reduced recess, although unsuccessful, won
support from such non-Labour members as Sir John Wardlaw-
Milne, Mr. Hore-Belisha, Sir William Davison, Commander
Bower, and Mr. Erskine Hill.

Another cause of uneasiness to members was the Government's
frequent resort to the use of secret sessions. During the 1939-1940

---

[1] *Round Table*, XXXIV (September, 1944), 356.
[2] 374 H.C. Deb., 5s., 39.
[3] *New Statesman and Nation*, XXII (20th September, 1941), 271.

session, ten parliamentary days were spent in secret session,[1] more than there had been in the entire four years of World War I. The fear was expressed that "if the habit of secret sessions grows the public may lose the sense of Parliament as its watchdog against arbitrary authority," and the view became freely expressed on all sides of the House that they should be terminated.[2] On 30th July, 1940, on a Government motion to go into secret session, the Whips were not put on, and 109 votes were cast against the Government.[3] The real fear of members was that secret sessions were undermining the informative function of the House and were preventing the public from hearing the Parliamentary barks.

There was some feeling in the House that the Government, fortified as it was with a ninety-nine per cent majority, should not needlessly restrict the expression of independent critical opinion by resorting to votes of confidence. Few members had any desire to overturn the Churchill Government, which was the overwhelming choice of both the House and the public. Since members did not wish to vote against the Government on matters of confidence, those who were critical of it on a particular issue usually contented themselves with speaking against it, but voted in the Government lobby.[4] There was, nevertheless, considerable sentiment that the Government ought to allow free votes on most issues so that it could get a fair picture of opinion in the House.[5] Labour members, especially, demanded from their leaders a considerable measure of freedom which should be used by them with a full sense of responsibility when they felt that criticism was in the national interest. In this demand they achieved some success,[6] although, as has been noted in connection with the "MacDonald Bill," the Prime Minister, on occasion, apparently acted contrary to the wishes of the Parliamentary Labour Party in this respect.

[1] Sir W. Ivor Jennings, "Parliament in Wartime, IV," *Political Quarterly*, XII (1941), 65.

[2] "In Defence of Freedom," *New Statesman and Nation*, XX (3rd August, 1940), 101.

[3] Sir W. Ivor Jennings, "Parliament in Wartime, III," *Political Quarterly*, XI (1940), 366.

[4] On the vote of confidence in January, 1942, Mr. Hore-Belisha, Mr. Granville, and Sir Henry Morris-Jones, three National Liberals who normally supported the Government, voted for the Government and then felt it necessary to assert their independence to criticize by resigning from their party. See *Round Table*, XXXII (March, 1942), 291.

[5] In reply to a member's question whether a free vote would be allowed on a particular issue, the Prime Minister replied: "All votes in this House are free in one sense: people are free to vote according to their consciences. . . . It is quite true that they are sometimes given some assistance in discerning which is the right Lobby" (399 H.C. Deb. 5s., 378).

[6] See *New Statesman and Nation*, XXI (22nd March, 1941), 291.

The Liberal Party, too, remained cool to the Government's invocation of votes of confidence.[1]

Confronted with a Government which it had vested with great emergency powers, the House of Commons thus attempted, in the first instance, to guard its own vantage position. Guided by the principle that Parliament should be jealous of its powers and should surrender no more of them than the requirements of the emergency demanded, members proceeded to consider each situation as it arose, to determine whether the particular incursion into parliamentary rights was a legitimate one. On each occasion in which members thought the prerogatives of the House were threatened, parliamentary criticism was voiced, and, in some instances, it is evident that Ministers modified their plans in response to the criticism. On balance, then, the House achieved considerable success in its determination to preserve itself as an independent forum for the expression of critical opinion. In evaluating the degree of success which parliamentary efforts achieved in preserving the British legislature as a relatively independent critical body, however, it must be noted that the Government appeared to share the House's belief that "the Government must secure the enthusiastic support of the House of Commons because it must have the enthusiastic support of the people."[2]

From the beginning, the Government indicated a willingness to co-operate with the House, to consult with it, and to give it opportunity to express itself.[3] The Emergency Powers (Defence) Acts contained provisions for parliamentary control which had been absent from DORA. In addition, Mr. Churchill, on several

---

[1] On 31st January, 1942, the Prime Minister wrote to Sir Archibald Sinclair, Leader of the Parliamentary Liberal Party: "I must draw your attention to the voting of the Liberal Party in the House on the Vote of Confidence. Out of a total of twenty, six abstained or were absent, leaving fourteen to represent the party. Of these fourteen three were Ministers. . . . You also have an Under-Secretaryship in the Lords. This is a lot of sail to carry on so small a hull. . . ." Winston S. Churchill, *The Hinge of Fate* (Boston: Houghton Mifflin Co., 1950), 71-72.

[2] Mr. Leslie Hore-Belisha, 25th June, 1940, as cited by Sir W. Ivor Jennings, "Parliament in Wartime, III," *Political Quarterly*, XI (1940), 363.

[3] The Prime Minister, on 19th December, 1942, wrote to the Leader of the House and to the Chief Whip: "It is in the interest and privilege of the House to receive full statements on public affairs from the Executive. . . . In time of war it is more important than in time of peace. The House would be ill served and would rightly take offence if statements, instead of being made to Parliament at the end of Questions, were handed to the Press. . . . The fact that the House is nearly always filled during such a statement and empties at its close is a very fair indication of what the ordinary silent Member feels. . . . Question time is one of the most lively and vital features of Parliamentary life." Churchill, *The Hinge of Fate*, 917-918.

C

occasions, expressed his appreciation of the services of the House of Commons, as may be seen from the following statement:

> I think I have said before that to try to carry on a war, a tremendous war, without the aid and guidance of the House of Commons would be a superhuman task. I have never taken the view that the Debates and criticisms of this House are a drag and a burden. Far from it. I may not agree at all with the criticism—I may be stunned by it, and I may resent it; I may even retort—but at any rate Debates on these large issues are of the very greatest value to the life-thrust of the nation, and they are of the very greatest assistance to His Majesty's Government.[1]

Mr. Churchill's tributes to a free Parliament were no doubt somewhat exaggerated in the face of the fact that he controlled ninety-nine per cent of the votes. The war-time Parliament operated under many handicaps—the absence of many of its members, secret sessions, and the absence of a formal Opposition. It demonstrated, however, a strong determination to retain its critical and informative functions to the greatest extent possible under the circumstances. The vitality of private members, coupled with the existence of a desire on the part of the Government to utilize and benefit from parliamentary criticism, enabled the House of Commons to maintain itself as a forum for criticism and the presentation of grievances. The manner in which members of Parliament used their opportunities to hold the war-time Government accountable will be considered in the next three chapters.

---

[1] 368 H.C. Deb. 5s., 257.

CHAPTER III

REGULATION 18B:
A CASE STUDY IN PARLIAMENTARY
CONTROL

BY VIRTUE of the broad purposes of the Emergency Powers (Defence) Acts, the British Government was empowered to make regulations which cut deeply into the basic liberties of its subjects. Professor Laski has suggested that the essence of modern war is "the effort to break the will of your enemy," and that, to that end, "the ability to maintain national unity is essential."[1] Enough was known of the potentialities of fifth columnists even before the lessons of Norway, Holland, and France were impressed, and the British Government accordingly determined to make provision, under its emergency powers, against any undermining of the national morale and the national war effort. Drastic limitations were imposed upon the most basic liberties of the subject. Detention of individuals on political grounds was authorized under Regulation 18B; Government control of the press was provided for by Regulations 2C and 2D; and many of the guarantees of free speech were removed by Regulations 39B and 39BA.

While Parliament had authorized Government interference with all of these liberties, it felt a special responsibility to insure that the Government should exercise its powers in this realm only under the closest supervision. Parliament was not ready to accept governmental action in this area which, in its opinion, went beyond the reasonable necessities of even an extremely serious situation. Mr. Churchill told the House of Commons in 1940 that the British people had made "immense surrenders of their hard-won liberties," and that "Parliament stands custodian of these surrendered liberties."[2] Accordingly, the House attempted to scrutinize closely each new demand for powers which would

[1] Harold J. Laski, "Civil Liberties in Great Britain in Wartime," *Bill of Rights Review*, II (Summer, 1942), 243.

[2] Cited by Captain Bernays, 401 H.C. Deb. 5s., 2028.

restrict the liberty of the subject, and to watch vigilantly the Government's exercise of each power which it possessed in this field.

Regulation 18B represented the most serious restriction imposed upon individual liberty in war-time Britain. Desiring to forearm itself against the activities of potential quislings, the Government listed, as one of the purposes for which it asked regulation-making power, the detention of persons "whose detention appears to the Secretary of State to be expedient in the interests of public safety or the defence of the realm." The first group of defence regulations, made on 25th August, 1939 and published on 1st September, included Regulation 18B, which gave the Secretary of State power to detain "any particular person . . . if satisfied . . . that it is necessary to do so."[1] Provision was made for an appeal to an Advisory Committee, but the recommendations of the Committee were not to be binding on the Home Secretary.

A World War I precedent existed for the exercise of such power. By Regulation 14B, made under DORA, the Secretary of State was given the power to detain a person in the interests of the public safety or the defence of the realm "in view of the hostile origins or associations of the person, but only upon the prior recommendation of a competent naval or military authority or of an advisory committee." The House of Lords, in Zadig's case,[2] had upheld the regulation saying, per Lord Finlay, L.C., that it might be necessary in a time of great public danger to entrust great powers to His Majesty in Council, and that "one of the most obvious means of taking precautions against dangers such as are enumerated is to impose some restriction on the freedom of movement of persons whom there may be any reason to suspect of being disposed to help the enemy."

Because the liberty of the individual to remain free of detention or imprisonment, except on conviction for a statutory offence, as determined by regular judicial procedure, had been for many centuries perhaps the most basic of British liberties, it was evident from the beginning that the House of Commons regarded 18B with great apprehension. While recognizing the necessity of the

[1] S.R. & O., 1939, No. 978.
[2] *Rex v. Halliday, ex parte Zadig*, 1917, A.C. 260.

Government's having to detain without trial in some cases, members felt that such a drastic power should be accompanied by special safeguards. On 24th August, 1939, the day upon which the Emergency Powers (Defence) Bill was introduced in the House of Commons, Mr. Kingsley Griffith, commenting upon the Government's request for detention power, said:

> Those words rather make me tremble for my own security, in case the Home Secretary took an adverse view of me. That is obviously a very extensive power indeed, and since it is discretionary I am wondering whether it is not possible to adopt in regard to that . . . a procedure whereby there would be some kind of judicial consideration of the cases of people who were detained without trial. The liberty of the subject is so important that even in these times of emergency I think it is right we should deal with it extremely tenderly.[1]

On 31st October, 1939, Mr. Dingle Foot moved a prayer of annulment against several regulations, including 18B. The general criticism was that the powers which the Government was claiming were too broad and thus liable to abuse. Mr. Herbert Morrison, then in opposition, sounded the keynote of this argument when he said:

> I am not going to use the argument usually put forward as a matter of courtesy that we do not believe the present Minister would be wicked but that we are afraid his successors might be. I think that any Minister is capable of being wicked when he has a body of regulations like this to administer. . . . Therefore, let us put aside the cant in which we engage that we are sure the present Home Secretary would not do wrong, but that we are not so sure of his successors. We believe that the present Home Secretary is capable of being wicked, and, therefore, the House should be guarded and careful as to the powers they give to him. . . .[2]

The special need for safeguards in connection with 18B was stressed by several members. Mr. Kingsley Griffith said that "everybody must be disconcerted by the absoluteness of the terms

[1] 351 H.C. Deb. 5s., 72.
[2] 352 H.C. Deb. 5s., 1846-1847.

of Regulation 18B" and called it "the most dangerous of all."[1] Mr. Holdsworth stated that the regulation entailed "a Gestapo power," and urged that the Advisory Committee be made an effective restraint.[2] It was further stated that the regulation permitted the Home Secretary to treat the people as though they were "criminals"[3] and "natives in Bengal."[4] Sir Archibald Southby urged the Home Secretary, Sir John Anderson, to reconsider the regulations without pressing the House to a division "in view of the effect that it would have abroad."[5] Some index to the amount of opposition which developed to the regulations and to the Home Secretary's stand on them can be gathered from the fact that the Home Secretary's reply lasted one hour and twenty-two minutes and was interrupted forty-eight times. The Lord Privy Seal, Sir Samuel Hoare, finally intervened in the debate, saying that "it was obvious . . . that there are anxieties about certain of these regulations lest they should be abused and lest they might go too far." That being so, Sir Samuel added, it was the Government's duty to take note of such criticism, and to formulate regulations which would command the general assent of the House.[6] Accordingly, he proposed that representative members from all sides of the House should consult with the Government with a view towards revising the regulations in question. Until the new regulations should be issued, the existing regulations would have to remain in force so that the Government would not be faced with a vacuum in certain areas. Hoare's proposal was agreed to by all sides, and Mr. Foot withdrew his prayer, after a debate which had lasted over four hours.

An informal conference between certain members and the Government took place, and on 23rd November, 1939, an amended regulation 18B was issued, which began:

> If the Secretary of State has reasonable cause to believe any person to be of hostile origin or association or to have been recently concerned in acts prejudicial to the public safety or

---

[1] *Ibid.* 1837-1838.

[2] *Ibid.*, 1882-1883.

[3] Mr. Kirkwood, *ibid.*, 1887.

[4] Dr. Edith Summerskill, *ibid.*, 1868.

[5] *Ibid.*, 1898.

[6] *Ibid.*, 1899.

the defence of the realm or in the preparation or instigation of such acts, and that by reason thereof it is necessary to exercise control over him, he may make an order against that person directing that he be detained.[1]

The terms of the amended 18B indicated that a considerable number of changes had been made. In the first place, specific grounds for detention ("hostile origin or association" or being "recently concerned in acts prejudicial . . . or in the preparation or instigation of such acts") were laid down; secondly, the vague direction to the Home Secretary that he be "satisfied" was replaced by a requirement that he have "reasonable cause to believe"; thirdly, the chairman of the Advisory Committee was required to inform the detainee of the grounds for his detention and to provide him with sufficient details to allow him to attempt to make a defence; fourthly, the detainee was given the right to make written objections to the Home Secretary; and, fifthly, the Home Secretary was required to inform Parliament, by monthly reports, of the number of detentions he had made and the number of cases in which he had not followed the Advisory Committee's advice.

On 22nd May, 1940, the grounds for detention under 18B were broadened by a new defence regulation which permitted the Home Secretary to detain any person whom he had reasonable cause to believe was a member of, or had been active in furthering, any organization which the Home Secretary was satisfied was either "subject to foreign influence or control," or controlled by persons who "have or have had associations with persons concerned in the government of, or sympathies with the system of government of, any Power with which His Majesty is at war."[2] The grounds for detention were later again broadened by another defence regulation to include action or words "expressing sympathy with the enemy," or indicating likeliness to assist the enemy.[3]

It should be noted that, in spite of the modifications of the original regulation, detention under 18B was still a discretionary political act. No provision was made for any appeal to, or review

[1] S.R. & O., 1939, No. 1681.
[2] S.R. & O., 1940, No. 777, II.
[3] S.R. & O., 1940, No. 1682, II.

by, a judicial tribunal, and the Home Secretary was in no way bound to accept the advice of the Advisory Committee. It should be further noted that the Advisory Committee was in no sense a judicial body, although its chairman, Mr. Norman Birkett, K.C., continued to serve in that capacity following his becoming Mr. Justice Birkett. All members of the Advisory Committee were appointed by the Home Secretary.[1]

It had been contended by Mr. Dingle Foot and Mr. Kingsley Griffith, among others, during the debate on 31st October, 1939, that 18B, in effect, abolished *habeas corpus*, since no provision for judicial scrutiny of detention was included. The Habeas Corpus Act, however, had not been suspended in either World War I or World War II, and "it was open to the subject to challenge detention by application for a writ of *habeas corpus*."[2] During World War I, however, in the Zadig case, in which detention under 14B had been challenged, Lord Finlay, L.C., stressing that the defendant was charged with no crime, stated that "it seems obvious that no tribunal for investigating the question whether circumstances of suspicion exist warranting some restraint can be imagined less appropriate than a Court of law."[3]

Several *habeas corpus* proceedings were instituted by detainees under 18B. In the first such case,[4] a Mr. Lees, who had been detained on the basis of his association with the British Union of Fascists, denied such association and challenged the possession by the Home Secretary of "reasonable cause" to order the detention. The Home Secretary submitted an affidavit stating that, after careful consideration of confidential reports, he believed he had reasonable cause for detaining Lees. The Home Secretary's affidavit was accepted by the court, which held that it would not inquire into the Home Secretary's reasons.

In another case concerning application for *habeas corpus*,[5] a Captain Budd was detained on the ground of hostile association. The details later given to Captain Budd indicated that the charges against him were based upon his association with the British

---

[1] Other members included Sir Walter Monckton, who was available to act as Chairman; Professor Collinson, Sir Arthur Hazlerigg, Mr. J. J. Mallon, and Miss Violet Markham.
[2] E. C. S. Wade and G. G. Phillips, *Constitutional Law* (3rd ed.; London: Longmans, Green & Co., 1946), 358.
[3] *Rex v. Halliday, ex parte Zadig*, 1917, A.C. 260, at 269.
[4] *Rex v. Home Secretary, ex parte Lees*, 1 K.B. (1941), 72.
[5] *Rex v. Home Secretary, ex parte Budd*, 2 All E. R. (1941), 749.

Union of Fascists. The court awarded him his *habeas corpus*, but a few days later he was again detained and charged with membership in the British Union. A second application for *habeas corpus* was refused by the court on the ground that the Home Secretary's affidavit could not be questioned by the judiciary.[1]

The issue in *Stuart v. Anderson*[2] was false imprisonment. The plaintiff contended that since his name had been placed on a detention order applying to 343 others, the Home Secretary could not have devoted careful consideration to his particular case, and could not, therefore, have had "reasonable cause" to order his detention. The court rejected Stuart's plea, saying that it had no power to review the Minister's decision and no proof that the Home Secretary had not carefully considered each particular detention.

The most significant decision which emerged from the many cases which arose under 18B was that delivered by the House of Lords in *Liversidge v. Anderson*,[3] in November, 1941. The case turned on the question of whether the phrase "has reasonable cause to believe" permitted any judicial determination of the validity of the Home Secretary's action. The Lords of Appeal, over the dissent of Lord Atkin, held that it did not. Lord Maugham stressed the point that the Home Secretary was not acting judicially, and that it would, therefore, "be strange if his decision could be questioned in a court of law." It seemed "reasonably clear" to Lord Maugham, with regard to the meaning of the disputed phrase, that "if the thing to be believed is something which is essentially one within the knowledge of A. B. or one for the exercise of his exclusive discretion, the words might well mean if A. B. acting on what he thinks is reasonable cause (and, of course, acting in good faith) believes the thing in question." Lord Macmillan pointed out that war did not relieve the courts of their duty to protect the liberty of the subject, but, under the terms of the regulation, the matter was one, he thought, "of opinion and policy, not of fact." Quoting the opinion of Lord Finlay, L.C., in Zadig's case with approval, Lord Macmillan

---

[1] There is an interesting account of Captain Budd's various encounters with the Home Secretary and the Courts in Sir Carlton Kemp Allen, *Law and Orders* (London: Stevens & Sons Ltd., 1945), 245-246.

[2] 2 All E. R. (1941), 665.

[3] A. C. 206 (1942).

concluded that "a decision on this question can manifestly be taken only by one who has both knowledge and responsibility which no court can share." Lord Wright believed that the word "reasonable" implied "instructed and intelligent care and deliberation," but felt that, in this case, it meant only that "the Minister must not lightly or arbitrarily invade the liberty of the subject." The Minister must, Lord Wright added, "be reasonably satisfied before he acts, but it is still his decision and not the decision of anyone else." Lord Romer agreed that in cases where an Act of Parliament is capable of more than one interpretation the courts should normally prefer "that construction which is the least likely to lead to an invasion of the liberty of the subject." But, in times of great national emergency, he believed, "the courts should . . . prefer that construction which is least likely to imperil the safety of this country." Like Lord Macmillan, he quoted Lord Finlay with approval, and concluded that he could not believe "that the legislature or the framers of the regulation ever intended to constitute the courts of this country the ultimate judge of the matters in question."

Lord Atkin's dissent was a spirited defence of the liberty of the subject. The question, for Lord Atkin, was "whether the words 'If a man has' can mean 'If a man thinks he has,' " and he was of the opinion that they could not. In English law, Lord Atkin averred, "reasonable cause" had always included the possibility of judicial review. Stating that he had "listened to arguments which might have been addressed acceptably to the Court of King's Bench in the time of Charles I," Lord Atkin concluded that the only authority he could recall "which might justify the suggested method of construction" was the exchange between Alice and Humpty Dumpty over the meaning of words, in *Through the Looking-Glass*.[1]

Lord Atkin's dissent found much support in letters to the editors in the various newspapers, for, as Sir Cecil Carr has said, "British public opinion may be relied upon to take the side

[1] "There's glory for you!" "I don't know what you mean by 'glory,'" Alice said. Humpty Dumpty smiled contemptuously. "Of course you don't—till I tell you. I meant, 'there's a nice knock-down argument for you!' " "But 'glory' doesn't mean 'a nice knock-down argument,' " Alice objected. "When *I* use a word," Humpty Dumpty said in a rather scornful tone, "it means just what I choose it to mean—neither more nor less." "The question is," said Alice, "whether you *can* make words mean so many different things." "The question is," said Humpty Dumpty, "which is to be Master—that's all." (Lewis Carroll, *Through the Looking-Glass*.)

of anybody who may seem to be the victim of an arbitrary officialism."[1] It appeared to many, both inside and outside of Parliament, that the effect of the decision in *Liversidge v. Anderson* was to give "to executive discretion an almost unlimited charter,"[2] and it indicated to most that "it was to the House of Commons, not to the courts, that the people of Britain had to look for any relief from arbitrary action in wartime England."[3]

Since the modifications of 18B resulting from Mr. Foot's prayer of 31st October, 1939, critical members of the House of Commons had not been reluctant to ventilate their concern over the administration of the regulation. It has already been noted that, in the dark days of May, 1940, following the collapse of France, the grounds for detention under 18B had been widened.[4] But even in such adverse circumstances, this had not been done without public debate and private consultation.[5] In the face of imminent invasion, and under the broadened grounds for detention, large numbers of persons were detained during May, June, and July, 1940. By August, 1,428 persons were in detention, the largest number held in custody at any one time during the entire life of the regulation.[6] The large number of detentions had resulted in the development of a backlog of cases to be heard by the Advisory Committee, and this matter was raised in an adjournment debate by Mr. Stokes on 10th December, 1940. Mr. Mander informed the House that there were then approximately 300 persons who had been in detention for more than three months without having had their cases considered by the Advisory Committee, and he charged that such a situation constituted an abuse by the Home Secretary of the powers which the House had given him.[7] The Home Secretary, Mr. Herbert Morrison, replied that if members had accepted an exceptional regulation "they must swallow some of the exceptional procedure that follows from it." He reminded

[1] Sir Cecil Carr, "A Regulated Liberty," *Columbia Law Review*, XLII (March, 1942), 354.

[2] Allen, *Law and Orders*, 243.

[3] Clinton L. Rossiter, *Constitutional Dictatorship* (Princeton: Princeton University Press, 1948), 198.

[4] See p. 39.

[5] Jennings, "The Rule of Law in Total War," *Yale Law Journal*, L (January, 1941), 385.

[6] Mr. Herbert Morrison, 400 H.C. Deb. 5s., 2380.

[7] 367 H.C. Deb. 5s., 882.

the House that Regulation 18B was "not classical liberalism at all" but "war legislation and state security" and that there was "no use in mixing the two things." Mr. Morrison concluded that he welcomed the discussion and was proud "that in the midst of this struggle . . . the British House of Commons can spare a day for the discussion of the rights, liberties, convenience, and happiness of even the least popular of His Majesty's subjects".[1]

It had been decided by the Home Office to close some of the detention camps and to transfer many of the detainees to more comfortable quarters in the Isle of Man.[2] However, on the second reading of the Isle of Man (Detention) Bill on 25th March, 1941, several members expressed concern that those detainees who were transferred to the Isle of Man from the mainland might thereby lose some of their legal rights. Although the writ of *habeas corpus* lay in the Isle of Man, there was some doubt whether it could be enforced, and members viewed with suspicion any attempt by the Government to place British subjects beyond the jurisdiction of British courts. The Government assured the House that such removal to the Isle of Man would not divest the detainees of any of the rights which they enjoyed on the mainland. Considerable concern had previously been shown, in the form of Questions, over the fact that the recommendations of the Advisory Committee were not always followed by the Home

---

[1] 367 H.C. Deb. 5s., 869, 873, 879-880.

[2] Some notion of the Government's interest in the comfort of 18B detainees can be gathered from the following memorandum written by the Prime Minister to the Home Secretary on 22nd December, 1940:

"It must be remembered that these political *détenus* are not persons against whom any offence is alleged, or who are awaiting trial or on remand. They are persons who cannot be proved to have committed any offence known to the law, but who because of the public danger and the conditions of war have to be held in custody. Naturally I feel distressed at having to be responsible for action so utterly at variance with all the fundamental principles of British liberty, *habeas corpus* and the like. The public danger justifies the action taken, but that danger is now receding.

"In the case of Mosley and his wife there is much prejudice from the Left, and in the case of the Pandit Nehru from the Right. I particularly asked that the rigorous character of the latter's imprisonment should be removed. In foreign countries such people are confined in fortresses—at least, they used to be when the world was still civilized.

"These reflections led me to look into the details of Mosley's present confinement, as well as others of that category. Does a bath every week mean a hot bath, and would it be very wrong to allow a bath every day? What facilities are there for regular outdoor exercise and games and recreation under Rule 8? If the correspondence is censored, as it must be, I do not see any reason why it should be limited to two letters a week. What literature is allowed? Is it limited to the prison libraries? Are newspapers allowed? What are the regulations about paper and ink for writing books or studying particular questions? Are they allowed to have a wireless set? What arrangements are permitted to husbands and wives to see each other, and what arrangements have been made for Mosley's wife to see her baby, from whom she was taken before it was weaned?

"I should be grateful if you would let me know your own view upon these matters." Winston S. Churchill, *Their Finest Hour* (Boston: Houghton Mifflin Co., 1949), 703.

Secretary, and this point was raised during the Isle of Man debate. Mr. Morrison's admission that, out of a total of 1,729 detentions up to March, 1941, he had differed from the recommendations of the Advisory Committee in fifty-five cases[1] led some members to say that the Advisory Committee was no check at all if its advice could be disregarded so frequently, and caused Earl Winterton to term the Home Secretary "a complete dictator".[2]

The grievance, which had been growing among members of the House, came to a head in November, 1941, when the House of Lords announced its decision in *Liversidge v. Anderson*. The judicial safeguard which many had hoped for, not only with regard to 18B, but also in connection with the defence regulations generally, had apparently not materialized, and the House of Lords decision appeared to be a sort of statement of abdication by the courts. It seems certain that many members believed that the revised wording of 18B, after the informal conference in November, 1939, had been meant to guarantee some sort of judicial scrutiny of the Home Secretary's actions.[3] No record of those conversations, however, is available, and hence much difference of opinion developed concerning the precise intentions of the conferees in making the change in wording.[4] In any case, the effect of the House of Lords' pronouncement was to increase the anxiety of many members over the Home Secretary's exercise of the far-reaching powers. On 11th November, 1941, Commander Bower, at Question Time, asked the Prime Minister whether, in the light of the Liversidge decision, the Government would introduce legislation to provide safeguards against abuse by the Home

---

[1] 370 H.C. Deb. 5s., 511.   [2] *Ibid.*, 518.

[3] Mr. Sydney Silverman has revealed: "... when the House of Commons substituted ... the words 'reasonable cause to believe', we all thought that was giving the courts a power to control what happens. That is why we altered it." *Third Report from the Select Committee on Procedure* . . . , H.C.R. 189-1, Session 1945-46 (London: His Majesty's Stationery Office, 1946), 275.

[4] C. K. Allen, like Lord Atkin, finds it significant that "Parliament used a form of words ['reasonable cause'] which has a perfectly clear and definite meaning in our law." "Regulation 18B and Reasonable Cause," *The Law Quarterly Review*, LVIII (April, 1942). Cf. however, the following interpretation of Lord Chorley: "The fact of the matter is, that when the Government agreed early in the war to amend the wording of the regulation as first issued, *viz.* 'if satisfied . . . that it is necessary' to 'if the Secretary of State has reasonable cause to believe' they gave too much away. It is surely obvious that if the question of whether the Home Secretary had reasonable cause can be tested in the courts the matter is, in effect, taken out of his hands, for every decision he takes under the regulation becomes appealable, all the evidence must be passed upon in public, and much of the emergency value of 18B is lost. Had *Liversidge v. Anderson* gone the other way the result would have been an amendment of the regulation so as to bring it into accord with the needs of the situation." Lord Chorley, "Law-Making in Whitehall," *Modern Law Review*, IX (April, 1946), 40.

Secretary of his powers of arrest and detention. The Prime Minister replied that the Government proposed neither to introduce any such legislation nor to abandon any of its powers.[1] As opposition to the administration of the regulation grew, it was stated in Parliament that the matter would be raised on the Debate on the Address, and, in anticipation of strong criticism from the House, the Prime Minister sought to ameliorate the conditions of detainees and to improve the administration of the regulation.[2]

On 26th November, 1941, Sir Irving Albery moved an amendment to the Address which referred to "the grave concern now felt in this House at the abolition of any judicial safeguard for the liberty of the subject against arbitrary acts of the Executive" and asked for "some modification of the Defence Regulations which, whilst still permitting the Executive to arrest and detain on suspicion, would provide that beyond a definite period the continued detention of any person shall be subject to a right of appeal to an independent tribunal".[3] There was agreement among members that it was necessary for the Home Secretary to detain persons on suspicion, but the aspect of the situation which bothered many was that the Minister was able to hold people in detention for an indefinite period without there being any real check upon his actions. The Government had long contended that a real check existed in the Home Secretary's responsibility to the House, but this point was disputed by several members. Flight-Lieutenant Boothby (now Sir Robert) said that it was "a complete fallacy to suggest that any real power is exercised

---

[1] 374 H.C. Deb. 5s., 2040.

[2] Memorandum from the Prime Minister to the Home Secretary, 15th November, 1941: "I shall be glad to know what action you have taken about enabling the twelve couples of married internees to be confined together. Now that order has been restored in the Isle of Man there would be no particular reason against their going there. If not there surely must be some prisons in England in which arrangements could be made for reasonable association of husband and wife.

"Is it true that when aliens are interned husband and wife are interned in one place ? If so it seems invidious to discriminate against those of British nationality.

"Feeling against 18B is very strong, and I should not be prepared to support the regulation indefinitely if it is administered in such a very onerous manner. Internment rather than imprisonment is what was contemplated.

"Sir Oswald Mosley's wife has now been eighteen months in prison without the slightest vestige of any charge against her, and separated from her husband.

"Has the question of releasing a number of these internees on parole been considered, or on condition of their finding sureties for good behaviour, etc. ? I should be glad if you would make proposals to the Cabinet before the debate in the House takes place." Winston S. Churchill, *The Grand Alliance* (Boston: Houghton Mifflin Co., 1950), 835.

[3] 376 H.C. Deb. 5s., 776.

by members of this House over the Executive",[1] and Mr. Sydney Silverman contended that it was "perfectly idle" to say that the Home Secretary was responsible in any real sense to the House for the administration of 18B.[2] Mr. Boothby, making reference to the detention of Captain Ramsay to support his claim, charged that "if Charles James Fox had been alive today and had made any of the series of speeches he made during the Napoleonic Wars, he would have been in Brixton jail after the first speech".[3]

The interpretation which the Government and the House of Lords had given to the words "reasonable cause to believe" was challenged, and the Home Secretary replied that if the words had been intended to provide judicial review, his predecessor would not have accepted that meaning, and that if the parliamentary conferees had desired to impose a recourse to the courts, "they would have insisted upon an explicit answer on that point".[4] Mr. Morrison informed the House that, out of a total of 1,769 detentions which had been ordered up to November, 1941, 1,106 persons had been released, leaving 663 persons in detention at that time.[5] He had rejected the recommendations of the Committee in eighty-nine cases.[6] Mr. Morrison also told the House that it was his policy, and that of his predecessor, Sir John Anderson, to institute criminal prosecutions in the regular law courts whenever there was sufficient evidence to warrant such prosecution.[7]

Most speakers had made it clear that they did not intend to press for a divison, since the Debate was on the Address, and that they hoped the Government would meet the views of the House without a vote. Mr. Morrison, however, stated that he would not be willing to continue in his task if his powers were curtailed. If there was material opposition to the regulation, Mr. Morrison continued,

> . . . it would be better for the House to divide now in order that the country may know where we all stand on this vital issue. . . . Moreover, it is not right that I should be left in any

---

[1] *Ibid.*, 828.　　　　　　　[2] *Ibid.*, 839.　　　　　　　[3] *Ibid.*, 830.

[4] *Ibid.*, 857. The Attorney-General told the House that the modified words of the regulation were designed to make clear to the Home Secretary "not that there is an alteration in the legal position in the sense that they give resort to the courts, but that this is a matter to which he must direct his personal judgment, and of which he must personally weigh the pros and cons". (*Ibid.*, 816.)

[5] *Ibid.*, 848-851.　　　　　　[6] *Ibid.*, 853.　　　　　　　[7] *Ibid.*, 849.

uncertainty as to the opinion of the House . . . I therefore say that if there is a material challenge, it would be better to divide. [An hon. Member: "Will there be a free vote?"] There will be no free vote. It will be a vote on the Address.[1]

No division took place and the amendment was negatived. Mr. Ernest Evans probably voiced the majority opinion of the House when he said:

> In view of the decision of the House of Lords, Parliament is the only body which can exercise any authority at all on the Home Secretary. . . . This is his job; it is the job we have put upon him. We must not give him any pretext to run away from that job by leasing this matter, on the authority of some appeal tribunal. It is essential, in dealing with the liberties of the subject, that we should hold the Home Secretary responsible, that his shall be the final responsibility and that Parliament, and this House in particular, in future, shall exercise even more vigilance than has been the case in the past in seeing that he does that job effectively and well.[2]

Members who were critical of the administration of 18B utilized another occasion, the debate on Supply, to continue their pressure for additional safeguards. On 21 July, 1942, Commander Bower, in Committee of Supply, introduced a motion to reduce the Home Secretary's Salary by £100 in order to draw the attention of the House to the administration of 18B. It was contended that the Advisory Committee was "in no sense a court of appeal", but merely "the creature of the Home Secretary",[3] and that the House could exercise no control over the Home Secretary in individual cases, since it did not have sufficient knowledge of the circumstances to judge whether or not the powers had been abused.[4] It was charged that the Home Secretary had, in fact, abused his powers, and the case of Mrs. Wilmot Nicholson, wife of Admiral Nicholson, was cited to substantiate the point. Mrs. Nicholson had been detained on 26th May, 1940, and her case had been reviewed in October, 1940. In February, 1941, she had been tried *in camera*, on charges that were not made

---

[1] *Ibid.*, 861.   [2] *Ibid.*, 814-815.
[3] Commander Bower, 381 H.C. Deb. 5s., 1428.
[4] Commander Sir Archibald Southby, *ibid.*, 1447.

public, by a regular court, and had been acquitted. She had been immediately returned to detention. In October, 1941, her case was reconsidered by the Advisory Committee, which informed her that she was being detained on the same charges of which the court had acquitted her. In January, 1942, she was informed that she would not be released. The charge that the Home Secretary had abused his powers was disputed by several members, one of whom pointed out that when Mr. Morrison became Home Secretary in October, 1940, there had been 1,381 persons in detention under 18B, while at the end of May, 1942, there were only 546.[1]

The major grievance of several members and the Home Secretary's response to it are illustrated clearly in the following exchange:

MR. HERBERT MORRISON: The constitutional position is that I am alone responsible for the administration of the matter, and the House must deal with me. If we get into the field of the relations between the Advisory Committee and the Minister, the House will be dealing with the Advisory Committee and the Advisory Committee will be placed in very great difficulties.

SIR IRVING ALBERY: What the right hon. Gentleman has just said brings out the major part of our grievance. How can we deal with him when we have no knowledge of the evidence on which he acts or of what evidence is available?

MR. MORRISON: I quite agree that there is a difficulty. This House is not a specific court of appeal against the Home Secretary in individual cases. It cannot be, and if the House tried to be, it would find itself in difficulties. A debate in this considerable assembly as to whether Mr. X or Mrs. Y or Miss A should be released would be impossible as an operative decision. What the House must do is to keep a watch on the Home Secretary, to have a Debate, to look for cases where in their judgment he has gone wrong, if they can get evidence that he has———[Interruption.] I know the limitations of the House. I agree that it is not altogether cricket, but I cannot help it. Having watched the Home Secretary's actions and had a Debate, the House can come to a broad

[1] Mr. Ivor Thomas, *ibid.*, 1441-1442.

decision whether or not he is on the whole fairly and prudently administering the Regulations. That is what the House can do. I do not want to deceive the Committee. These are exceptional powers which are confined to an individual. That individual has a terrible responsibility and a heavy task. It is not a job I would want to run after or a job that has great pleasure in it, but I discharge it with interest and conscientiousness, knowing all the time that this exceptional authority has been given to me by Parliament and that I must be careful and restrained in its use. I do not want to boggle the issue. The only thing that the House can do is to watch the general administration and pounce on the Home Secretary if it becomes convinced that he has not discharged this responsibility. Then the House must either reduce his powers or in a perfectly clean and understandable fashion place the responsibility for decision somewhere else.[1]

Mr. Morrison said that he had considered the proposals which members had made that the Advisory Committee should have the final power to make decisions concerning detention, but had come to the conclusion that "if the Committee were executive, the Home Secretary could not be held responsible for the internal security of the country". Such a system, he added, "would not fit in with Parliamentary institutions, because the more exceptional power you give to a Minister in time of war, the more it is essential that Parliament should be the master of that Minister and that he should feel himself accountable to it for its administration".[2] With regard to the case of Mrs. Nicholson, the Home Secretary replied that he had given the case "very careful consideration," and was "satisfied that she is rightly detained".[3] The motion was defeated by a vote of 222 to 25, after a debate covering more than ninety columns of Hansard.

Another 18B detention case evoked criticism in the House of Commons in January, 1943. Thomas Wilson had been detained in April, 1940, on the ground of "acts prejudicial", and, in June, 1940, had written to the courts asking to be tried for a specific offence. An official of the Home Office had intercepted and suppressed the letter. Upon release from detention in

[1] 381 H.C. Deb. 5s., 1508-1509.
[2] Ibid., 1511.   [3] Ibid., 1508.

January, 1943, Mr. Wilson had immediately asked the King's Bench to take action against the Home Secretary for contempt of court. In a strongly worded statement, Mr. Justice Humphreys said that "one of the inalienable rights which every British subject has, when he is detained in custody . . . as the result of the opinion of a Secretary of State under . . . 18B . . . is to come to this court and ask that his case may be considered by the court". He warned that "if any case is brought before me hereafter in which any person—I care not how high his position and how great his fame—be found to have interfered with that right of one of His Majesty's subjects, I think I should have no difficulty in putting in force . . . the great powers of this King's Bench Division by imprisoning such a person for contempt of court".[1] On 21st January, 1943, two questions were put to the Home Secretary about the Home Office's action in the Wilson case, and Sir Henry Morris-Jones called the Home Secretary's attention to a motion on the Order Paper which referred to the alarm with which the House viewed "the intervention of an unnamed official at the Home Office whereby a citizen was deprived of his inalienable right of application to the court".[2] At the end of Questions, Mr. Morrison made a lengthy statement to the House, stating that the mistake had been due entirely to error in judgment, and that he did not believe any disciplinary action was necessary. He assured the House that steps had been taken to insure that a similar mistake would not recur, and apologized for the occurrence of "this grave error".[3]

A somewhat similar incident, involving the interception and suppression of a letter written by Admiral Sir Barry Domvile to the editor of *The Times*, was raised by Sir Irving Albery at Question Time on 28th January, 1943. Detainees had, from the beginning, been allowed to correspond with their families, and, since October, 1940, had been allowed to communicate with members of Parliament. The sending out of matter for publication was, the Under Secretary for the Home Department answered, quite different from the writing of letters to individuals, and Admiral Domvile's letter had been suppressed because

---

[1] Cited by Allen, *Law and Orders*, 248.

[2] 386. H.C. Deb. 5s., 285.   [3] *Ibid.*, 286-287.

"detention necessarily involves the curtailment of many activities, including propaganda activities".[1]   Sir Irving Albery expressed dissatisfaction with this answer and announced that he would raise the matter on the Adjournment as soon as possible.

Sir Barry's letter, a strong protest against regulation 18B, was the subject of the Adjournment Debate on 10th February, 1943. The debate itself wandered far from the question of Domvile's letter, and ranged over the whole area of 18B, including its administrations, conditions of detention, and the merits of Admiral Domvile's detention.   Sir Irving Albery contended that writing to the press was a basic civil liberty,[2] and Sir Archibald Southby charged that the Home Secretary's action undermined freedom of expression and opinion.[3]   Mr. Pickthorn said that 18B was the "most important subject which the House of Commons can discuss",[4] and Mr. Muff recounted his experiences in visiting detention camps.   The Under Secretary replied that the contents of Admiral Domvile's letter had nothing to do with its interception, adding that "if the letter had been nothing more than to say that Admiral Sir Barry Domvile had heard the cuckoo on 15th April, the letter would have been intercepted in exactly the same way".[5]   It would be impracticable, he said, for the Home Office to exercise a censorship over material written by detainees for publication, and therefore the decision had been made to allow no such correspondence at all.   He pointed out that the number of persons then detained under 18B was in the neighbourhood of five hundred, and that the Home Secretary was "endeavouring to release . . . every individual who can be released without danger to the state".[6]

Criticism of 18B was renewed on 15th July, 1943, on the annual debate to continue the Emergency Powers Act for another year.   Mr. Stokes questioned "whether it was ever the intention of this House that the Home Secretary would ever go against the recommendations of the Advisory Committee",[7] and Mr. Pickthorn contended that detention under 18B was "an infinitely worse fate than death."[8]   Much of the discussion centred around

---

[1] *Ibid.*, 599.
[2] *Ibid.*, 1378.
[3] *Ibid.*, 1382.
[4] *Ibid.*, 1390.
[5] *Ibid.*, 1404.
[6] *Ibid.*, 1403.
[7] 391 H.C. Deb. 5s., 454.
[8] *Ibid.*, 462

the difficulties which 18B detainees encountered when seeking employment after release, since their detention was recorded on their identity cards, and thus a stigma remained with them.[1] The Home Secretary reported that there were, on 30th June, 1943, only 429 persons in detention, as compared with 529 on 30th June, 1942. Of the 429, 286 were detained because of hostile origins or associations, 55 for acts prejudicial, and 88 because of membership in the British Union. Since 18B had been instituted, the Home Secretary told the House, he had accepted the recommendation of the Advisory Committee in ninety-five per cent of the cases. In sixty-one cases he had declined to follow the Committee's recommendation for release and in seventeen cases he had ordered release against the recommendation of the Committee.[2]

By the end of September, 1943, the Home Secretary was able to report that sixty-four persons had been released between the middle of July and the end of September, thereby leaving 364 persons still in detention.[3]

Perhaps the strongest popular and parliamentary outcry over 18B developed in November, 1943, over the release of Sir Oswald and Lady Mosley. The parliamentary background of this event is worth noting, since it explains to some extent the heatedness of the reaction to the Mosleys' release, and indicates also that party considerations had become involved in Parliament's appraisal of the regulation and its administration. Opposition to the original form of 18B had been voiced by members of all parties, and Mr. Herbert Morrison had strongly attacked the original regulation.[4] After the formation of the Coalition Government and Mr. Morrison's appointment to the Home Office, however, parliamentary criticism of 18B tended to come mostly from Conservative members. While a few Labour members, notably Mr. Richard Stokes and Mr. Sydney Silverman, initiated and supported criticism of the regulation and its administration, the bulk of criticism came from Conservatives such as Sir Archibald Southby, Earl Winterton, Commander Bower, Sir Irving Albery, Mr. Boothby, and Mr. Pickthorn. This group of members had shown considerable interest in the detentions of such persons as

[1] Mr. Boothby, *ibid.*, 471.   [2] *Ibid.*, 501–502.
[3] 392 H.C. Deb. 5s., 1033.   [4] See p. 37.

Captain Ramsay, Admiral Domvile, and Mrs. Nicholson. As the number of releases of 18B detainees was greatly increased after Morrison's assumption of the Home Secretaryship, some members of the Labour Party appeared to believe that Morrison was being unduly influenced by Conservative pressure in Parliament.[1] Other Labour members apparently believed that Morrison was being unduly attacked by some of the Conservatives, and thought it was their duty to rally to his support.[2] As will be noted at a later stage of this study, the Coalition had become restless by 1943, and party differences were beginning to show themselves. It was into this atmosphere of increasing party tension that the Mosley affair broke.

Sir Oswald Mosley, leader of the British Union of Fascists, and his wife had been among the first to be detained under 18B. Mosley had suffered from recurrent attacks of phlebitis during his detention. In June, 1943, his condition became aggravated, and in November of that year a medical board, made up of the Medical Commissioner of Prisons, two prison medical officers, and two outside specialists (Dr. Geoffrey Evans and Lord Dawson of Penn), reported to the Home Secretary that "if Sir Oswald Mosley remains under conditions of prison life there will be substantial risk of the Thrombo-phlebitis extending and thus producing permanent damage to health and even danger to life."[3] After weighing the security factors, the Home Secretary decided to act upon the medical opinion, and, while Parliament was in recess, he ordered the release of the Mosleys. His action precipitated a storm of protest in the country which was reflected in the House of Commons.

Dr. Haden Guest (Labour) laid the groundwork for the

---

[1] Mr. Tom Driberg, M.P., wrote: "Recent releases follow a revived Parliamentary clamour by Tories of the extreme Right; but Morrison would no doubt claim that he is guided rather by the change in the military situation. . . . It is noteworthy that these gentlemen have only agitated on behalf of upper-class detainees; nobody bothers about the wretched little East End shopkeeper whose head may have been turned by Fascist propaganda because he has had an unfortunate experience with some Jewish business rival." *New Statesman and Nation*, XXVI (14th August, 1943), 101.

[2] On the motion to reduce the Home Secretary's salary, 21st July, 1942, Morrison had been defended by some Labour back-benchers. Another indication of this attitude may be seen from the following statement which Mr. McGovern (ILP) made on 16th June, 1944: "I regret that there is a tendency on the part of a number of Members to look at a question of this kind from the point of view of who is the Minister who is being assailed, instead of from that of the principle. One hears Labour Members saying, 'We must defend Morrison.' But Morrison is not being challenged as Morrison, or as a member of the Labour Party. He is being challenged as a member of the Executive. . . ." (400 H.C. Deb. 5s., 2357.)

[3] Herbert Morrison, *Prospects and Policies* (New York: Alfred A. Knopf, 1944), 126.

parliamentary discussion of the case by asking the Home Secretary, at Question Time on 23rd November, 1943, why the Mosleys had been released, since there were adequate medical services available to detainees. Mr. Morrison replied that Britain's national fortunes had improved to such an extent that it had been possible to release several former members of the British Union, but that he would not have released Sir Oswald Mosley merely on that basis. The additional factor which had led him to his decision was eminent medical opinion that continued detention would endanger Mosley's life. Adequate control was being exercised over Mosley; he was, among other things, forbidden to travel more than seven miles from his country house, was required to report in person to the police once a month, and was forbidden to engage in political activity, write for publication, or to associate with former members of the British Union.[1] Mr. Shinwell (Labour) asked for a general debate on Mosley's release in view of its effect on public opinion, and Mr. Attlee announced that the Government would provide time for such a debate if there was general interest.

The Prime Minister had anticipated that Mosley's release would raise controversy.[2] In spite of the fact that differences arose in the Cabinet over Morrison's decision, Mr. Churchill assured the Home Secretary of his full support,[3] and advised him to make his case before Parliament in terms of "health and humanity" and "the great principle of *habeas corpus* and trial by jury, which are the supreme protection invented by the British people for ordinary individuals against the State".[4] By the time the parliamentary storm broke, the Prime Minister was in Cairo, conferring with President Roosevelt and Chiang Kai-shek. The demands of strategic global planning, however, did not prevent his keeping in touch with Morrison on the Mosley affair.[5] While at Teheran, Churchill learned from Attlee that the Cabinet had

[1] 392 H.C. Deb. 5s., 1431.
[2] Winston S. Churchill, *Closing the Ring* (Boston: Houghton Mifflin Co., 1951), 679.
[3] *Ibid.*, 680.   [4] *Ibid.*, 679.
[5] Mr. Churchill, from Cairo, sent the following memorandum to Morrison on 25th November, 1943: "In case there is a debate on an amendment to the Address to terminate 18B, I would strongly counsel the line that we very much regret having to be responsible for such powers, which we fully admit are contrary to the whole spirit of British public life and British history. These powers were conferred on us by Parliament because of the dire peril of the State, and we have to administer them in accordance with the principles of humanity,

[*Continued overleaf*

agreed to support Morrison's decision, and was informed also that Parliament was considerably agitated.[1] From Teheran, on 29th November, 1943, the Prime Minister counselled Morrison that "considering you are supported by the Cabinet, and by me as Prime Minister, you have no choice whatever but to fight the matter through" and predicted that the Home Secretary would "no doubt be supported in any direct issue by a very large majority".[2]

The fourth day of the Debate on the Address, 1st December, 1943, was allocated to the release of the Mosleys, and an amendment to the Address was laid down which regretted "the decision of your Majesty's advisers to release Sir Oswald Mosley, which is calculated to retard the war effort and lead to misunderstanding at home and abroad." The debate, which covered eighty-three columns of Hansard, centred around the effect that the release was having on public opinion. It was charged that the Home Secretary's action had created "scepticism and cynicism,"[3] a "deep revulsion of feeling on the part of people of all kinds . . . classes and political parties,"[4] and "a considerable amount of feeling which doubts the *bona fides* of the Government as a whole in their onslaught upon Fascism."[5] Mosley's release had led to the feeling that there was "one law for the rich and another for the poor,"[6] and no subject "for many months has raised more agitation."[7]

In response to these criticisms, the Home Secretary reiterated

---

but all the time we desire to give back these powers from the Executive to Parliament. The fact that we have gained great victories and are in a much safer position makes the Government the more desirous of parting with exceptional powers. The time has not yet come when these can be fully dispensed with, but we can look forward to that day.

"On no account should we lend any countenance to the totalitarian idea of the right of the Executive to lock up its political opponents or unpopular people. The door should be kept open for the full restoration of the fundamental British rights of *habeas corpus* and trial by jury on charges known to the law. I must warn you that departure from these broad principles because the Home Office have a few people they like to keep under control by exceptional means may become a source of very grave difference between us and the totalitarian-minded folk. In such a quarrel I am sure I could carry the majority in the House of Commons and the mass of the nation. Anyhow, I would try. It seems to me you have a perfectly good line in deploring the fact that such powers are thrust on you and in proclaiming your resolve to use them with the utmost circumspection and humanity. Do not quit the heights." Churchill, *Closing the Ring*, 680.

[1] *Ibid.*, 841.　　　　　　　　　　[2] *Ibid.*

[3] Mr. Parker, 395 H.C. Deb. 5s., 403.

[4] Mr. Greenwood, *ibid.*, 455.

[5] Mr. Moelwyn Hughes, *ibid.*, 413.

[6] Mr. Woods, *ibid.*, 398.

[7] Sir Percy Harris, *ibid.*, 418.

his acceptance of outstanding medical opinion as the basis of his action, but admitted that he "could have handled it better from what one might call the public relations angle."[1] Hitting back at some of the previous criticism he had received concerning the administration of 18B, Mr. Morrison stated:

> If you say that I am to administer this Regulation as a politician, that I am to keep this man in because I hate him or disagree with him, and that I am to let the other man out because I have sympathy with him—and that is, you know, the argument behind this—Sir, if the House of Commons wants that done, it will kindly proceed to frame the Regulation under which it can be done, and I wish it luck in framing it, and if it is to be a principle of our administration that the Home Secretary has to release or detain according to opinion and according to likes and dislikes, or according to mobs, then I say that even though the House of Commons gives me that power, it can find another Home Secretary. I will not do the job in such a way. There is too much of a party political element in the desires about the administration of this Regulation, too much of the unjudicial, and a bit of mob hysteria.[2]

The Home Secretary indicated that he was "a bit hurt" by Mr. Arthur Greenwood's suggestion that his decision in the Mosley case had been influenced by social considerations, and said that he did "not give twopence for the influence of the upper classes."[3]

"If you want 18B administered in such a way . . . that I must be indifferent to the health, or even the death, of a detainee," Mr. Morrison concluded, "I say to my critics . . . let them draft . . . either an amendment to the Defence Regulations or an amendment to the law that will give me the necessary directions".[4] The amendment to the Address was defeated, 327 to 62, and Mr. Churchill, from Teheran, sent Mr. Morrison his congratulations, saying that "your courageous and humane discharge of

---

[1] Mr. Herbert Morrison, *ibid.*, 465.

[2] Morrison, *op. cit.*, 124.

[3] *Ibid.*, 130.

[4] 395 H.C. Deb. 5s., 469.

your most difficult and disagreeable functions will gain its reward in the respect of the British nation."[1]

Critical sentiment concerning the administration of 18B persisted in the House during 1944. In February, two motions, one urging general reconsideration of the regulation and the other calling for the establishment of a judicial tribunal to determine "reasonable cause" were put forward, and the Government was repeatedly asked to assign time for a consideration of the proposals.[2] On 13th June the Leader of the House announced that a day for a debate on both proposals would be made available in Committee of Supply. The debate, which took place on 16th June, 1944, and which covered 101 columns of Hansard, was on the motion for a reconsideration of 18B "with a view to the . . . transfer to a judicial tribunal . . . [of] final responsibility for determining whether there is reasonable cause for detention".[3] The gist of the criticism was, again, that the Advisory Committee constituted no safeguard and that, in individual cases, the House had no effective control over the Minister. The Home Secretary once more stressed his responsibility to the House, and again reminded members that the only way for the exceptional powers of 18B to be administered was "to place the responsibility fairly on the shoulders of the Minister, hold him accountable to Parliament, [and] watch him with care." The system was, he admitted, "not 100 per cent foolproof," but was the best guarantee the House could have under the circumstances.[4] He revealed that, on 31st May, 1944, there were 226 persons detained under 18B, and that there had been only seven new detentions since July, 1943, as compared with 210 releases.[5] The motion was defeated, 135 votes to 31.

On 26th September, 1944, the Home Secretary informed the House of his decision to release Captain Ramsay from detention. Because of the success of the armies of the United Nations, Mr. Morrison said, he believed that it was legitimate to undertake the risk that Ramsay might "be tempted again to engage in

---

[1] Churchill, *Closing the Ring*, 681. Mr. Churchill ends his discussion of the Mosley affair by saying that "people who are not prepared to do unpopular things and to defy clamour are not fit to be Ministers in times of stress."

[2] Mr. Pickthorn, 3rd February, 1944, 396 H.C. Deb. 5s., 1411; Sir A. Southby, 16th March, 1944, 398 H.C. Deb. 5s., 405; Mr. Manningham-Buller, 20th April, 1944, 399 H.C. Deb. 5s., 377.

[3] 400 H.C. Deb. 5s., 2317.

[4] *Ibid.*, 2390-2391.   [5] *Ibid.*, 2380.

irresponsible and mischievous activities,"[1] and therefore Captain Ramsay was being unconditionally released. Mr. Morrison indicated that circumstances were not sufficiently propitious to release all of those who had been detained under 18B for hostile origin or associations or for acts prejudicial, but he told the House that a new review of all detentions had been undertaken, and that all except fourteen of those detained because of membership in the British Union had been released.[2] The announcement of Ramsay's release evoked hostile comment from a few Labour members, and Mr. Gallacher (Communist) was ordered to withdraw from the remainder of the day's sitting because of his refusal to retract remarks about his newly-released colleague which were deemed "unparliamentary" by the Speaker. Mr. Leach, however, told the Home Secretary that many members were satisfied with his "courageous interpretation of and his rightful exercise of his powers under 18B."[3]

The short discussion of Captain Ramsay's release marks the end of parliamentary discussion of 18B during war-time. In June, 1944, the Allied invasion of Normandy had taken place; in August, Paris had been liberated, and in September the American First Army had crossed the German frontier. As the prospect of early German defeat became clear, the release of persons detained under 18B was accelerated, and by early November, less than one hundred persons remained in detention.[4] On 8th May, 1945, President Truman and Prime Minister Churchill proclaimed the end of the war in Europe, and on 9th May, Mr. Morrison told the House of Commons that 18B had been that day revoked by Order-in-Council and that he had authorized the immediate release of all persons still detained under the regulation.[5]

Thus, after a life of some five-and-a-half years, one of the most severe restrictions upon traditional British liberties came to an end. From its inception to its demise, 18B was never popular. The constant criticism and vigilance exhibited by the House of Commons with regard to the regulation and its administration reflected the anxiety which the general public experienced in contemplating the drastic powers which had been entrusted in

---

[1] 403 H.C. Deb. 5s., 42.
[2] Ibid., 43.
[3] Ibid., 48.
[4] 404 H.C. Deb. 5s., 951-952.
[5] 410 H.C. Deb. 5s., 1909.

18B to the executive. Almost every member shared Sir John Mellor's sentiment that 18B "was accepted by Parliament as an unpleasant, disagreeable, inevitable necessity in time of war".[1] Members of Parliament took seriously their function as guardian of "surrendered liberties." While it is true that some partisanship entered into parliamentary discussions of the administration of the regulation[2]—that some members of the Conservative Party appeared to show undue concern for some of the more affluent or socially eminent persons detained, and that some Labour members appeared to permit their hostility to political Rightism to colour their judgment of the same individuals, as seen especially in the Mosley and Ramsay cases—the wide margins of support which the Home Secretary received each time the administration of 18B was challenged indicated that the great majority of members believed that the regulation was necessary and was being applied fairly by both Sir John Anderson and Mr. Morrison. Neither Home Secretary had an easy task. To Sir John, in the dark days of the early summer of 1940 when German invasion seemed imminent, fell the task of ordering the bulk of the detentions made under the regulation. To Mr. Morrison, called upon to administer the regulation for almost four-and-a-half years after the imminent threat of invasion had passed, fell the job of providing for state security in the face of constant parliamentary nudging which sometimes seemed to grasp insufficiently the nature of the constitutional problem involved.

By and large Parliament took a reasonable and constitutionally-sensible attitude towards 18B. Nevertheless, many of the debates indicated that some members, by their insistence that the ultimate decision as to whether or not a person should be detained should be entrusted either to the courts or to the Advisory Committee, betrayed a lack of appreciation not only of the basic

---

[1] 414 H.C. Deb. 5s., 2125.

[2] An element of partisanship also entered into Cabinet discussions of the regulation. Mr. Churchill wrote to Mr. Morrison on 12th January, 1941: "I do not see why, if Mosley is confined, subversives and Communists should not be equally confined. The law and the regulations ought to be enforced against those who hamper our war effort, whether from the extreme Right or the extreme Left. That is the position which the Conservative Party adopt, and I think it is a very strong one, and one which the country as a whole would approve. I know it is your wish to enforce an even justice and if you bring the matter before the Cabinet I am sure you will receive full support. 'Sauce for the goose is sauce for the gander.'" *The Grand Alliance* (Boston: Houghton Mifflin Co., 1950), 724-725.

assumptions of parliamentary government but also of the nature of the powers which 18B encompassed. The power contained in 18B was the very drastic power which every constitutional state must have when it finds itself in such dire straits that its survival is imminently threatened—the power to forearm itself against the commission of sabotage and other acts prejudicial to national security by detaining those persons believed by those responsible for the national welfare and survival to be likely to engage in such activities. The purpose of detention is preventive. The basis upon which such detentions are ordered—suspicion and reasonable belief—is not similar to the type of evidence which is necessary for conviction in a court of law, and, therefore, as British courts have recognized in both World Wars, it is not possible for the judiciary to review the reasonableness of the executive's exercise of a discretionary, political power to detain persons when such detention is deemed, by the political branches of the government, to be necessary in the face of pressing public danger.[1] Critics of the *Liversidge v. Anderson* decision "did not always appreciate that it was Parliament which had expressly created the power of the executive to intern suspects without trial

---

[1] My belief is that the position taken by the British courts on this point is the correct one. I am aware that there is a considerable amount of contrary opinion, especially in American legal and judicial expressions. Nevertheless, American courts have not, in actual time of war, affirmed such contrary opinion except in one instance, and it is noteworthy that, in that instance, the Supreme Court was unable to apply it successfully. (*Ex parte Merryman*, Fed. Case No. 9487, 1861.) The ringing defences of the judicial right to pass upon the reasonableness of military action in detaining citizens in time of war, as expressed in *Ex parte Milligan* (4 Wallace 2, 18 L. Ed. 281 [1866]) and in *Duncan v. Kahanamoku* (327 U.S. 304 [1946]) were delivered after the fighting had ceased.

The attitude of the British courts has been, moreover, substantially supported by Mr. Justice Holmes's opinion in *Moyer v. Peabody* (212 U.S. 78 [1909]). Professor Charles Fairman has contended, however, that *Moyer v. Peabody* does not state the prevailing American view, and that "it is of the very essence of the rule of law that the executive's *ipse dixit* is not of itself conclusive of the necessity." (See "The Law of Martial Rule and the National Emergency," *Harvard Law Review*, LV [1942], 1272.) Fairman believes that *Moyer v. Peabody* was correctly "toned down" by Chief Justice Hughes in *Sterling v. Constantin* (287 U.S. 378 [1932]). (See Charles Fairman, *American Constitutional Decisions* [Rev. ed.; New York: Henry Holt & Co., 1950], 290.)

Nevertheless, American experience in connection with the internment of Japanese-Americans in World War II is more instructive of the realities of preventive detention than is the citing of decisions rendered in the calm aftermath of hostilities or in the peace-time circumstances of industrial strife. The constitutional question of the ability of the political branches of government to order the detention by the military of American citizens of Japanese ancestry was side-stepped by the Court in *Hirabayashi v. U.S.* (320 U.S. 81 [1943]), and in *Korematsu v. U.S.* (323 U.S. 214 [1944]). These decisions, according to Professor Edward S. Corwin, "go beyond the doctrine of the minority in Milligan's case, that Congress may in time of war authorize martial law, for while they in effect concede this, they prettify the concession by further permitting Congress to throw over martial law the sanctifying aegis of civil authority" (*Total War and the Constitution* [New York: Alfred A. Knopf, 1942], 98).

In addition, the Court refused to examine the relocation programme, in the light of military necessity, saying, per Mr. Chief Justice Stone in *Hirabayashi v. U.S.* (320 U.S. 81 [1943], at 102) that it was "enough that circumstances within the knowledge of those charged

[Continued overleaf

during the period of the war".[1]   Regulation 18B was, as Mr. Morrison informed the House, not "classical liberalism at all," but "state security." Some members of Parliament, however, had difficulty in appreciating the distinction.[2]

The constitutional issue of ministerial responsibility was also inadequately appreciated by those members who pressed for the Advisory Committee's assuming executive functions. Under the doctrine of ministerial responsibility, the Home Secretary was accountable for home security, and he could not share that responsibility with others who were not accountable to the House of Commons. Had the Home Secretary been forced by Parliament to act upon the recommendation of the Advisory Committee (or the courts), and had an 18B detainee, released upon such advice, then committed an act of sabotage, the Home Secretary would, nevertheless, have remained responsible, and, would, in all likelihood, have lost his job for having been negligent in providing for internal security. Hence, Mr. Morrison, who was strongly aware of his constitutional responsibility, occasionally became impatient with the apparent inability of some members to grasp the full implications of the concept of ministerial responsibility.

An additional factor, however, caused Mr. Morrison to guard jealously his prerogatives under 18B.   Recognizing the violence

---

with the responsibility for maintaining the national defence afforded a rational basis for the decisions which they made," and that whether the Court would have made the same decision was "irrelevant" while the Court, in *Ex parte Endo*, (323 U.S. 298 [1944]), held that Miss Endo, an American citizen whose loyalty was conceded by the War Relocation Authority, could not be detained in a relocation centre, it is significant to note, as Professor Corwin has pointed out, that "the right of the authority to detain Japanese-Americans whose loyalty was not yet established (to whose satisfaction is not indicated) was . . . inferentially conceded" (*Total War and the Constitution*, 99).

In the light of the Court's inability, in actual time of war, to perform those functions which its peace-time pronouncements promise, the following words of Mr. Justice Jackson, dissenting in *Korematsu v. U.S.*, reveal a realistic appraisal which is worth much consideration: "But I would not lead people to rely on this court for a review that seems to me wholly delusive. The military reasonableness of these orders can only be determined by the military superiors. If the people ever let command of the war power fall into irresponsible hands, the courts wield no power equal to its restraint. The chief restraint upon those who command the physical forces of the country, in the future as in the past, must be their responsibilities to the political judgments of their contemporaries and to the moral judgments of history." (323 U.S. 214 [1944], at 248.)

[1] Sir Cecil T. Carr, "A Regulated Liberty," *Columbia Law Review*, XLII (March, 1942), 353.

[2] Some British lawyers have also shared this difficulty. C. K. Allen, for example, is perturbed that "responsible persons and journals have justified all the severities of Regulation 18B as 'acts of war'—a doctrine which implies that England has lived for five years under martial law and which betrays a significant decay of constitutional principles. The notion that because a country is at war it has the right to conduct 'acts of war' on its own citizens is something never before heard of in our history." (*Law and Orders*, 250-251.)

done by the drastic powers contained in the regulation to the tradition of *habeas corpus*, and recognizing also the unpopularity of the regulation, the Prime Minister had never been fond of it. As early as December, 1940, Mr. Churchill indicated that, while he believed that the public danger justified 18B, he thought that the danger was receding.[1] In November, 1941, he informed the Home Secretary that, in view of the strong feeling against 18B, he would "not be prepared to support the regulation indefinitely if it is administered in such a very onerous manner."[2] As time progressed, Mr. Churchill became even more outspoken. On 25th November, 1943, the Prime Minister wrote to Mr. Morrison: "I am convinced 18B should be completely abolished. . . . However, as these views conflict with the line you have adopted I shall not press them at this stage".[3] On the basis of this and other evidence,[4] it would appear that Mr. Morrison was the leading Cabinet proponent of the retention of 18B. Mr. Morrison had given much thought to the problem of what a constitutional democracy must do to preserve itself in times of crisis and had studied the history of Weimar Germany with great interest. At the Annual Meeting of the Society of Labour Candidates, on 26th October, 1941, he told his audience that "the greatest trouble with the Weimar Republic was the weakness of the democratic leadership, the feebleness of the parliamentary institutions and the unwillingness of Governments to govern." His development of this theme sheds interesting light on his attitude towards 18B:

> Because the German Governments of that period were afraid to govern, political confusion extended and constitutional government and liberty went down under an illegal assault from quarters which should never have been permitted to become so menacing. So it has been in other countries where governments were soft with Fascist fifth-column elements. Country after country has found itself stabbed from

---

[1] Churchill, *Their Finest Hour*, 703.

[2] Churchill, *The Grand Alliance*, 835.

[3] Churchill, *Closing the Ring*, 680.

[4] "Mr. Morrison was so completely convinced of the strength of his case that he would not be willing to continue in office without the powers originally granted to Sir John Anderson. . . ." H. R. G. Greaves, "Parliament in Wartime," *Political Quarterly*, XIII (January-March, 1942), 87.

behind because their governments were not willing to face up to the necessity of denying liberty of action to those who were determined to use that liberty of action for the purpose of destroying liberty altogether . . . I shall be as delighted as anybody else when the day comes that Defence Regulation 18B and others can be dropped. But I warn the country against the efforts of certain reactionary elements—helped at times quite unconsciously by progressives—to spread the idea that, even in the face of our enemies' fifth-column techniques, we can afford to be without emergency powers, or that if we have them we should not use them. That view is, to say the least of it, a great mistake. It was just such combinations of reactionaries on the one hand, and well-meaning but rather foolish people who thought they were upholding liberty on the other, that led to the ruthless destruction of liberty in Germany . . . Britain must not go the way of the Continental victims of Nazi fifth-column activity.[1]

Thus, the lessons which Mr. Morrison believed he had learned from Weimar, added to his strong sense of the constitutional responsibility of ministers, caused him to withstand much of the pressure and many of the suggestions put forward by Parliament and the Prime Minister for modification or abandonment of 18B.

Regulation 18B was administered under the continuous scrutiny of the House of Commons, and parliamentary criticism achieved considerable success in causing the executive to correct abuses which occurred in the exercise of the regulation. Perhaps the most striking example of parliamentary influence was the success which the House of Commons achieved in securing, in the autumn of 1939, a modification in the wording of the original regulation. While the new form of the regulation did not succeed in securing judicial review of the Home Secretary's actions (although, on the basis of available evidence, this was apparently the intent of some of the members who participated in its framing), parliamentary action on that occasion undoubtedly impressed upon the Home Secretary the House's deep concern over the regulation. The parliamentary protest against the three-month delays between detention and hearing which ensued after the

[1] Morrison, *op. cit.*, 120-121.

large-scale detentions in the summer of 1940 resulted in remedial action by the Home Office. Similarly, Parliament's demonstration of concern for the conditions of detention caused the Government to take hasty action to improve the welfare and comfort of detainees. A joint parliamentary-judicial growling over the interception by the Home Office of a detainee's appeal for a writ of *habeas corpus* led the Home Secretary to apologize to the House for the incident and to take steps to prevent a recurrence.

All of the foregoing represent rather clear-cut instances of the success of parliamentary criticism based upon significant and well-founded grievances. In assessing the role of Parliament, however, it seems necessary to note the relative paucity of abuses and grievances which accrued from the exercise of the great powers of 18B. Considering the proximity of Great Britain to actual theatres of military operations, the imminence of German invasion in 1940, and, later, the crucial role of Britain in the mounting of the Allied invasion of the continent, it is noteworthy that the total number of detention orders made under 18B was 1,857.[1] During the first three years of the war, detention orders were made against 1,816 persons,[2] of whom 1,335 were detained in May, June, and July of 1940.[3] It seems likely that, under the grave stress of conditions immediately following the fall of France, something less than meticulous attention may have been directed towards individual detentions. Nevertheless, by August, 1942, 1,301 persons had been released,[4] and with improvements in British national fortunes, the number of persons in detention dwindled appreciably. Each of the detainees was accorded an opportunity to appear before the Advisory Committee, and it has been reported that Mr. Morrison "himself repeatedly scrutinized every dossier of every individual brought to his attention under Regulation 18B".[5] Hence, the contention that detentions under 18B were characterized by "recklessness"[6] is not substantiated by the evidence.

---

[1] 414 H.C. Deb. 5s., 2130.
[2] 414 H.C. Deb. 5s., 2130.
[3] 381 H.C. Deb. 5s., 1516-1517.
[4] 414 H.C. Deb. 5s., 2130.
[5] Maurice Edelman, *Herbert Morrison* (London: Lincolns-Prager Publishers Ltd., 1948), 60.
[6] Allen, *Law and Orders*, 241.

Writing several years before World War II, Professor Laski stated that he knew of "no case where the state [had] exercised extraordinary power outside of the normal process of law in which that power [had] not been grossly abused." In a later war-time edition of the book, however, Laski noted in a footnote to the above sentence that "the war of 1939 [had] provided a notable exception to this judgment of 1930" in that Mr. Herbert Morrison had exercised special powers in the domestic field "with great imaginative wisdom".[1] If it is admitted that 18B was administered well and that abuses in its exercise were minimal, much of the credit must go to Parliament. The knowledge that many members of Parliament focused their attention on 18B and its administration caused Sir John Anderson and, later, Mr. Morrison to administer the regulation with the greatest circumspection. It was, above all, the day-to-day confrontation with vigilant members of Parliament which caused the Home Secretary to be sensitive to their grievances and to be mindful of his daily responsibility to the House of Commons. An awareness that a vigilant legislature was ready and eager to do daily battle in the interests of the principle of individual liberty forced the Government to limit its activities to those required by necessity alone, and prevented the Government from utilizing the criterion of convenience or from wandering from the rigid confines to which Parliament expected adherence.

The history of 18B is instructive. The high stakes for which modern wars are fought have cultivated the perfection of the techniques of sabotage and subversion, and modern states, if they seek to survive, must act to ward off fifth-column activities. When war has actively begun, or when the threat of it is imminent, it is necessary for constitutional states to practice preventive detention against those whom the responsible authorities believe might engage in such activities. Since those detained will have committed no crime, they cannot be tried in a court of law. Courts can honour applications for the writ of *habeas corpus* and can examine whether or not detentions have been made in accordance with the statutory requirements. Both British and American experience in World War II, however, reveal that courts will

---

[1] Harold J. Laski, *Liberty in the Modern State* (revised edition, New York: Viking Press, 1946), 90.

not challenge the discretionary judgments of the executive which the legislature has authorized.

To prevent discretionary power from becoming arbitrary power, even in war-time, is the task of the constitutional state. Discretionary power need not be arbitrary power and may be exercised in a constitutional manner if there are regularized restraints upon the wielders of power and if the Government is responsible to the governed. When courts are unable to provide an effective restraint upon executive power, the legislature must step forward to assume the task. The British legislature appreciated its function, and performed it with diligence. Parliament was the restraint upon those who administered the great powers of 18B, for it was to Parliament that the Government was accountable. The most important consideration, however, was that Parliament never permitted the Government to forget this fact.

CHAPTER IV

PARLIAMENT AND CIVIL LIBERTIES IN WAR-TIME

WHILE the detention of individuals without judicial trial, authorized by Regulation 18B, was perhaps the most severe limitation which emergency powers placed upon civil liberties in war-time Britain, the Government, faced generally with the nature of modern war, and, more particularly, with the imminence of enemy invasion, imposed other significant restrictions upon traditional British liberties. Parliament was, in consequence, forced to extend its scrutiny over a wide range of governmental activities which touched upon some of the most basic liberties of the individual.

Under the broad powers granted by the Emergency Powers (Defence) Act, the Government thought it necessary to make several regulations limiting freedom of discussion. Restrictions upon freedom of discussion were necessary, according to the Government, in the first place, in order to prevent useful information from reaching the enemy, and, in the second place, in order to curtail the expression of certain opinions believed likely to undermine public morale. The need for some sort of censorship, especially concerning military matters, was generally recognized and accepted. Concern was shown, however, over the restrictions upon opinion. Among the first batch of regulations laid before the House in October, 1939, were several which made inroads into the free expression of opinion. By Regulation 39A it became an offence to attempt to cause disaffection among persons in the armed forces. Under Regulation 39B(1) it was an offence to endeavour "to influence" public opinion in a manner likely to be prejudicial to the defence of the realm or to the efficient prosecution of the war. Regulation 39B(2) empowered the Secretary of State to prevent or restrict the publication of matters which might be prejudicial to the defence of the realm, and Regulation 39B(3) stated that any person who had offended against censorship provisions could be forbidden to publish any newspaper in the

United Kingdom. The National Council for Civil Liberties immediately warned that Regulation 39B was capable of very grave abuse and was especially likely to be misinterpreted with regard to pacifist activities. In the first few weeks of the existence of the regulation there developed more than forty cases of police intimidation against pacifist organizations, in which the police stated that they believed such propaganda was an offence under the regulation. The National Council for Civil Liberties presented information on these cases to Mr. Attlee, the Leader of the Opposition, on 31st October, 1939.[1] The prayer of Mr. Dingle Foot on 31st October, 1939, which has been mentioned above in connection with Regulation 18B,[2] was also directed against these regulations. Sir Stafford Cripps asked the Home Secretary if it would be creating "disaffection" under Regulation 39A by telling soldiers that the allowance for their families was not sufficient and the Home Secretary replied that it might be so.[3] The Home Secretary's statement that the Attorney-General was to judge offences under Regulation 39B was challenged by Sir Stafford, who contended that the question of what is likely to be prejudicial to the defence of the realm was of a political nature, and therefore not one for the Attorney-General to decide.[4] Mr. Bevan suggested that a recent broadcast of the Archbishop of Canterbury in which he inveighed against evacuation might be an offence against Regulation 39B,[5] and Mr. Attlee summed up most criticism by pointing out that it was the generality and extensiveness of the regulations that caused alarm among members.[6] The Home Secretary promised that the Government would consider the insertion of limiting words in the regulations to bring them into accord with the sentiments of the House, and the revision of the regulations was referred to an all-party conference.

As a result of the conference, substantial modification of the original regulations was achieved. The phrase "seduce from duty" replaced the more ambiguous words "cause disaffection" in Regulation 39A.[7] Regulation 39B(1) was modified so that

[1] Ronald Kidd, *British Liberty in Danger* (London: Lawrence and Wishart, 1941), 217-218.
[2] See pp. 37-38.
[3] 352 H.C. Deb. 5s., 1868.
[4] *Ibid.*, 1892-1893.
[5] *Ibid.*, 1873.
[6] *Ibid.*, 1870.
[7] S.R. & O., 1939, No. 1681, I, 811.

propaganda was no longer an offence unless carried on "by means of any false statement, false document, or false report." It was also stipulated that the accused person might plead in defence that he had "reasonable cause to believe that the statement, document, or report was true." The effect of the amendment was "to draw a distinction between a statement of an unpopular *opinion* and the mis-statement of actual *fact*."[1] The general powers of censorship under Regulation 39B(2) were abolished by the new regulations of 23rd November, 1939. Instead, the Home Secretary was authorized to censor the publication of matter which might be prejudicial to the good relations of the United Kingdom with foreign countries or to any transactions contemplated between the Government of the United Kingdom and persons in other countries.[2] This modification resulted only in the censorship by the War Office of outgoing mails. Regulation 39B(3) was entirely abolished by the new regulations.

From the end of November, 1939, then, there was no general censorship in Great Britain. A system of voluntary censorship was established under Regulation 3, however. By the terms of this regulation, it was an offence to obtain, publish, or possess information relating to certain subject matters (principally military) or information "which would or might be directly or indirectly useful to an enemy." The regulation further provided, however, that a person should not be guilty of an offence against the regulation "in respect of anything done by him if he proves that it was done under any authority or permission granted by or on behalf of His Majesty."[3] Thus no prior restraints on publication existed, although newspapers might be prosecuted in courts of law for violating the provisions of Regulation 3. In practice, most editors submitted news stories about which there might be doubts for prior approval.[4]

An incident in the first days of the war indicated the concern which Parliament showed for the freedom of the press. On the evening of 11th September, 1939 (more exactly, in the early hours of 12th September), police, under orders from the Ministry of

---

[1] Kidd, *op. cit.*, 219.

[2] S.R. & O., 1939, No. 1681, I, 811.

[3] S.R. & O., 1940, No. 384, II, 13.

[4] Kidd, *op. cit.*, 220.

Information, began to seize all issues of morning papers carrying the news that British troops had landed in France. The news, which had been broadcast by the Paris Radio, had been approved for publication by the War Office on the evening of 11th September. Before midnight, however, the Ministry of Information withdrew approval, and the police were dispatched to confiscate all newspapers carrying the announcement. At 2.55 a.m. the Ministry of Information issued a new statement authorizing publication of the news of the landing of the British troops.[1] On 13th September, during a general debate on the war situation, Mr. Arthur Greenwood, the acting Leader of the Opposition, raised the matter in the House of Commons, terming it "a completely intolerable situation," "not intelligent censorship," and an "extraordinary example of crass stupidity and vacillation."[2] Sir Archibald Sinclair, Leader of the Parliamentary Liberal Party, thought the incident was "a shocking muddle",[3] and a debate ensued which complained of the operations of the Ministry of Information and of restrictions on news issued to the press. Sir Samuel Hoare, Lord Privy Seal, replying for the Government, apologized for the "misunderstanding" and promised that a similar incident would never recur.[4]

Until May, 1940, the British press operated only under the system of voluntary censorship which resulted from Regulation 3. Restrictions were imposed only on factual material likely to be of value to the enemy. On 9th May, 1940, however, the Home Secretary, Sir John Anderson, announced that a new group of defence regulations had been made which were "designed to check the spread of propaganda calculated to undermine the resolution of the people to prosecute the war to a successful issue."[5] Under one of the new regulations, 2c, the systematic publication of matter calculated, in the opinion of the Home Secretary, to foment opposition to the war became an offence. Any newspaper considered guilty of such publication should first be warned by the Home Secretary. If such publication were persisted in, the Government should prosecute the newspaper

[1] See Francis Williams, *Press, Parliament and People* (London: W. Heinemann Ltd., 1946), 3-6, for a graphic account of this incident.

[2] 351 H.C. Deb. 5s., 664-665.

[3] *Ibid.*, 678.   [4] *Ibid.*, 687.

[5] 360 H.C. Deb. 5., 1381.

concerned in a court of law. The penalty for such offence was seven years imprisonment or a fine of £500 or both.[1] Before agreeing to the regulation, the House of Commons insisted that no prosecutions under it should be undertaken without the consent of the Attorney-General. Although some fear was expressed that the new regulation contained power to punish "honest and clean" minority opinion,[2] the fact that the Home Secretary revealed that he had consulted with a representative group of members of Parliament in framing the new regulation, coupled with his assurance that there was "no question of punishing people who honestly express minority opinions".[3] led the House to accept the regulation without further discussion.

Events were moving rapidly, however, and the days immediately following the adoption of Regulation 2C saw the German armies race through Belgium, the Netherlands, and France. The belief that the invasion of Great Britain was imminent led the Government to seek even more drastic powers over the press. On 29th May the Government issued Regulation 2D which provided that if the Home Secretary were satisfied that any newspaper was systematically publishing material calculated to foment opposition to the war, he might suppress the newspaper immediately by executive order, without recourse to any court of law.

Although members of the House of Commons were acutely aware of the imminence of German invasion, they, nevertheless, demonstrated grave concern over the extensive powers for which the Government was asking under Regulation 2D. On 25th June, Mr. Hore-Belisha intimated that the rigorous press censorship in France had contributed to the downfall of that country,[4] and on 3rd July, Sir Henry Morris-Jones asked the Prime Minister for an assurance that the press would be permitted to express a completely free opinion about all aspects of the conduct of the war. Mr. Attlee, the Lord Privy Seal, replied that the Government intended to interfere as little as possible with the liberties of the press, but that he could not give an assurance that the publication of statements "which either give information of value

---

[1] S.R. & O., 1940, No. 680.
[2] 360 H.C. Deb. 5s., 1384.
[3] Ibid., 1382, 1384.
[4] 362 H.C. Deb. 5s., 305.

to the enemy, or are calculated to impede our war effort by weakening the resolution of the public" would not be interfered with.[1]

Parliamentary anxiety over Regulation 2D came to a head on 31st July, 1940, when Mr. Sydney Silverman moved a prayer urging that the regulation be annulled. Strong opposition to the absence of any right of appeal to the courts from the Home Secretary's determination was voiced by members of all parties.[2] Although the Home Secretary stated that a safeguard existed "in the exercise of vigilance by the House of Commons",[3] and the Attorney-General contended that if an appeal to the courts were granted, the House would be unable to criticize the Home Secretary's actions,[4] most members who participated in the debate were unimpressed with the efficacy of the parliamentary safeguard and insisted that the only effective protection against the Home Secretary's discretionary power lay in an appeal to a court of law. Mr. Kenneth Lindsay referred to a "growing feeling" that the House was "not quite prepared at every point to trust the Executive",[5] and Major Milner suggested that the Home Secretary had committed a breach of agreement with the House by modifying Regulation 2C without consulting Parliament in advance.[6] During a debate which lasted for two-and-a-half hours, only two back benchers supported the Government.[7] Impressed with the gravity of the situation, the House approved the regulation, but only by a vote of 98 to 60, the narrowest majority received by the Government on an unsuccessful prayer throughout the war. It appears certain that members accepted Regulation 2D with great reluctance and only with the understanding that the Home Secretary had given assurance that the powers would be used only in an extremely grave situation.[8] Further, they appeared to believe that, once the imminent threat

[1] 362 H.C. Deb. 5s., 835-836.

[2] Among those who opposed the regulation were Commander King-Hall, Mr. Kenneth Lindsay, Sir George Hume, Mr. Noel-Baker, Sir Richard Acland, Mr. Pickthorn, Major Milner, Mr. Glenvil Hall, Mr. Vernon Bartlett, Mr. Lipson, Mr. Etherton, Sir Henry Fildes, Mr. Edmund Harvey, Mr. Shinwell, and Mr. Wilfrid Roberts.

[3] Sir John Anderson, 363 H.C. Deb. 5s., 1321.

[4] Sir Donald Somervell, *ibid.*, 1335.

[5] *Ibid.*, 1329.   [6] *Ibid.*, 1329-1330.

[7] Sir Joseph Nall, *ibid.*, 1338-1339; Mr. Thurtle, *ibid.*, 1342.

[8] Harold J. Laski, *Freedom of the Press in Wartime* (London: National Council for Civil Liberties, n.d.), 1.

of invasion had passed, the Government would revert to Regulation 2c.[1]

On the basis of this understanding, therefore, it was with considerable surprise and alarm that many members learned of the Government's use of Regulation 2D to suppress the *Daily Worker* and the *Week* in January, 1941. Both were publications of the British Communist Party, and had opposed the prosecution of the war. The suppression of the *Daily Worker* and the *Week* was coupled with reports that other editors had been privately warned by the Government,[2] and many felt that an undesirable amount of caution in the expression of opinion characterized the press.[3] It was not denied by parliamentary critics that the two Communist papers had been engaged in "the systematic publication of material calculated to foment opposition to the war". It was, rather, the procedure which the Government had followed which caused alarm. Nearly eight months had elapsed since Regulation 2D had been introduced, and many members felt that the imminent danger which might have justified its use had passed. The general line of criticism which developed in the House of Commons on 28th January, 1941, on Mr. Bevan's motion expressing regret at the Home Secretary's action was, therefore, that the Government should have proceeded under 2c, rather than under 2D. Mr. Bevan contended that 2D had been justified to the House on the sole ground that it "might be needed in circumstances of direct peril arising out of physical invasion",[4] and charged that the Government had "broken faith with the House of Commons".[5] Sir Richard Acland stated that the making of Regulation 2D had, in the first place, been "an extreme breach of courtesy to . . . members", since members had been consulted on the making of 2c, but not on 2D.[6] Sir Percy Harris charged that the procedure under 2D savoured "much too much of the Gestapo" and suggested that the regulation should be amended.[7] Sir Richard and Sir Percy, among others, expressed concern at

---

[1] Francis Williams, *op. cit.*, 33.

[2] Laski, "Civil Liberties in Wartime." *Bill of Rights Review*, II (Summer, 1942), 247; Sir Richard Acland, 363 H.C. Deb. 5s., 1327.

[3] See, for example, Jennie Lee, *This Great Journey* (New York: Farrar and Rinehart, Inc., 1942), 255-256.

[4] 368 H.C. Deb. 5s., 465.   [5] *Ibid.*, 476.

[6] *Ibid.*, 482.   [7] *Ibid.*, 506.

the Government's determination to treat the issue as a matter of confidence.[1]   The Home Secretary, Mr. Herbert Morrison, defended his action by stating that there was still danger of invasion and that, under such circumstances, the courts were too slow and ineffective. Mr. Morrison assured the House that the Government would not use its powers to prevent the press from criticizing the Government, but only to prevent attempts by the press to sabotage the war effort. The freedom of the press, he concluded, remained secure because he had to justify his actions to the House of Commons.[2] Mr. Bevan's motion was defeated, 323 to 8.

A second application by the Government of Regulation 2D in March, 1942, again evoked considerable parliamentary criticism. On 19th March, 1942, the Home Secretary had warned the editor of the *Daily Mirror* that Regulation 2D would be used against the newspaper if it persisted in following the policy it was then pursuing. The immediate cause of the Home Secretary's action appears to have been the publication, on 6th March, of a cartoon which depicted a wrecked seaman clinging precariously to a raft in a turbulent sea. The caption stated simply: "The price of petrol has been raised by a penny (official)." The leading article in the same issue was an attack upon the administration of the army. The *Daily Mirror* had for some time been conducting in its pages a campaign against the "old school tie" influence at the War Office and in the army. The paper, with a daily circulation of a million and a half copies, was popular among soldiers because of its stand as the soldiers' advocate. It was reported that several members of the Cabinet had long viewed the *Daily Mirror* with disfavour, and that the issue of 6th March particularly disturbed the Prime Minister, who interpreted the cartoon and its caption to imply that seamen's lives were being risked in order that the oil companies might receive larger profits. Mr. Churchill is reported to have believed that both the cartoon and the leading article were calculated to cause alarm and despair, and accordingly he demanded that the newspaper should be suppressed.[3]

---

[1] *Ibid.*, 479–480; 507.   [2] *Ibid.*, 516.

[3] Francis Williams, *op. cit.*, 35. Mr. Morrison's biographer says that Churchill wanted the *Daily Mirror* to be banned outright and that Mr. Morrison "actually had intervened in order to protect the paper from suppression." (Maurice Edelman, *Herbert Morrison* [London: Lincolns-Prager Ltd., 1948], 60.)

The decision to proceed against the *Daily Mirror* under Regulation 2D, some twenty-two months after the regulation had been formulated for use in only extremely grave emergency, caused concern both outside and inside of Parliament. It was reported that some members of the Cabinet were not happy with the Prime Minister's decision,[1] and *The Times* expressed the alarm of the newspaper world when it condemned the Government's action by saying: "Anything that tends to impede or impair the free play of opinion, may do grave disservice to the State, especially in time of war, and recoil disastrously upon the Administration that imposes it".[2]

A debate on the Government's use of Regulation 2D against the *Daily Mirror* took place in the House of Commons on 26th March. Mr. Wilfrid Roberts reminded the Home Secretary that the regulation had been approved during a moment of grave crisis by only 38 votes, and asked for an assurance that the regulation would not be employed again.[3] Sir Irving Albery suggested that the Prime Minister transform his verbal respect for liberty into action in the present case, [4] and Mr. Bevan questioned the competency of Mr. Morrison to exercise discretionary powers.[5] Mr. Barnes charged the Home Secretary with a breach of the understanding that Sir John Anderson had given the House in connection with the use of the regulation,[6] and Mr. Silverman asked that the Whips be taken off so that Members could avail themselves of an opportunity to express their real sentiments on the issue.[7] The Home Secretary replied that if he had proceeded under 2C the House would not have been able to criticize his action since the case would have been *sub judice*. He preferred to utilize Regulation 2D because his decision entailed "a broad judgment of public policy" and "there is no better and no more immediate and swifter tribunal to deal with it than the House of Commons".[8] No modification of the Government's action was obtained and the editor of the *Daily Mirror* therefore had no choice but to change the newspaper's policy in accordance with the Government's directions.

---

[1] Francis Williams, *op. cit.*, 37.
[2] Cited *ibid.*, 38.
[3] 378 H.C. Deb. 5s., 2234-2235.
[4] *Ibid.*, 2243.
[5] *Ibid.*, 2252-2253.
[6] *Ibid.*, 2266-2267.
[7] *Ibid.*, 2303-2304.
[8] *Ibid.*, 2285.

Regulation 2D was used only on these two occasions, and Regulation 2C was not employed at all. While it has been reported that during March, 1942, the Government seriously contemplated the possibility of imposing a political censorship on the British press,[1] no such action was taken. Members of Parliament continued, meanwhile, to attempt to secure the lifting of the ban on the *Daily Worker*. In March, 1942, the Parliamentary Liberal Party declared itself against the suppression of the *Daily Worker* and asked Sir Archibald Sinclair to press the matter on the Cabinet.[2] Labour members continued to express their dissatisfaction with the ban, and in May, 1942, the Labour Party Conference passed a resolution asking that the proscription be removed. It was, accordingly, "extremely difficult for Labour and Trade Union Ministers to be members of a Government which refuse[d] a desire so strongly expressed by the constituent bodies of the working-class movement",[3] and in August, 1942, the Government announced its decision to allow the reappearance of the *Daily Worker*.

Other Government attempts to restrict freedom of opinion in the interest of national morale encountered significant opposition in the House of Commons, causing the Government to modify its actions to a large degree. Perhaps the most far-reaching attempt by the Government to restrain the free expression of opinion was Regulation 39BA, made in June, 1940, which provided that "any person who publishes any report or statement relating to matters connected with the war which is likely to cause alarm or despondency shall be liable on summary conviction to imprisonment for a term not exceeding one month or to a fine not exceeding fifty pounds, or to both". The regulation further provided that it should be good defence for the accused to prove "that he had reasonable cause to believe that the report or statement was true" and "that the publication thereof was not malicious".[4] Several prosecutions were soon instituted under the new regulation, and the zeal with which constables and the courts directed themselves to enforcing the regulation caused alarm in Parliament and among

---

[1] Francis Williams, *op. cit.*, 63.
[2] *New Statesman and Nation*, XXIII (21st March, 1942), 190.
[3] *Ibid.*, XXIV (29th August, 1942), 136.
[4] S.R. & O., 1940, No. 938, II, 55.

the public.[1] It was reported that "a host of informers immediately sprang up", some actuated by "stupid zeal" and others "by motives of political prejudice".[2] Persons relaying rumours that parachutists had landed were fined as much as £30,[3] and proceedings were instituted against an individual who had "stated in a shop that Baldwin and Chamberlain had sold the country and should be shot".[4]

Soon after the regulation came into force the Ministry of Information began a campaign of "Silent Columns". Its purpose, as expressed by its motto—"if you must talk, talk victory"—was apparently to prevent the spread of alarm and despondency by discouraging virtually all expression of opinion. To some members of the public "the spectacle of a Ministry of Information begging that nobody should tell anybody anything . . . was rich comedy",[5] but Parliament immediately protested at this effort to suppress discussion of the war. As members became aware also of the heavy sentences being imposed by the magistrates under Regulation 39BA, they voiced their concern in the House of Commons. On 23rd July, 1940, the Prime Minister informed the House that the original notion of the "Silent Columns" was "well meant" but that "in black and white it did not look by any means so attractive and seemed to suggest that reasonable and intelligent discussion about the war ought not to take place". Accordingly, said the Prime Minister, the "Silent Columns" had passed into "innocuous desuetude". He went on to assure the House that the Home Secretary would review all sentences imposed by the courts under Regulation 39BA and stated the Government's belief that sentences "should be reduced or remitted wherever it is clear that there was no evil wish or systematic purpose to weaken the national defence".[6] Asked if the Government would consider

---

[1] It was reported in the *Daily Mail* that the chief constable of Derby had stated: "I've killed Communism and the Fascists in this town and I intend to stop anything else that may be tried to persuade people to express their views, however patriotic the real motive may be." Quoted in *New Statesman and Nation*, XX (10th August, 1940), 131.

[2] Kidd, *op. cit.*, 232.

[3] *Round Table*, XXX (September, 1940), 892.

[4] In this case, "Mr. Blades, K.C., maintained that there was no evidence to show that alarm was caused. If the defendant had stated that Baldwin and Chamberlain had been shot, instead of should be shot, there would be a cause for alarm and despondency." *New Statesman and Nation*, XX (27th July, 1940), 83.

[5] W. N. Ewer, "The Ministry of Information," *Political Quarterly*, XII (1941), 94.

[6] 363 H.C. Deb. 5s., 597-598. See also the Prime Minister's memorandum to the Home Secretary, dated 19th July, 1940, on this point (Churchill, *Their Finest Hour*, 646-647).

withdrawing or amending the regulation, the Prime Minister indicated that it would not. Continued criticism in the House, however, during which it was contended that the carrying out of the regulation "causes ridicule throughout the country,"[1] caused the Home Secretary to announce on 8th August, that he had issued a circular for chief constables advising them before submitting cases for prosecution under Regulation 39BA, to consider whether they could not be properly dealt with by a warning.[2] On 15th August, in answer to a question whether the Government would consult with members with a view towards amending Regulation 39BA, the Home Secretary replied that in view of the steps he had taken he did not believe that further difficulties would be encountered concerning the administration of the regulation. However, in the event that new difficulties should arise, he assured the House that arrangements for consultation with members for the purpose of amending the regulation could be made.[3] The need for such consultations did not arise, since the regulation soon fell into disuse. There had been seventy-four prosecutions instituted under the regulation from its inception on 11th June up to 25th July,[4] and some indication of its abeyance may be gathered from the fact that in the following nine months only thirty-one new prosecutions were instituted.[5]

Members of the House of Commons exhibited further concern over what they considered other attempts by the Government to restrain the free expression of political opinion. In the summer of 1940 several members showed apprehension over the existence of the Home Security Committee, headed by Viscount Swinton. A veil of secrecy surrounded the operations of the committee, but it was admitted by the Prime Minister that its function was to deal with fifth-column activities.[6] Mr. Russell Strauss reflected the suspicions of some members when he asked if the Swinton Committee was in any way responsible for the police searches of the homes of Trade Unions officials and he questioned the reason for

[1] Mr. Ammon, 25th July, 1940, 363 H.C. Deb. 5s., 965.

[2] Sir John Anderson, 364 H.C. Deb. 5s., 407.

[3] Sir John Anderson, 15th August, 1940, *ibid.*, 987-988.

[4] 363 H.C. Deb. 5s., 965.

[5] Herman Finer, "The British Cabinet, the House of Commons and the War," *Politica Science Quarterly*, LVI (September, 1941), 355.

[6] Mr. Churchill, 363 H.C. Deb. 5s., 1153.

the prohibition that no newspaper might mention the committee without special permission.[1]   The Prime Minister refused to answer questions concerning the committee, pleading that "it would not be in the public interest to give any information on the subject."[2] Further questions were asked concerning the membership and salaries of the committee, and, several members expressing dissatisfaction with the Government's reply, Mr. Stokes announced that he would raise the matter on the Adjournment.[3] Further pressure from members to extract information on the membership, salaries, and operations of the committee[4] caused the Prime Minister to retort that he "would answer no further Question, at any time . . . whether it is convenient or easy . . . to answer them or not" about the Swinton Committee.[5] Mr. Bevan charged that the Prime Minister had "inadvertently missed the whole point of the criticism" and he called attention to the "widespread dissatisfaction in the country about the composition of this committee".[6] In spite of the Government's determined refusal to provide information on the Swinton Committee, the persistent criticism of the House was apparently successful, since the committee was soon disbanded.[7]

The acute suspicion with which members regarded any action by the Government which tended ot curtail the free expression of opinion brought the Ministry of Information under especially heavy fire from the House. The influence of the House in assigning the Ministry's "Silent Columns" to "innocuous desuetude" has already been noted. The activities of the Home Intelligence Division of the Ministry, in particular, came under suspicion. The function of the Home Intelligence Division was to keep a finger on the public pulse by receiving reports from persons throughout the country on people's reactions to the news or to new Government regulations. These reports were then circulated to the various Ministers "for their information in case anything appeared that was of departmental interest or that disclosed criticism in a particular area that could be remedied by departmental action".[8]

[1] *Ibid.*, 1154.   [2] Mr. Churchill, *ibid.*, 603.
[3] 364 H.C. Deb. 5s., 414-416, 8th August, 1940.
[4] Mr. Mander, Mr. Stokes, Mr. Hopkinson, 15th August, 1940, 364 H.C. Deb. 5s., 958-962.
[5] Mr. Churchill, *ibid.*, 963.
[6] *Ibid.*   [7] Finer, *op. cit.*, 357.
[8] Francis Williams, *op. cit.*, 120-121.

Almost immediately the press, with the *Daily Herald, Daily Express*, and *Daily Mirror* taking the lead, denounced the Ministry for its use of inquisitorial methods, and the *Daily Herald* coined the term "Cooper's Snoopers" to describe the men and women engaged in submitting reports to the Ministry. The charge made against the "Snoopers" was that "they knocked at people's doors, asked questions about morale of a nature frequently regarded by those questioned as attempts to trap them into making indiscreet remarks against the Government, and then reported their highly-coloured and biased findings to the Minister of Information, Mr. Duff Cooper, who rushed off to the Cabinet with them".[1] Sir Archibald Southby led the attack on "Cooper's Snoopers" in the House of Commons on 31st July, 1940. The methods used by the Ministry to determine the state of public opinion were described by various members as "wanton spying"[2] and "a waste of public money",[3] and it was intimated that the Ministry was attempting to usurp Parliament's function of representing public opinion.[4] The following day the matter was raised on the Adjournment. The debate, which lasted over two hours, was devoted in large part to a discussion of the merits of scientific public opinion analysis. The Minister of Information informed the House that the interviewers were not employees of the Ministry, but were employees of the War-Time Social Survey, set up under the auspices of the National Institute of Social and Economic Research. He stated further that only two per cent of the people visited had objected to being questioned, and that the names of persons questioned were not revealed to the Government. The Minister found considerable support for his project among members of the House, and the majority apparently believed that the project contained no real threat to expression of opinion or to the functioning of Parliament.[5]

The Ministry of Information came under further parliamentary criticism for certain of its actions concerning broadcasts on

[1] *Ibid.*, 119. Sir Richard Acland reported the following titbit as an example of the opinions relayed to the Ministry of Information: "The Prime Minister is a very nice gentleman; he takes such an interest in the war, doesn't he ?" (363 H.C. Deb. 5s., 1530).

[2] Sir A. Southby, 363 H.C. Deb. 5s., 1216.

[3] Mr. Lyons, *ibid.*   [4] Mr. Granville, *ibid.*

[5] Francis Williams reports that after Mr. Duff Cooper left the Ministry of Information there was an attempt to revive the charge and to rechristen those engaged on the project "Bracken's Trackers." "But the alliteration," Mr. Williams says, "was not so good and it did not catch on" (Francis Williams, *op. cit.*, 119).

the radio. Before the war, the British Broadcasting Corporation, operating under a Royal Charter, was theoretically responsible to the Postmaster General. In practice, however, the Postmaster General had not sought to influence the B.B.C., and the determination of its policies and operations was left to a seven-man Board of Governors appointed by the Government. With the coming of war, the number of Governors of the B.B.C. was reduced to two, both of whom were Conservatives, and responsibility for its policy and operation was transferred to the Minister of Information, who began to exercise his power of control by passing upon policy and programming. One such exercise of control over programming, was the Minister's decision to ban a broadcast by the Glasgow Orpheus Choir because its director, Sir Hugh Roberton, was a pacifist. On 11th March, 1941, a motion, carrying more than forty signatures and protesting against the ban on the choral broadcast, was put down in the House of Commons.[1] In response to criticism from the House on 12th March over the discrimination practised by the B.B.C. and over the composition of its Board of Governors, Mr. Duff Cooper, the Minister of Information, said it was the policy of the B.B.C. "not to invite to the microphone persons who have taken part in public agitation against the national war effort,"[2] and announced his agreement with the Governors' belief that "not everybody has a right to expect the privilege of exercising free speech through the B.B.C".[3] It was reported that Mr. Duff Cooper's attitude had caused in Parliament "a growing uneasiness about the arbitrary procedure at the B.B.C.",[4] and had also disturbed the Government.[5]

Realizing that a parliamentary storm was brewing, Mr. Duff Cooper told the House that the Government was willing to consider the possibility of reorganizing and increasing the Board of Governors,[6] and on 20th March the Prime Minister announced that artists would not be banned from the B.B.C. because of their political connections.[7] After a further debate in the House on

---

[1] 369 H.C. Deb. 5s., 1148-1150.
[2] *Ibid.*, 1270.   [3] *Ibid.*, 1271.
[4] *Spectator*, CLXVI (14th March, 1941), 271.
[5] *New Statesman and Nation*, XXI (15th March, 1941), 263.
[6] 369 H.C. Deb. 5s., 1272.
[7] 370 H.C. Deb. 5s., 284.

25th March on the exclusion policy of the B.B.C., the Government responded to parliamentary pressure by announcing, on 1st April, 1941, its decision to increase the Board of Governors from two to six members.[1]

One of the most striking instances of the success of Parliament in its role as watchdog over individual liberties occurred in the summer of 1940. On 16th July, 1940, Sir John Anderson introduced the Emergency Powers (Defence) (Number 2) Bill for its Second Reading. The bill was to provide for the establishment of special courts to try civilians in certain areas which might be designated as "war zones" by the Home Secretary in a state of grave emergency. Because of the seriousness of the military situation, Sir John urged that the bill be passed in all its stages in both Houses on that day. The novel judicial system, he pointed out, was to operate only in areas where, due to attempted invasion or severe air attack, the ordinary judicial machinery would be inadequate. Under the regulations to be made pursuant to the bill, the civilian nature of the courts would be stipulated. The regulations would further provide, he asserted, that suitable men of judicial rank should be selected by the Lord Chancellor to act as presidents of the special war-zone courts, that the courts should be empowered to deal with offences of all kinds, that the ordinary rules of evidence should apply, and that offenders should have legal representation. There was to be no provision for trial by jury, and while the courts were to be empowered to impose any sentence authorized by law, including the death sentence, there was to be no right of appeal to any higher court.

Many members listened in shocked amazement as the Home Secretary recited the plans he intended to enact by the bill. Mr. Hore-Belisha immediately asked why the safeguards mentioned by the Home Secretary were not included in the bill,[2] and another member asked if the Home Secretary was "sure he [was] dealing with the right bill".[3] Mr. Shinwell noted that there was nothing in the bill itself which indicated that the courts would

---

[1] The four new members—Dr. J. J. Mallon and Sir Ian Fraser, both former Governors of the B.B.C., and Lady Violet Bonham Carter, a leader of the Liberal Party, and Mr. Arthur H. Mann, former editor of the *Yorkshire Post*—were people "of progressive mind, in whom the public might have confidence" (Finer, *op. cit.*, 359).

[2] 363 H.C. Deb. 5s., 68.

[3] Mr. Glenvil Hall, *ibid.*

actually be civil in nature.[1] Mr. Lees-Smith expressed the concern of many members when he stated that "the whole content of this bill is in the regulations, and the House has not seen the regulations".[2] "It is all very well," another member added, "for anybody to come before this House and say 'I have a Bill which entitles me to cut off your head, but I can assure you that I am only going to cut your toe nails' . . . but I do not think we ought to leave it quite like that".[3] Sir Archibald Southby thought that the judicial system of the country ought not to be changed by unseen regulations in an afternoon,[4] and Mr. Glenvil Hall did not know of any other Minister "who introduced a bill of such magnitude, hoped to carry it through all its stages in a single afternoon, and yet did not once refer to the actual provisions of the bill he was introducing".[5]

After members had engaged in nearly five hours of critical comment, Sir John Anderson asked that the House vote to commit the bill to committee stage for further consideration. He assured the House that amendments would be introduced in committee to make it clear that the courts to be established under the bill were to be civil rather than military and to meet the other concerns of the House, and he promised to discuss the terms of the regulations with a representative group of members before formulating them. Even with these concessions, sixteen members voted against the motion to commit the bill to committee stage.[6]

The committee stage was held on 23rd July, and the Home Secretary introduced amendments which he thought would satisfy the desires of the House. It was immediately evident, however, that Sir John's amendments did not go far enough to meet the wishes of many members. Mr. Aneurin Bevan introduced an amendment to limit the powers of the Home Secretary to making only one set of regulations under the bill. Sir John Anderson, he charged, was not "a good House of Commons man",[7] and "experience during the last nine months has taught us that, after the House has parted with powers to the executive, those powers

---

[1] *Ibid.*, 69.   [2] *Ibid.*, 77.

[3] Mr. Kingsley Griffith, *ibid.*, 81.

[4] *Ibid.*, 96.   [5] *Ibid.*, 97.

[6] The vote was 124-16. One Conservative, 2 Liberal, 10 Labour, 2 Independent Labour Party, and 1 Independent voted against commitment.

[7] 363 H.C. Deb. 5s., 729.

have been gravely abused by the executive".[1]   Mr. Bevan's amendment was supported by members from all sides of the House,[2] and, in response to this feeling, the Home Secretary indicated that he would consult a representative group of members before changing the initial regulations or before making subsequent regulations.[3]   Accordingly, Mr. Bevan withdrew his amendment.

Major Milner then proposed that the right to legal representation be accorded to the accused by the statute itself rather than by regulation under the statute. Support for the Milner amendment was voiced by members of all parties.[4] Sir John Anderson continued to oppose the amendment, believing that the matter could be adequately handled by regulation, and Mr. Bevan warned that if the Home Secretary persisted "in the mood of which he is now the victim he will find himself up against the wishes of the committee".[5] Finally, the Attorney-General intervened to state that the Government would attempt to insert words to meet the wishes of the committee in the House of Lords.

At the end of three-and-a-half hours of debate, the Chief Whip intervened to say that, before the debate, he had made enquiries and had been informed that the bill would be passed that day within two-and-a-half or three hours. Since the debate had already exceeded that time and some twelve amendments still remained on the paper, he suggested he had better move progress in order to avoid an all-night sitting. Accordingly, progress was reported and the decision was taken to continue discussion the following day.[6]

The mood of the House on 16th July and 23rd July had been perhaps best expressed by Sir Archibald Southby in his statement that "we are not so afraid of Hitler that we cannot take time to discuss things quietly".[7] The mood continued on 24th July, when Mr. Edmund Harvey moved an amendment providing for

---

[1] *Ibid.*, 731.

[2] Mr. Kenneth Lindsay, Mr. Richard Stokes, Mr. Edmund Harvey, Mr. Sydney Silverman.

[3] 363 H.C. Deb. 5s., 729.

[4] Captain W. T. Shaw, Mr. Edmund Harvey, Sir A. Southby, Mr. Glenvil Hall, Mr. Sydney Silverman, Mr. Aneurin Bevan, Mr. Stephen, Mr. Ernest Evans.

[5] 363 H.C. Deb. 5s., 754.

[6] *Ibid.*, 759.   [7] *Ibid.*, 758.

some statutory opportunity of review in all the decisions of the special courts. "It is desirable," Mr. Harvey stated, "that Parliament should secure this as a right of the subject."[1]   Five members, from all sides of the House, then supported Mr. Harvey's amendment.[2]   The Home Secretary resisted the amendment, saying that the Government did not want any sort of judicial review of the sentences.   The Government had, however, no intention of excluding the Prerogative, and, therefore, in cases involving the death penalty there would be an automatic review by the Home Secretary.   The position which Sir John Anderson adopted did not satisfy many members, and it was contended by one member that the Home Secretary desired to deprive citizens of their rights of *mandamus* and *certiorari*.   If this was the case, the member continued, the House "will not let him have the bill this week or next".[3]   Five other members then made speeches attacking the adequacy of the Prerogative as a safeguard, and supporting the amendment.[4]   The Home Secretary then replied that he might, by regulation, provide for the establishment of a committee with legal experience to give advice to the Home Secretary in reviewing these cases.[5]   This concession, however, did not satisfy the House, and another five members made speeches supporting the Harvey amendment.[6]   The Attorney-General then intervened in the debate and gave an undertaking that the Government would be willing to consider in the House of Lords whether words could be inserted in the bill which would satisfy the demand of the House for a review by a judicial body of cases involving the death penalty and other serious sentences.   Under further pressure from members, the Attorney-General formally accepted the Harvey amendment.[7]

During the entire debate on 24th July, which lasted more than two-and-a-half hours, only one member made a speech supporting the Government.[8] With the end of the debate in sight,

---

[1] *Ibid.*, 832.

[2] Mr. Messer, Sir I. Albery, Mr. Silverman, Sir A. Southby, and Mr. Hannah.

[3] Mr. E. Evans, 363 H.C. Deb. 5s., 841.

[4] Mr. Bevan, Mr. Stephen, Colonel Gretton, Mr. Lees-Smith, and Mr. Pritt.

[5] Sir John Anderson, 363 H.C. Deb. 5s., 861.

[6] Mr. Levy, Sir R. Acland, Mr. Naylor, Mr. Goldie, and Mr. Lyons.

[7] Sir Donald Somervell, 363 H.C. Deb. 5s., 871-873.

[8] Rear-Admiral Beamish.

several members took the opportunity to express their concern with the bill, even as amended. One member desired "to protest most strongly against the way this bill has been introduced, altered, pushed through the House, and all attempts at improvements stone-walled by the Ministers in charge, in a shocking way."[1] Another member predicted that the House would "look back with a little shame as well as regret" at the bill.[2]

On 1st August, 1940, the Home Secretary brought the bill, with the amendments which had been made in the House of Lords, into the House for final consideration. By the amendments, all death sentences were to be automatically reviewed by a tribunal composed of three persons of high judicial experience, and Sir John Anderson indicated that by regulation he would make provision for the review "of cases in which there are sentences less than the death sentence".[3] Several members refused to participate in the formality of thanking the Home Secretary for his concessions. One member suggested that "we may congratulate ourselves on our part in having brought about this desirable state of affairs",[4] and another member reiterated that members were "determined to preserve the democratic practice and procedure of this House, and its overriding authority".[5] Mr. Glenvil Hall wound up the debate with the following words:

> The House will watch the Regulations with some care, because frankly there has grown up recently a suspicion that the Executive is attempting to take more power than it needs to take even in this time of dire peril. This Bill is a good example of the Executive attempting to take to itself more authority than it should take. Although the Home Secretary has met us in a full and frank way, we must still remember that he would not have done so had the House not forced him to do it. Therefore, although we are grateful to him for meeting us and keeping his word to us, nevertheless we have to realize that what thanks are due are due to the House as a whole and not to the Government.[6]

[1] Mr. Glenvil Hall, 363 H.C. Deb. 5s., 904.

[2] Mr. Silverman, *ibid.*, 904-905.

[3] *Ibid.*, 1439.

[4] Mr. Shinwell, *ibid.*

[5] Major Milner, *ibid.*, 1445.

[6] *Ibid.*, 1446.

One other significant event—the internment of enemy aliens by the Government—accorded Parliament further opportunity to act as watchdog over individual liberties. Although certain limitations upon the activities of aliens were imposed by the Alien Registration Act, 1914, and the Alien Registration (Amendment) Act, 1919, which were both in force when war broke out in 1939, the Crown, under the Prerogative, had the right to expel, intern, or control in any other way, at its discretion, all enemy aliens.[1] At the outbreak of war there were some 74,200 aliens of German and Austrian origin in Great Britain,[2] but since many of them were refugees from the Nazi regime, the Chamberlain Government decided to screen all enemy aliens carefully before ordering the internment of any of them. Accordingly, 112 tribunals, composed of men with legal experience who were appointed by the Home Secretary in consultation with the Lord Chancellor, were established to give each enemy alien an individual hearing. After examination, each enemy alien was to be placed in one of three categories: A, B, or C. Those found to be convinced supporters of the enemy cause were placed in category A and were interned. Enemy aliens about whom there were doubts were placed in group B, and were allowed to remain at liberty with some restrictions. Class C aliens, because they were refugees from Hitler or had otherwise shown evidence of strong hostility to Nazi Germany, were free from both internment and special restrictions. An appeal to the Home Secretary from the classification of the tribunal was provided. By January, 1940, the tribunals had completed their examination of the enemy aliens, and, as a result of such examination, only 486 persons had been interned,[3] while approximately 64,000 persons were placed in category C and thus exempted from both internment and restrictions.[4] Some dissatisfaction over the apparent confusion and inconsistency on the part of the tribunals in assigning persons to the B classification developed,[5] and a review of all B classifications

---

[1] E. C. S. Wade and G. Godfrey Phillips, *Constitutional Law* (4th edition; London: Longmans, Green & Co., 1950), 189. See also *Rex v. Vine Street Police-Station Superintendent ex parte Liebmann*, 1916, 1 K.B., 268.

[2] F. Lafitte, *The Internment of Aliens* (London: Penguin Books, 1940), 62.

[3] *Spectator*, CLXIV (19th January, 1940), 63.

[4] Lafitte, *op. cit.*, 63.

[5] Sir Cecil Thomas Carr, *Concerning English Administrative Law* (New York: Columbia University Press, 1941), 101.

was begun in May, 1940, by new regional committees. Before
the review was completed, the Government had drastically
modified its policy towards enemy aliens.

British public opinion appears to have been favourable to
refugees until May, 1940, although as early as January, 1940,
several newspapers, principally the *Sunday Express* and the *Daily
Sketch*, had begun to urge the Government to "intern the lot." By
the late spring, with heavy fighting taking place in Belgium,
Holland, and France, the campaign to "intern the lot" was
accelerated in the press, found some expression in Parliament,[1]
and did not leave the public unaffected.[2] In this atmosphere of
increasing xenophobia, Sir John Anderson, on 12th May, declared
the coastal area from Inverness to eastern Dorset to be a
"protected area" and ordered the internment of all German and
Austrian males in the area between the ages of sixteen and sixty.
A few days later all German and Austrian males from sixteen to
sixty in the B category were interned. On 27th May, the internment of approximately 3,000 women in class B was ordered, and
during the first week in June, 300 persons between the ages of
sixty and seventy in group B were interned. On 10th June following Italy's entrance into the war, about 4,100 Italian men and
women were interned, including all Italian males between the
ages of sixteen and seventy who had resided in the United Kingdom for less than twenty years. By the middle of June some 7,000
men and 3,800 women were said to be in internment camps.[3]

On 21st June, with the collapse of France, the Home Secretary
decided on a policy of "general internment." All chief constables
were authorized to arrest for internment any class C German or
Austrian about whom they might have doubts with regard to
national security, and a few days later the internment of all class
C men under seventy (with certain exceptions, such as invalids
and key workers) was ordered. By the middle of July, two-thirds
of all the male Austrians and Germans who had been in Great
Britain at the outbreak of war had been interned.[4]

---

[1] Colonel Burton, 360 H.C. Deb. 5s., 33; Captain Shaw, 361 H.C. Deb. 5s., 295-296.

[2] One observer of the prevailing attitude towards enemy aliens wrote that "the animus
displayed against them is quite the most unpleasant feature of the present outcry." (Dingle
Foot, "The Law and the Quislings," *Spectator*, CLXIV [3rd May, 1940], 620.) See also
Norman Bentwich, "England and the Aliens," *Political Quarterly*, XII (January-March, 1941).

[3] Lafitte, *op. cit.*, 72.   [4] *Ibid.*, 74.

At the peak of the internment policy the number of enemy aliens interned was approximately 27,000.[1] It was perhaps inevitable that the internment of such a number of persons in so relatively short a time should have resulted in certain administrative errors and shortcomings. Even before the policy of "general internment" was undertaken, the Prime Minister, on 4th June, admitted that the Government had not been able to "draw all the distinctions" which it would have preferred to make.[2] After the adoption of the "general internment" policy, some elderly Germans, Austrians, and Italians who had lived in Great Britain for forty years were interned, and only rarely did those in charge of internment segregate Fascists from anti-Fascists.[3] Occasionally, tragic errors were committed.[4]

This drastic action on the part of the Government evoked much hostile comment in Parliament and in the press. The *Manchester Guardian, News Chronicle, New Statesman and Nation*, and *Spectator* were forthright in their condemnation of the Government's policy. From the second week in May until 10th July, only three sitting days of Parliament were free from Questions directed by members to the Government with regard to the policy and its administration. The Government's action in ordering the internment of so large a proportion of the German and Austrian aliens was difficult for many members to comprehend in the light of the statement of the Under-Secretary for Home Security on 29th May that he could not "recall any case since the beginning of the war of anything which could be described as a hostile act" being attributable to Germans or Austrians residing in Great Britain.[5] Although the Home Secretary had stated on 4th July that it was "the plain truth" that "nearly all the aliens who were placed in category C were placed there because on investigation it was found that they were themselves the victims of those who are the common enemy",[6] the Under Secretary, a few days later,

[1] 367 H.C. Deb. 5s., 502.

[2] 361 H.C. Deb. 5s., 798.

[3] Harold J. Laski, "Civil Liberties in Great Britain in Wartime," *Bill of Rights Review*, II (Summer, 1942), 245-246.

[4] Gaetano Antonio Pacitto, a naturalized British subject, was seized on 10th June. He was sent to Canada aboard the ill-fated *Arandora Star*, and drowned. 365 H.C. Deb. 5s., 237.

[5] Mr. Peake, 361 H.C. Deb. 5s., 522.

[6] 362 H.C. Deb., 5s., 995-996.

declared that there was "no prospect at present of any review covering general policy".[1] It became known early in July that many of the interned males were being sent to Canada in the company of military prisoners of war, and, on 3rd July, news of the torpedoing and sinking of the *Arandora Star*, en route to Canada with 1,500 German and Italian internees, was revealed. Public and parliamentary indignation at the Government's handling of enemy aliens came to a head.

On 10th July, 1940, the Government's policy towards enemy aliens was brought up on the Adjournment and discussed for almost six hours. Miss Eleanor Rathbone said that many members had wanted to raise the matter for some time, but had been restrained "by a reluctance to give publicity to a matter which reflects unfavourably on our country's reputation for humanity, liberality, and efficiency".[2] Members were disturbed over the misery and fear which refugees were suffering, and were concerned because no clear-cut responsibility for the policy and its administration appeared to exist. The War Office claimed responsibility for male internees, the Home Office for female internees, and both disclaimed responsibility for sending internees overseas, contending that that decision had been made by a committee of the Cabinet, presided over by the Lord President of the Council.[3] The major criticism of members was that the Government had been stampeded into the policy of "general internment" by certain newspapers and by a panic-stricken public.[4] In the face of criticism from all sides of the House,[5] the Home Secretary stated that arrangements were being made to exempt from internment certain categories of persons whose work was of special value to the war effort. The Home Secretary's statement did not satisfy the House. It was reported that there was still "a strong feeling on all sides over the treatment of refugees and aliens."[6]

On 23rd July, in response to five questions on the Order Paper seeking information on the Government's proposals for dealing with internees, Sir John Anderson announced his modified policy. He admitted that, due to the great urgency of the "general

---

[1] *Ibid.*, 1150.   [2] *Ibid.*, 1211.   [3] *Ibid.*, 1218.

[4] Major Cazalet, *ibid.*, 1209; Colonel Wedgwood, *ibid.*, 1246.

[5] Viscount Wolmer, Mr. Graham White, Mr. G. R. Strauss, Mr. Wilfrid Roberts, Mr. Silverman, Mr. Sorensen, and Mr. Noel-Baker.

[6] *Spectator*, CLXV (19th July, 1940), 51.

internment" policy, mistakes had been made and persons had been detained who should have been exempted under the instructions. Retrospective effect would be given to the instructions so that all ill and infirm persons might be released. In addition, there would be an enlargement of exempted categories "to include particularly those who can render service of special value or make a significant contribution to the war effort." The categories would be announced in a forthcoming White Paper. A committee, under the chairmanship of Mr. Justice Asquith, and including Sir Herbert Emerson and Major-General Sir Neill Malcolm, both of whom were experienced in the handling of refugees, was to be set up to advise the Home Secretary on categories for exemption. The Home Secretary promised a better treatment of the interned aliens, and said that the Home Office was to assume full responsibility for internment camps and for the selection of aliens to be sent overseas.[1]

Parliament did not find Sir John's statement of policy satisfactory. It was followed by ten supplementary questions, and would have been followed by more had not the Speaker intervened in order to permit the day's business to proceed. In addition to releasing those who should not have been interned in the first place, the policy appeared to establish a utilitarian criterion for release, which many members found unpalatable. "Instead of having categories to be left out of unjust imprisonment," one member remarked, "there should be categories to be retained in imprisonment".[2] Another member believed that "men should be let out of the internment camps because they are innocent and not because they are useful".[3] Questions about alien internment continued to be put to the Home Secretary daily, and from 10th July to 22nd August, only one sitting day was free from discussion of aliens. On 25th July, for example, there were eight questions concerning aliens on the Order Paper. The White Paper, which contained eighteen categories of release, was presented to the House of Commons on 31st July, and met, according to one member, "with almost universal reprobation".[4]

[1] 363 H.C. Deb. 5s., 587-588.
[2] Colonel Wedgwood, ibid., 589.
[3] Mr. Rhys Davies, 364 H.C. Deb. 5s., 1530.
[4] Mr. Wedgwood, 363 H.C. Deb. 5s., 1382.

Sections of the press believed that the Government's policy and actions indicated that it was indifferent to public opinion on the alien issue.[1]

Parliamentary indignation at the slowness of release and the utilitarianism of the new policy culminated in a three-and-a-half hour debate on the summer adjournment on 22nd August, 1940. There was much criticism of the White Paper. It was contended that it did not matter how many categories of exemption there were if, in fact, people were not being released,[2] and that even the existence of war and overworked officials did not warrant the introduction of the "Bengal touch in British administration".[3] Sir John Anderson defended the policy of "general internment" as a military and security necessity,[4] but announced several new concessions which were to be made on the basis of the recommendations of the Asquith Committee. The maximum age of internment was to be reduced from seventy to sixty-five; employers of at least twelve British subjects were to be eligible for release, as were persons who had British-born or -naturalized sons serving in His Majesty's Forces; the release of scientists, researchers, and academicians was no longer to be confined to persons whose work was held to be a direct specific contribution to the war effort; and a new category of exemption was to be established to provide for persons who had taken a prominent and public part in opposing the Nazi system and who were actively friendly to the Allied cause. Eligibility under the new category was to be determined by a special tribunal, appointed by the Home Secretary, which would study the writings, speeches, and political activities of the aliens. The Chairman was to be a person of legal experience, and the other members were to be people with a knowledge of the politics of Germany and Austria.[5] The Home Secretary revealed that there had been 805 releases made under the categories of the White Paper.[6]

A revised White Paper, containing nineteen categories of exemption, was issued on 26th August, 1940. By 17th September,

---

[1] *Spectator*, CLXV (23rd August, 1940), 183.

[2] Major Cazalet, 364 H.C. Deb. 5s., 1532.

[3] Mr. Rhys Davies, *ibid.*, 1530.   [4] *Ibid.*, 1542.

[5] *Ibid.*, 1551. The tribunal consisted of Sir Cecil Hurst, Chairman, Sir Andrew McFadyean, Dr. R. W. Seton-Watson, and Mr. Ivone Kirkpatrick.

[6] *Ibid.*, 1430.

2,516 enemy aliens had been released,[1] and, on 19th September, Sir John Anderson told the House that he would give "most sympathetic consideration" to any recommendations which the Asquith Committee might make concerning the release of aliens of long residence in Great Britain, but that "a general policy of releasing those with long residence against whom nothing is known could not be justified".[2] On 3rd October, Mr. Morrison succeeded Sir John Anderson as Home Secretary. By 5th October, 4,603 enemy aliens had been released from internment.[3] Parliamentary dissatisfaction continued, however, and on 9th October Mr. Glenvil Hall warned the new Home Secretary that there was "a rising feeling" which might "burst its banks if something is not done".[4] On 17th October, the Home Secretary answered eleven questions with regard to alien internment, and on that day a new White Paper was issued which added four new categories of exemption. Mr. Morrison told the House, on 26th November, that male internees under fifty-five years of age would be eligible for release if they demonstrated their loyalty to the Allied cause by enlisting in the Pioneer Corps, a part of the British Army.[5]

By the beginning of December, 1940, the release of almost 8,900 German, Austrian, and Italian internees had been authorized,[6] and Parliament appears to have been generally satisfied with the progress of releases. Members were still concerned, however, with the treatment of aliens who remained in detention and, on 3rd December, one day of the Debate on the Address was devoted to that topic. Mr. Morrison was urged to remedy the administrative errors which had developed. He replied that he had told the Home Office staff that the House of Commons was "in a nasty temper" about the alien situation,[7] and informed the House that, although security had to be the balancing factor, he was proceeding with releases as quickly as possible.[8]

Little more was heard in Parliament about the internment of aliens. The answers to occasional parliamentary questions revealed that in the middle of January, 1941, 9,816 aliens had been released, while 17,940 still remained interned.[9] By June,

[1] 365 H.C. Deb. 5s., 102.
[2] Ibid., 184-185.
[3] Ibid., 263.
[4] Ibid., 365.
[5] 367 H.C. Deb. 5s., 80-81.
[6] Ibid., 651.
[7] Ibid., 457.
[8] Ibid., 464.
[9] 386 H.C. Deb. 5s., 1436.

1941, 16,694 had been released[1] and by November, 1941, 9,019 remained in internment, while some 18,000 had been released.[2] On 1st January, 1943, the number of interned enemy aliens was 6,123.[3]

While the Government's handling of the internment of enemy aliens has been called "perhaps the worst blot on the British record in the second World War",[4] it would perhaps not be inappropriate to say that Parliament experienced its "finest hour" on that occasion. Credit for the amelioration of the great hardships suffered by refugees must be given to both Parliament and the press who reversed a xenophobic trend in British public opinion and forced the Government to take remedial action. It seems undeniable that, in the words of one who experienced internment as an enemy alien, "the debates on the topic in question, held in both the House of Commons and the House of Lords, during this critical period of British history, will forever remain on record as evidence of the high achievement of the 'mother' and 'teacher' of parliaments in maintaining freedom of speech and opinion, even in a time of utmost emergency".[5]

It is significant that most of the parliamentary activity described in this chapter occurred in the summer of 1940, the period when Great Britain stood in greatest danger of German invasion. The continent had been overrun, and only the narrow channel separated Britain from the victorious German armies. Expecting invasion momentarily, the British Government felt obliged to exercise many of the broad powers which Parliament had granted it for such a contingency, and, thereby, to infringe upon some of the basic civil liberties of the individual. The summer of 1940 was a period in which the maxim *inter arma leges silent* might well have been descriptive of the reality, for the discretionary powers of the Government might, in such an extremely desperate situation, have become arbitrary powers. Such was not the case, however. The laws were not silent and

---

[1] 372 H.C. Deb. 5s., 1124.

[2] 374 H.C. Deb. 5s., 2073-2074.

[3] 386 H.C. Deb. 5s., 1436.

[4] Clinton L. Rossiter, *Constitutional Dictatorship* (Princeton: Princeton University Press, 1948), 200.

[5] Maximilian Koessler, "Enemy Alien Internment: with Special Reference to Great Britain and France," *Political Science Quarterly*, LVII (March, 1942), 101.

the Government was not uncontrolled because Parliament was able to check the Government's use of its powers by reminding the wielders of power that they were accountable to Parliament.

The proper role of a legislature in a crisis situation of grave proportions is not easy to determine. It must not nag; it must not be unrealistic in its demands; at the same time, it must not render itself impotent by allowing the executive a completely free hand in the management of national survival. The British Parliament came close to finding the solution of this problem. It recognized, as one member of Parliament put it, that "some freedoms must be surrendered for the duration of the war, but [that] others are part of the very objects and aims of the war to preserve and vindicate."[1]   It grasped, moreover, the intimate connection between, and the indivisible nature of, the basic civil liberties, and realized that freedom of press, speech, and Parliament were all part of the same parcel, and that an infringement upon any one of them undermined the efficacy of the others. If any illustration of the validity of this thesis is needed, the alien internment situation is evidence. Free parliamentary debate and a free press to report it were able to influence the Government to such an extent that "the worst blot" on the Government's record was rather quickly eradicated.

Awareness of Hitler engendered neither a fear psychosis nor lockjaw. Few in Parliament equated unpopular opinions with disloyalty; few were so panic-stricken as to be indifferent to the plight of 27,000 interned enemy aliens; few were so daunted as to think that survival required the total suppression of individual liberty. Parliament was steadfast and indefatigable in its determination to maintain the essential liberties which can be maintained in war-time. Back-benchers of all parties understood their task, and addressed themselves to it with vigour. They asked almost four thousand questions in the House of Commons in the three-month period, June through August, 1940.[2] Day after day, private members rose from the back benches and bombarded Ministers with questions designed to remind the executive that basic liberties were not to be sacrificed. Thus, Ministers could not plead ignorance of the sentiments of the House, nor could they

[1] Kenneth Lindsay, "Parliament in War," *Spectator*, CLXV (30th August, 1940), 215.

[2] *Spectator*, CLXV (30th August, 1940), 211.

forget their responsibility to Parliament. Parliament insisted that Ministers take heed of its grievances. The unfamiliarity of Sir John Anderson, in the key position of Home Secretary, with Parliament and its methods and traditions demonstrated that "a Minister who cannot persuade the House he is right must make concessions to the feelings of the House".[1] Sir John brought to the Home Secretaryship a great store of administrative experience gained from a long and distinguished career as a civil servant and imperial administrator, but he did not appear to develop the ability to sense the real sentiment of the House. His relations with Parliament during the critical summer of 1940, especially in connection with the alien internment issue, very likely contributed to his transference from the Home Office[2] to the Lord Presidency of the Council.

All of this parliamentary activity had its results. Not only did Parliament force the Government to modify its original regulations imposing restrictions upon speech and opinion; it also carefully watched the administration of the watered-down, though still potent, regulations, and thereby prevented cabinet, constables, and courts from being too zealous in applying them. Parliamentary criticism caused the Government to abandon the Swinton Committee and the "Silent Columns." Criticism in Parliament also contributed to the ending of discrimination by the B.B.C. Occasionally, Parliament became angry, as, for example, when Government action threatened the independence of the press, or when the Government appeared callous toward the individual, as in the war-zone courts and alien internment situations. The Government was impressed with parliamentary demonstrations of "nasty temper," and took appropriate action to mollify it.

In the final analysis, Parliament was successful in protecting individual liberties because back-benchers of all parties concentrated their energies on that task, and because the Government realized the need of carrying the House with it at every stage. Since the Government needed almost unanimous popular

---

[1] W. Ivor Jennings, "Parliament in Wartime, III," *Political Quarterly*, XI (1940), 354.

[2] Argus, "Friendly Enemy Aliens," *Contemporary Review*, CLIX (January, 1941), 53. Mr. Churchill, commenting on the replacement of Sir John Anderson by Mr. Morrison, "thought it would be a help to have a long-trained Parliamentarian at the Home Office" (Churchill, *Their Finest Hour*, 369).

backing in order to prosecute the war successfully, it could not afford to ignore the grievances which ordinary members of Parliament expressed.

CHAPTER V

TECHNIQUES OF PARLIAMENTARY CONTROL IN WAR-TIME

ALTHOUGH Parliament achieved a considerable degree of success in protecting individual liberties from unnecessary executive encroachments, many members, nevertheless, remained concerned about the over-all effectiveness of the House of Commons as a restraint upon the Government. As one observer has noted, parliamentary criticism was "much more effective than a strictly logical assessment of the balance of power between the Executive and the House of Commons would suggest."[1] After the transfer of most of its legislative powers to the executive in August, 1939, and, more especially, after the formation of the Coalition Government in June, 1940, Parliament appeared to be left with only a very short lever with which to try to bring pressure against the Government. Fortified with a 99 per cent majority in the House, the Government could make every issue a matter of confidence and could expect to carry the House, since few members realistically contemplated any alternative to the Churchill Government.

"Experience in the present war", Lord Sumner wrote at the end of World War I, "must have taught us all that many things are done in the name of the Executive in such times purporting to be for the common good, which Englishmen have been too patriotic to contest."[2] Similarly, in the early period of World War II, members of Parliament were too patriotic, or too impressed with the terrible nature of the enemy force, to be very fastidious in their attitude towards the broad question of executive-legislative balance. From the granting of emergency powers to the executive in August, 1939, until the end of 1942, the House of Commons did not overtly concern itself much with the general issue of constitutional equilibrium. In connection with the

[1] Francis Williams, *Press, Parliament, and People* (London: W. Heinemann Ltd., 1946), 107.

[2] *Attorney-General v. De Keyser's Royal Hotel* (1920), A.C., 563.

Government's use of 18B, many members expressed the belief that parliamentary control over the executive was illusory, and the Government's determination to make such issues as the administration of 18B, the suppression of the *Daily Worker*, and the proceedings against the *Daily Mirror* matters of confidence also evoked some parliamentary alarm over a shifting of the balance in favour of the executive. For the most part, however, until 1943 Parliament concentrated on remedying specific grievances as they arose and contented itself with safeguarding basic liberties. Members who were concerned over the upsetting of the constitutional balance which they saw in the practice of delegating wide emergency powers to the executive, motivated by a desire not to embarrass the Government while the country was in grave danger, permitted their fears to recede to a state of suspension until such time as more propitious national fortunes might grace their grievances with a greater sense of relevancy. Until 1943, parliamentary opportunities to raise the general issue of legislative-executive relations were, for the most part, allowed to pass. In July, 1942, for example, on the motion for the continuance of the Emergency Powers (Defence) Act for another year, members permitted the occasion for a prolonged debate in the area of emergency powers and delegated legislation to lapse, and the only words spoken at that time consisted of the seven-line speech of the Under-Secretary for the Home Department.

Until 1943, also, the right to pray against defence regulations was invoked relatively infrequently. The significance of the prayers laid down during the first three years of the war should not be minimized, but the sparsity of prayers prior to 1943 is also noteworthy. From August, 1939, to the end of 1942, six prayers to annul defence regulations were moved, whereas the same number of prayers was put forward during the first four months of 1943. An analysis of the first six prayers reveals a great deal about parliamentary interests during the period, and also gives some indication of the effectiveness of the prayer as a technique of parliamentary control. Two of the prayers were directly concerned with executive infringements upon basic liberties. The first, Mr. Dingle Foot's on 31st October, 1939, against Regulations 18B, 39A, 39B and others, was withdrawn when the Government agreed to an informal conference with members to modify the regulations in order to make them acceptable to the House.[1] The second prayer, that of Mr. Sydney Silverman on July 31st, 1940, against Regulation 2D, called forth strong opposition to the regulation from members of all parties, and was pressed to a division which the Government won by only thirty-eight votes.[2] This was the narrowest Government majority on a prayer throughout the war. A third prayer, put down by Dr. Edith Summerskill on 15th December, 1942, might also, for purposes of this analysis, be placed in the civil liberties category. Dr. Summerskill's prayer was against Regulation 33B, which provided for compulsory treatment of any individual who had infected two other persons with a venereal disease. Dr. Summerskill opposed the regulation because she thought that it did not go far enough, and would probably affect only prostitutes. Much support for her motion, however, came from members who believed the regulation was a meddlesome interference with individual liberty. The prayer was defeated, 245 votes to thirty-one.[3]

Of the remaining three prayers, two were protests against the use of defence regulations for purposes thought not to have been contemplated by Parliament when passing the enabling statute. On 1st April, 1941, Mr. Magnay prayed against Regulation 42BA, which permitted the opening of theatres and music halls on Sunday. The general parliamentary objection was that authorizing the Sunday opening of theatres and music halls was not sufficiently closely connected with the prosecution of the war to warrant its being done by regulation rather than by statute. The Government decided to allow a free vote, and members took advantage of their freedom from the whips by carrying the prayer by a vote of 144-136.[4] On 14th October, 1942, Mr. Craven-Ellis moved a prayer against the Defence (Amalgamation of Police Forces) Regulations which empowered the Home Secretary to amalgamate certain local police forces. The Parliamentary objection was that the powers granted to the Home Secretary by

---

[1] See pp. 37-38.   [2] See p. 73

[3] 385 H.C. Deb. 5s., 1807-1888.

[4] The *Economist* called the House's action "a disgraceful exhibition and the best possible argument for dissolving the 1935 Parliament at the earliest convenient moment" (CXL [5th April, 1941], 443). See also Tom Harrisson, "The House of Commonsense," *New Statesman and Nation*, XXI (12th April, 1941), 380-381, for an analysis of the vote and of public opinion on the issue.

the regulations were far too wide, and that, by virtue of them, he might establish a national police force, an action not contemplated by Parliament under the Emergency Powers (Defence) Act. The Home Secretary promised the House that he would consult with local authorities before making any amalgamation orders and assured members that he did not intend to set up a national police force. On the basis of the assurances, the prayer was withdrawn.[1]

The sixth prayer was concerned with property rights. Mr. Spens, on 6th August, 1941, moved the annulment of Defence Regulation 78, which authorized competent Government authorities to dismiss any director or manager in a controlled industry if the competent authority believed that the director or manager was obstructing the Government controller for that industry. The regulation further authorized the competent authority to acquire all of the share capital of a controlled industry at a price to be determined either by the Treasury or by an accountant named by the Lord Chief Justice. Members objected on the grounds that the regulation gave the Government powers over property which were too drastic. Nevertheless, upon receiving assurance from the Government that the regulation would be used in only one or two cases, Mr. Spens withdrew the prayer.[2]

Each of the prayers prior to 1943 was motivated by a particular substantive grievance, and was directed towards the removal of such grievance. The first six prayers were not part of a concerted effort to reassert the position of the Parliament. The prayers which followed them, however, were to be differently motivated.

Professor Laski has written that "it is the genius of any legislative assembly to develop a personality of its own which it seeks, if it can, to maintain in independence of the executive power".[3] The calendar year 1943 witnessed the development in the House of Commons of a noticeable increase of interest in the constitutional position of Parliament *vis-a-vis* the executive. In a review of the activities of Parliament for the year 1943, one

[1] 383 H.C. Deb. 5s., 1696-1734.

[2] 373 H.C. Deb. 5s., 2050-2064.

[3] Harold J. Laski, "The War Cabinet and Parliament," *New Statesman and Nation,* XX (14th December, 1940), 612.

observer remarked that, during the year, the House of Commons had "grown conscious of its constitutional duty to supervise and check the executive."[1]   Members revived discussion of the problem of delegated legislation which had lain dormant since Mr. Dingle Foot's motion in 1937 that the power of the executive "has grown, is growing, and ought to be diminished", and many lent their support to Mr. Foot's sentiments.   Demands for more effective parliamentary control over the executive became commonplace in the House of Commons as grievances were increasingly aired.

The renaissance of parliamentary interest in controlling the executive was probably due to three factors.   First, there was a considerable amelioration of Britain's fortunes by 1943.   German invasion had become improbable, allied air supremacy was established, and allied forces were pursuing the retreating Axis forces in Tunisia.   The improvement in the British position appears to have established an atmosphere of sufficient optimism to permit many members of Parliament to feel that they could, in good conscience, pelter the Government with criticisms of the whole structure of delegated legislation under the emergency powers.

In addition, the inability or the unwillingness of the courts to restrain the executive's use of emergency powers had been realized for some time.   Although on two occasions the judiciary had invoked *ultra vires* against executive action under the Emergency Powers Act, by the end of 1941 the courts had given clear notice that neither Parliament nor the country should expect to look to them for relief against oppressive executive action.   In 1940, in the case of *Jones v. Farrell*,[2] Mr. Justice Bennett held that the section of Regulation 55 which authorized the Government to carry on an undertaking was beyond the power given the Government by the Emergency Powers Act to take possession or control of an undertaking, and hence was invalid.   The following year, however, in a case involving the validity of another defence regulation,[3] a higher court used the occasion to say that

---

[1] Onlooker, "Parliamentary Control of Delegated Legislation," *Journal of the Society of Clerks-at-the-Table in Empire Parliaments*, X (1941), 83. (The volume of the *Journal* for the year 1941 was not published until 1943.)

[2] 3 All Eng. Rep. 608 (1940).

[3] *Rex v. Comptroller General of Patents, ex parte Bayer Products, Limited* (1941), 2 K.B. 306.

Mr. Justice Bennett had been wrong in holding Regulation 55(4) to be *ultra vires* because he should have remembered that the enabling statute had provided that the specific powers granted by the act were not to limit the powers given to His Majesty in Council to make such regulations as appeared to him necessary and expedient for the general purposes of securing the public safety, the defence of the realm, etc. Lord Justice Clauson then proceeded to recite what appeared to be a judicial abdication statement:

> In my view this court has no right or jurisdiction to investigate the reasons which moved His Majesty to reach the conclusion that it was necessary or expedient to make the regulation. The legislature has left the matter to His Majesty and this court has no control over it. This court, in my view, has no duty and no right to investigate what was the advice which was given to His Majesty which moved him to the view that it was necessary or expedient for the purposes in question to make this regulation; and I know of no authority which would justify the court in questioning the decision which His Majesty has (as I understand it) stated that he has come to—that this regulation is necessary or expedient. If His Majesty has once reached that conclusion, that regulation is the law of the land, subject to this, that the Act specially provides machinery by which, if either House of Parliament is disposed to take a view differing from that upon which His Majesty has been pleased to act, the order can be annulled.[1]

In another case, arising under Regulation 55, [2] Mr. Justice Farwell held that the action of a controller of a Government-controlled enterprise, in directing the company to increase its bank overdraft, was *ultra vires*. The Government reacted to the decision by immediately issuing a new regulation, Regulation 78, which furnished it with the powers desired.[3]

What appeared to many to be the ultimate in judicial abdication came in the House of Lords' decision in *Liversidge v. Anderson*

---

[1] Sir Cecil T. Carr, "A Regulated Liberty," *Columbia Law Review*, XLII (March, 1942), 342, quoting from *Reports of Patent, Design and Trade Mark Cases* (1941) at 268–269.

[2] *John Fowler and Company (Leeds) v. Duncan* (1941) 2 All Eng. Rep., 577.

[3] A prayer was moved in the House of Commons against Regulation 78 on 6th August, 1941. See pp. 102.

towards the end of 1941.[1] Parliament, wishing to surround the executive's power to detain individuals under Regulation 18B with greater safeguards, had, in conference with the Government, substituted the words "has reasonable cause to believe" for "is satisfied" as the guide for the Home Secretary's actions in this area. It would appear that many members had believed that, in making this change, they were insuring a judicial check on the executive's action. In the Liversidge decision, however, the court held that the doctrine of *ultra vires* was not applicable even to "reasonable cause to believe," and that the direction to the Minister was still one of subjective determination.[2] The perturbation of the House of Commons at this decision has already been noted, and parliamentary appreciation of the far-reaching import of the Lords' pronouncement was a significant factor in arousing the House of Commons to seek further parliamentary safeguards against executive action.

The third explanation for the strong parliamentary activity beginning in 1943, which was aimed at strengthening the position of the House of Commons in relation to the executive, appears to be the realization that government by emergency powers was not likely to be limited to war-time. At Swindon, on 20th December, 1942, in his first speech after joining the War Cabinet, Mr. Herbert Morrison stated that "much of the social control of production which we have learned to accept and value during the war will need to be continued during the peace."[3] On 12th January, 1943, the Prime Minister outlined a comprehensive programme of social and economic legislation with which he believed the post-war Government would have to deal.[4] Later, Mr. Herbert Morrison indicated explicitly that he anticipated an increase in delegated legislation under emergency powers to handle reconstruction problems.[5]

The driving force of the increased parliamentary endeavour

---

[1] See pp. 45-46.

[2] C. K. Allen believes that "there is ground for thinking that *Liversidge v. Anderson* was an emergency interpretation of an emergency measure and is not likely in future to be applied generally to Statutory Instruments governed by this form of delegation." *Law in the Making* (5th ed.; Oxford: Clarendon Press, 1951), 541-542.

[3] Herbert Morrison, *Prospects and Policies* (New York: Alfred A. Knopf, 1944), 6.

[4] Winston S. Churchill, *The Hinge of Fate* (Boston: Houghton Mifflin Co., 1950), 958.

[5] Morrison, *op. cit.*, 48-55. Speech at Dundee, 3rd October, 1943.

to translate the legal supremacy of Parliament into effective supervision of the executive was a group of Conservative private members who styled themselves the "Active Back-Benchers". Organized informally under the chairmanship of Sir Herbert Williams, the group came into existence at the end of 1942 "as a result of strong objection which was being taken to certain Defence Regulations made under the Emergency Powers Act".[1] Its members embarked upon the task of examining each new defence regulation and all other Statutory Rules and Orders, which were at that time being issued at the rate of fifty or more a week. Sir Herbert Williams has described the activities of his group in the following words:

> We found there was a very wide field for activity. We forced debates on many of these Statutory Rules and Orders. We asked innumerable questions, and . . . continued . . . to seek every opportunity of raising the principles involved and frequently tabled amendments to Government Bills for the purpose of securing that delegated legislation was kept under proper control.[2]

The activities of these back-benchers caused one observer to comment that there had developed during 1943 "a new technique of vigilance".[3] In the wake of the onslaught upon delegated legislation by the "Active Back-Benchers", other private members began to voice anxiety over the threat to parliamentary supremacy which they saw in the practice. While some members attacked the whole principle of delegated legislation and agitated for its speedy demise, most of those who participated in the campaign directed their criticisms against specific aspects of the practice which they believed hindered the exertion of effective parliamentary control.

One of the grievances advanced most frequently and most vigorously was that the volume of the output of defence regulations and rules and orders made under them was so great as to preclude members from exercising anything approaching a continuing and comprehending examination upon which criticism of

---

[1] Sir Herbert Williams, "The A.B.B.s, *Journal of the Society of Clerks-at-the-Table in Empire Parliaments*, XIV (1945), 181.

[2] *Ibid.*   [3] Onlooker, *op. cit.*, 90.

the executive might be based. Up to the middle of February, 1943, for example, 318 Defence (General) Regulations and forty-three Codes of Defence Regulations dealing with special subjects such as finance and administration of justice had been made. In addition, the number of Statutory Rules and Orders made and in force under the defence regulations up to that date was in the neighbourhood of 2,100.[1] Members complained that the mere bulk of the regulations and orders made them "undigestible",[2] and it was contended that no member of Parliament could be "expected to winnow them all in order to disengage those which deserve special attention."[3] One member expressed "disgust at the large number of Regulations continually issued",[4] and another said that it was "physically impossible for the average member to carry out what is his plain duty".[5]

An additional source of grievance was that a large number of the orders made under the defence regulations were not laid before the House. Defence regulations themselves were to be laid before the House, and prayers for annulment might be moved against them. Some of the rules and orders made under the regulations had to be laid before the House although no prayers could be moved against them. Access to these rules and orders was difficult, however, since they were in fact placed in the library of the House, often under lock and key.[6] A large number of the orders were not required to be laid before the House at all, and it was contended that this practice made for the exaltation of the power of the bureaucracy at the expense of the House of Commons.[7]

In a lively debate on 19th January, 1943, an attack was made on several aspects of the process of emergency legislation. The immediate occasion of the debate was a prayer against an omnibus Order in Council which amended five existing defence regulations and brought three new regulations into existence. The Order in Council dealt with such diverse matters as civil defence, fire

---

[1] 386 H.C. Deb. 5s., 1935.

[2] Mr. de la Bere, 4th November, 1943, 493 H.C. Deb. 5s., 855.

[3] C. K. Allen, *Law and Orders* (London: Stevens & Sons Ltd., 1945), 91.

[4] Mr. Gledhill, 15th July, 1943, 391 H.C. Deb. 5s., 450.

[5] Commander Bower, 17th May, 1944, 400 H.C. Deb. 5s., 213.

[6] Allen, *Law and Orders*, 91.

[7] Mr. Levy, 2nd February, 1943, 386 H.C. Deb. 5s., 748.

prevention duty, the National Fire Services, pharmacists, penalties for illegal export of goods, and restrictions on appeals by charities. The mover of the prayer objected to the practice of incorporating such a variety of subjects in one Order in Council, and contended that if "there were one matter alone in this Order which was liable to abuse and to which objection ought to be made . . . it would be necessary to object to the whole Order".[1] An immediate concession on this point was given by the Home Secretary, who promised to discontinue the practice of amalgamating diverse regulations in the same Order in Council.[2]

Criticism was also directed at the bulk and unintelligibility of Statutory Rules and Orders. It was pointed out that, on that particular day, there were between eighty and one hundred regulations and orders laying on the Table.[3] Sir Herbert Williams charged that, in the absence of a formal Opposition, the task of examining such a large amount of subordinate legislation was too great for any individual member, but the Home Secretary denied that this was true.[4] It was alleged that, moreover, "order after order is being issued to-day that is quite unintelligible to highly qualified solicitors and barristers",[5] and that "no Member could understand more than two per cent of them unless he were prepared to spend hours and hours in the Library looking up the cross references."[6] On this grievance, also, members received an immediate concession from the Home Secretary, who promised that an explanatory memorandum would be affixed to regulations or orders which were difficult to understand.[7] During the entire debate, no private member spoke in support of the Government.

In spite of the Government's concession with regard to explanatory memoranda for complicated or technical regulations and orders, members continued to press for more intelligible subordinate legislation, and vied with each other in claiming credit for length of time spent in research in order to decipher the meaning of a piece of delegated legislation. Mr. Pritt appears

[1] Flight-Lieut. Raikes, 386 H.C. Deb. 5s., 149-151.
[2] Mr. Herbert Morrison, *ibid.*, 161-163.
[3] Flight-Lieut. Raikes, *ibid.*, 149.
[4] *Ibid.*, 157.
[5] Flight-Lieut. Challen, *ibid.*, 169.
[6] Mr. Levy, *ibid.*, 152.
[7] Mr. H. Morrison, *ibid.*, 161-163.

to have set something of a record in claiming that it took him eight hours to determine the effect of one Order in Council.[1] Many orders contained so many cross references[2] or such technical terms[3] that members could enliven the proceedings of the House considerably by merely reading the text of orders while, at the same time, striking a blow for parliamentary control.[4] "Occasionally," Sir Herbert Williams has revealed, "it happens in the House that the most effective way of criticizing an order is to read a few of the more important paragraphs and then innocently to ask the Minister what it all means".[5]

Even the Government's concession on explanatory memoranda later drew criticism from the House when a prayer was removed to annul the Defence (Fire Guard) Regulations in order to draw attention to the fact that the Home Office had issued a seventy-one page explanatory memorandum to elucidate one of the orders. Mr. Morrison agreed that it was "not easy to defend an Explanatory Memorandum which was issued for the purpose of simplifying and which contains more words than the number of words in all the orders which it explains".[6]

---

[1] 387 H.C. Deb. 5s., 1878, 25th March, 1943.

[2] C. K. Allen says that the following order (S.R. & O., 1216, 1943) is "something of a classic" but "by no means uncharacteristic":

"The Control of Tins, Cans, Kegs, Drums and Packaging Pails No. 5 Order, 1942 a), as varied by the Control of Tins, Cans, Kegs, Drums and Packaging Pails No. 6 Order, 1942 (b), the Control of Tins, Cans, Kegs, Drums and Packaging Pails No. 7 Order, 1942 (c), the Control of Tins, Cans, Kegs, Drums and Packaging Pails No. 8 Order, 1942 (d), and the Control of Tins, Cans, Kegs, Drums and Packaging Pails No. 9 Order, 1942 (e), is hereby further varied in the Third Schedule thereto by substituting for the reference 2A therein the reference 2A (i) and by deleting therefrom the reference 2B.

"This Order shall come into force on the 25th day of August, 1943, and may be cited as the 'Control of Tins, Cans, Kegs, Drums and Packaging Pails No. 10 Order, 1943,' and this Order and the Control of Tins, Cans, Kegs, Drums and Packaging Pails Nos. 5–9 Orders, 1942, may be cited together as the Control of Tins, Cans, Kegs, Drums, and Packaging Pails Nos. 5–10 Order, 1942–3."

The explanatory memorandum revealed that the order "enables tin plate to be used for tobacco and snuff tins other than cutter lid tobacco tins," (Cited by Allen, *Law and Orders*, 118–119.)

[3] Mr. Levy asked the Parliamentary Secretary to the Ministry of Food what was intended to be meant by the order (S.R. & O. No. 1445, 1943) which read: "Dogfish flaps sold separately shall not be regarded as fillets."

The Parliamentary Secretary: ". . . flaps, including dogfish flaps, are lugs or belly-walls. . . ."

Mr. Levy: "Does my right Hon. Friend not recognize that even the trade does not understand this ? Why not put it in plain and simple language, so that we can understand what it is all about ?"

The Parliamentary Secretary: "I do not think any language can be more plain and simple." (392 H.C. Deb. 5s., 1388.)

[4] Of the wording of one Order, Mr. Levy said: "If it were not so tragic, it would be comic. If you introduced this Order on a music-hall stage, it would run for a thousand nights." 386 H.C. Deb. 5s., 153.

[5] Williams, *op. cit.*, 182.

[6] 392 H.C. Deb. 5s., 1334–1335, 19th October, 1943.

A matter to which the House repeatedly called attention was delay by Government Departments in laying regulations and orders before Parliament. Under the terms of the Emergency Powers Act, regulations made thereunder were to be laid before Parliament "as soon as may be" after being made, and the twenty-eight day period during which Parliament might pray for an annulment was to begin only when the Order had been laid. In the meantime, however, the regulation was to have effect from the time it was made. The lack of any precise meaning to the phrase "as soon as may be" presented a problem which has not yet been solved to the complete satisfaction of Parliament. Instances were brought forward of delays in laying of over four months,[1] and the problem was, as expressed by one member, that "if Orders are to be held up for weeks before being placed on the Table, prosecutions may have taken place and individuals may have been sent to penal servitude for fourteen years while the House is waiting to examine the Orders".[2] An order prohibiting the transport of flowers by train was operative for a week before it was available in the Library of the House of Commons, and during that time, six persons were arrested and prosecuted for violating its provisions. In response to criticism, the Government announced that arrangements had been made to have new Statutory Rules and Orders delivered to the House daily instead of once a week.[3]

While delays in laying were considered "a minor constitutional outrage" since they deprived the House "of its opportunity of making a protest merely through idleness in tabling the Order",[4] a startling weakness in the chain of parliamentary control was revealed on 26th July, 1944, when the Home Secretary informed the House that there had been a failure to lay before Parliament several National Fire Service regulations made under the Fire Service (Emergency Provisions) Act of 1941. Some of the regulations had been issued as early as August, 1941,

---

[1] Mr. Levy, 19th January, 1943, 386 H.C. Deb. 5s., 152.

[2] Flight-Lieut. Challen, *ibid.*, 168.

[3] 378 H.C. Deb. 5s., 468, 2nd March, 1943. The Prime Minister demonstrated considerable annoyance at this particular order and told the Minister of War Transport "that some effort should be made to ease up this war on the flowers, in which your department is showing an undue relish." (Churchill, *The Hinge of Fate*, 935.)

[4] Sir H. Williams, 19th January, 1943, 386 H.C. Deb. 5s., 167.

and thus had been in force for nearly three years without Parliament's having had an opportunity to examine them. The regulations had been signed, sent to the Stationery Office to be printed, placed on sale, but, by an oversight, no copies had been sent to either House of Parliament. Mr. Morrison announced that the regulations were being laid before Parliament at once, and that the Government would introduce an indemnity bill to relieve the Home Secretary of any consequences which he might have incurred from his failure to submit the regulations to Parliament.

During the debate on the Indemnity Bill in August, 1944, the sentiment was expressed that Parliament had failed to develop adequate machinery of control to guarantee that the instructions were carried out. Mr. Morrison told the House that arrangements had been made to provide a double check against a recurrence of failure to lay, since "when Parliament has enacted that Regulations shall be laid, failure to comply with that enactment is a grave offence by the Minister responsible". In addition, he promised careful consideration by the Government of any parliamentary suggestion "to set it beyond doubt by some appropriate enactment that Regulations which are subject to a negative Resolution shall cease to be operative if they are not laid within a specified period".[1] After considerable comment on the lack of adequate parliamentary mechanisms of control and the expression by the Home Secretary of sincere regret at the incident, the House passed the Act of Indemnity[2] on the same day. Both the necessity for the Act and its precise effect have been questioned,[3] and the Home Secretary admitted that he did not know whether the regulations had been invalidated by his failure to lay them before Parliament. He believed that that was a question which only the courts could settle.

While members of Parliament were objecting to specific practices connected with widespread government by regulation, and gaining some successes from their efforts, there persisted the basic grievance that the structure of parliamentary control would remain weak so long as the basic responsibility for exercising it

[1] 402 H.C. Deb. 5s., 1218-1219.

[2] 7 & 8 Geo. 6, c. 35.

[3] See, for example, Allen, *Law and Orders*, 108-112.

rested on the individual member. In spite of the concessions made by the Government to make regulations and orders more intelligible or to reduce delays in laying, for example, the fact remained that the task of tracking down, studying, and reporting upon the uses to which the Government was putting its crisis powers was too onerous to be performed by members of Parliament acting as individuals. Accordingly, throughout 1943 and during the first half of 1944, there was ever-growing pressure in Parliament for the creation of machinery to aid Parliament in performing its job as watchdog. The institutional arrangement for which the House of Commons pressed was a Select Committee which should be charged with examining subordinate legislation and reporting abuses in it to the House. In its report in 1932, the Donoughmore Committee had recommended the establishment of Standing Committees in both Houses of Parliament to perform this function, but the suggestion had encountered considerable opposition, and no steps had been taken towards its realization.

During 1943, however, a concerted effort began in the House to convince the Government that such a mechanism was essential to its fulfilling its supervisory function. On 26th May, 1943, a prolonged debate on Major Petherick's motion "that Parliament should vigilantly maintain the ancient right and duty of examining legislation, whether delegated or otherwise" revealed much support for the establishment of a scrutinizing committee.[1] The debate on the Government's motion to extend the Emergency Powers Act for another twelve months, on 15th July, 1943, lasted over four hours, and one of the chief issues in the debate was the setting up of a Select Committee to scrutinize Statutory Rules and Orders. For the Government, Mr. Morrison resisted these early demands on the ground that such a Committee would interfere with the obligation which every member of Parliament had "to make himself reasonably skilled in these matters".[2] In addition, he argued that such an examination of subordinate legislation by a committee of the House would delay governmental action and,

---

[1] It is interesting to note that Colonel Sir Charles MacAndrew, later Chairman of the Select Committee on Statutory Rules and Orders, opposed the creation of such a Committee. "What chance would one Committee have of dealing with all these Regulations? The whole thing is perfectly nonsensical. . . . The present method of putting down a Prayer, although perhaps unsatisfactory, is the best way of dealing with matters of this kind." 389 H.C. Deb. 5s., 1629-1630.

[2] 386 H.C. Deb. 5s., 158.

if Ministers and Department officials had to appear to give testimony before the committee, "the strain would be too great and the delay too considerable".[1] Members such as Mr. Hugh Molson and Sir Herbert Williams disputed the validity of the Home Secretary's objections, and pointed to the fact that precedents for a scrutinizing committee existed in the Special Orders Committee of the House of Lords, which since 1925 had examined all departmental orders, rules, regulations, etc. requiring an affirmative resolution, and in the Ecclesiastical Committee of the House of Commons, which examined Measures passed by the Church of England Assembly requiring confirmation by the House. By the spring of 1944, sentiment in the House favouring the committee had grown to such an extent that Mr. Molson was able to obtain more than 140 signatures from members of all parties to his Motion on 17th May calling for the establishment of a Select Committee "to carry on a continuous examination of all Statutory Rules and Orders and other instruments of delegated legislation presented to Parliament".[2]

After a debate which covered ninety-seven columns of Hansard, Mr. Morrison announced that the Government was willing to see the establishment of an additional parliamentary safeguard over the executive, and, therefore, would view favourably the setting up of the Select Committee. In one important respect, the Government was willing to go beyond what was requested by the House, when the Home Secretary announced that "it would be undesirable for the Committee to draw the special attention of the House to any Regulation unless it has either heard an officer of the Department or seen a Memorandum put in by the Department."[3] The Committee, however, should not have the power to send for Ministers. The function of the Committee should be, according to the Home Secretary, "to protect the authority of Parliament and not the interests of a particular party or group,"[4] and the terms of reference should be such "that the Committee does not try to do the work of the courts of law".[5]

On 21st June, 1944, it was ordered by the House of Commons:

[1] 389 H.C. Deb. 5s., 1661.
[2] 400 H.C. Deb. 5s., 202.
[3] *Ibid.*, 269.   [4] *Ibid.*   [5] *Ibid.*, 274.

H

That a Select Committee be appointed to consider every Statutory Rule or Order (including any Provisional Rule made under Section 2 of the Rules Publication Act, 1893) laid or laid in draft before the House, being a Rule, Order, or Draft upon which proceedings may be taken in either House in pursuance of any Act of Parliament, with a view to determining whether the special attention of the House should be drawn to it on any of the following grounds:

(i) that it imposes a charge on the public revenues or contains provisions requiring payments to be made to the Exchequer or any Government Department or to any local public authority in consideration of any licence or consent, or of any services to be rendered, or prescribes the amount of any such charge or payments:

(ii) that it is made in pursuance of an enactment containing specific provisions excluding it from challenge in the courts, either at all times or after the expiration of a specified period:

(iii) that it appears to make some unusual or unexpected use of the powers conferred by the Statute under which it is made:

(iv) that there appears to have been unjustifiable delay in the publication of it:

(v) that for any special reason its form or purport calls for elucidation.[1]

It can be seen from the terms of reference that the committee was intended to concern itself only with procedural or constitutional aspects of delegated legislation. The purpose of the committee was to sift through the great bulk of Statutory Rules and Orders and to extract, for special parliamentary consideration, those which seemed to contain abuses of the powers which Parliament had granted, either by imposing charges, or requiring payments, or by otherwise making some unusual or unexpected use of the conferred powers, or those concerning which parliamentary or judicial control was made difficult or impossible by the unclarity of their form or purport, by delay in their publication, or by their containing provisions which excluded them from judicial challenge. It was not intended that the committee should

[1] 401 H.C. Deb. 5s., 310.

concern itself with the policy or merits of either the subordinate legislation or the statutes under which it was made. Since full discussion of policy and merits took place in the House at the time of the enactment of the parent statute, it was not considered desirable that the committee should revive such discussion by drawing the House's attention, on questions of merits, to the Statutory Rules and Orders which implemented the policies previously approved by Parliament. Since, as Sir Cecil Carr has said, "a Select Committee cannot relieve the responsible Minister of his responsibility to parliament," a report of the committee was intended only to have the effect "of waving a red light if something [was] detected of which parliament ought to take notice".[1] However, as Sir Cecil Carr has also pointed out, the term of reference which allowed the committee to report on "unusual or unexpected use" of a statutory power "permit[ted] the consideration of aspects not far removed from policy and merits".[2] Pressure for enlarging the committee's terms of reference in order to permit it to consider the policy and merits of subordinate legislation subsequently developed, and will be discussed at a later point.[3]

It should be noted that the committee was an instrument only of the House of Commons. Eleven members of Parliament, chosen to reflect the strength of the parties in the House, were named to the committee. The committee was furnished the assistance of the Counsel to the Speaker (Sir Cecil Carr), was empowered to meet while the House might be adjourned, and was charged with requiring the submission of oral or written testimony from the department concerned before drawing the attention of the House to any particular regulation or order.

The establishment of the scrutinizing committee constituted an important victory for the House of Commons in its war-time attempts to maintain itself as watchdog over the executive. It was another manifestation of the effectiveness of concerted back-bench activity, for Mr. Morrison later revealed that he had assented to the establishment of the committee not because he

[1] Sir Courtenay Ilbert and Sir Cecil Carr, *Parliament* (3rd ed. rev.; London: Oxford University Press, 1950), 73-74.

[2] *Third Report from the Select Committee on Procedure* . . . H.C.R. 189-1, Session 1945-46 (London: His Majesty's Stationery Office, 1946), 244.

[3] See pp. 162-163.

was convinced of the merits of the proposal, but only because he was impressed by the strength of sentiment in the House.[1] The setting up of the committee was the direct result of some eighteen months' pressure from members of Parliament, for the most part back-bench Conservatives, and marked the culmination during war-time of Parliament's bid to strengthen its hand against the executive. With the establishment of the committee, there existed for the first time a formal instrument through which Parliament might, depending upon the operation of the committee and the response of members to its recommendations, subject delegated legislation to closer scrutiny than had previously prevailed.

An analysis of the motions to annul defence regulations from January, 1943, until the end of the war also reflects increased parliamentary activity aimed at bringing delegated legislation under effective control. In the first place, members of the House of Commons showed a great deal more inclination to use the prayer as an instrument of parliamentary control. During the last twenty-eight months of the war, members put down more than twice as many prayers against defence regulations as they had during the first forty months of the war. While six prayers against defence regulations were moved up to the end of 1942, no less than fourteen were put forward between January, 1943 and May, 1945.

The content of the post-1942 prayers reflects Parliament's primary concern during the period. Seven, or one-half of the total number, were intended to draw attention to practices of the executive in the area of delegated legislation which were considered to impede effective parliamentary control. Four of these were protests against the practice whereby Ministers delegated to subordinates the powers which Parliament had delegated to the Ministers.[2] Members complained in each case that, as a result of the practice of sub-delegation, the actual wielder of power was too far removed from control by Parliament and that, accordingly, the power would not be used with a proper sense of

---

[1] *Third Report from the Select Committee on Procedure* (1946), 149.

[2] Regulations 18, 47A, 53, 60, and 78, 27th January, 1943 (Commander Bower); Regulation 14 of Defence (Armed Forces) Regulations, 10th February, 1943 (Charles Taylor); Regulations 42D, 60DAA, and 104A, 25th March, 1943 (Mr. Pritt); Regulations 55A, 8th July, 1943 (Sir Harold Webbe).

responsibility.   Each of the prayers was withdrawn after the Minister concerned had given satisfactory assurance that the sub-delegated powers would be exercised responsibly.

Two more of the seven prayers which were concerned with specific executive practices in the realm of delegated legislation have already been mentioned.   Mr. Raikes' prayer of 19th January, 1943, protesting against the practice of amalgamating several topically-unrelated defence regulations in the same Order in Council, was withdrawn after the granting of concessions by the Home Secretary,[1] and Sir Herbert Williams's motion on 19th October, 1943 to amend the Defence (Fire Guard) Regulations was withdrawn after it had served its purpose of calling attention to the issuance of a seventy-one page explanatory memorandum intended to clarify the regulations.[2]

The seventh prayer in this category was, in some respects, perhaps the most remarkable war-time prayer.   On 3rd February, 1943, Mr. Thomas Levy moved the annulment of an Order in Council amending Defence Regulation 70.   The existing regulation authorized the Minister of War Transport to make orders for the purpose of regulating traffic on highways, and the proposed amendment which was embodied in the Order in Council was intended to enable him to make orders "for removing or modifying, or for limiting the application of, any prohibitions or restrictions imposed by or under any Act."   The blank cheque nature of the request disturbed many members, and Mr. Aneurin Bevan thought that "it would be an excellent thing, a corrective for the Government and a reassertion of the authority of Parliament, if we chastized the Government on this occasion by compelling them to withdraw this Order and bring forward in precise and definite language an Order stating concretely what they wanted, and why, instead of conferring upon a Government Department powers more analogous to a dictatorship than to a democratic community".[3]   Under intense hammering, the Joint Parliamentary Secretary to the Ministry of War Transport confessed that "if hon. Members wanted to challenge the system of Orders in Council, this was a very good one for them to select, because the powers proposed in it are extremely wide",[4] and he

---

[1] See pp. 107-108.
[2] See p. 109.
[3] 386 H.C. Deb. 5s., 1011.
[4] Ibid., 1004-1005.

admitted that it was "very plain to everybody" that he had "not succeeded in convincing the House".[1]

Pleading urgent necessity, however, he promised to find a narrower and more restricted form of words if the House would agree to the withdrawal of the prayer. It is difficult to determine exactly what happened at this stage of the proceedings. Mr. Levy appeared satisfied to withdraw the prayer in the light of the promises received, but the House was apparently in such a state of confusion and excitement that a division on the prayer was ordered and, on the division on the motion to annul, everyone in the House, including Ministers, voted in the affirmative and the prayer was, therefore, carried unanimously.[2]

Of the remaining seven motions to annul defence regulations from January, 1943, until the end of the war, only two appear to fall directly into the "liberty of the subject" category. On 14th July, 1943, Mr. Levy prayed against an Order in Council which proposed to make it a criminal offence to trespass on any land used for growing crops. It was urged by several members that the Order unduly restricted the liberty of the subject, but the Minister firmly defended the Order and the prayer was negatived.[3] The second prayer directed against what was thought to be an interference with individual liberty was more significant and gave rise to a lively debate in the House. On 28th April, 1944, Mr. Aneurin Bevan moved the annulment of Defence Regulation 1AA which provided that persons who incited strikes without the approval of the trade unions should be liable to five years imprisonment. While some members considered the regulation to be an unnecessary limitation upon the liberty of the individual worker, others thought it was also a direct affront to Parliament since the Ministry of Labour had consulted the Trades Union Council, but not the House of Commons, in making it. A further element of contentiousness developed during the discus-

---

[1] *Ibid.*, 1012.

[2] Sir Herbert Williams has given his version of the incident: "We were never able to find out in the course of the debate what the real purpose of the Order was, but as far as I could discover it was to facilitate the dangerous driving of somewhat unusual military vehicles, which the American Forces had brought with them. . . . We ultimately got the Government Front Bench so rattled that when Mr. Speaker put the Question the Ministers inadvertently voted the same way as their critics. . . . The sequel was interesting, for, despite the great urgency which the Parliamentary Secretary had pleaded, nearly six months elapsed before the Ministry produced a very much milder Order, which was found to be reasonable." Williams *op. cit.*, 183.

[3] 391 H.C. Deb. 5s., 313-334.

sion. Since none of the Conservative members who usually participated in prayers and led the attack on delegated legislation had supported this prayer, Mr. Sydney Silverman, in an acrimonious exchange, accused the Conservatives of objecting to delegated legislation only when questions of property were involved. The prayer was defeated by a vote of 314 to twenty-three, in a division in which about seventy Labour members abstained from voting.[1]

Two of the prayers were concerned with property rights. Of these, one was withdrawn upon the granting of concessions by the Minister,[2] and the other was withdrawn upon the Minister's giving a satisfactory explanation of the necessity for the regulations.[3]

Of the three prayers moved against defence regulations during 1945, prior to the dissolution of the Coalition Government, two were the results of reports from the Scrutinizing Committee. The committee had drawn the special attention of the House to Regulation 68D, the purpose of which was to provide loans to hotel keepers at certain coastal holiday resorts in order to aid their rehabilitation, and to Regulation 60CAA, which over-rode the provisions of the Public Health (Preservation of Food) Regulation 1925 by modifying the nature and quantity of preservatives which could be used in certain foods. Both of these regulations had been reported by the committee because they appeared to make an "unusual or unexpected use" of the powers conferred by the Emergency Powers Act, and the movers of the prayers objected to the regulations on the same ground. The motion to annul Regulation 68D was negatived,[4] and the prayer against Regulation 60CAA was withdrawn after the mover expressed satisfaction with the Minister's explanation.[5]

The last war-time prayer against a defence regulation was Sir Herbert Williams's motion to annul the Defence (Good Friday and St. Patrick's Day) Regulations. The point at issue on this prayer was a question of policy, since the mover objected to the

---

[1] 399 H.C. Deb. 5s., 1061-1158.
[2] Regulation 54CA, 7th April, 1943.
[3] Regulation 73B, 399 H.C. Deb. 5s., 312-342, 19th April, 1944.
[4] 407 H.C. Deb. 5s., 1105-1133.
[5] 408 H.C. Deb. 5s., 349-352

Government's decision not to make Good Friday a holiday. The prayer was defeated, 79-19.[1]

After the establishment of the Scrutinizing Committee, the House directed its attention to the question of emergency powers and delegated legislation in the transitional period. Members were anxious to know the Government's views on the extent of emergency powers which would be needed during the post-war reconstruction period. On 14th July, 1944, the Under Secretary for the Home Department moved that the Emergency Powers (Defence) Act be continued for another year, and made a short speech which revealed none of the Government's intentions concerning the post-war use of emergency powers. He suggested that the motion provided a suitable occasion for members to discuss any aspects of the application of emergency powers in which they were interested, and it immediately became clear that members were interested only in discovering the Government's plans for post-war emergency powers. While most members who spoke accepted the necessity of some post-war controls, especially over the economy, they demanded that Parliament be given an opportunity to review the entire scope of emergency powers in order to determine which should be retained and which should be ended.

The Government was warned by several members that Parliament would not tolerate the continued use of the Emergency Powers (Defence) Act for peace-time purposes, and the Government was asked to give assurances that completely new emergency legislation would be enacted and was urged to set up a committee of Ministers to enquire into what controls would be necessary after the war. It was further urged that the findings of such a committee should be reported to the House in the form of a White Paper. Mr. Morrison responded to the debate by saying that, while it would be premature for the Government at that time to try to enumerate a policy in connection with post-war emergency powers, it would, nevertheless, be the duty of the Government "to sweep away all restrictions which can safely and without social disadvantage be dispensed with" and "to come to Parliament and to consult Parliament and to give the House the fullest opportunity of reviewing the whole position and considering the

[1] 409 H.C. Deb. 5s., 341-358.

extent and nature of the emergency powers which ought to be continued".[1]

The War Cabinet had, in fact, been devoting some attention to the problems which would have to be faced in the wake of the war. Since October, 1943, Ministers had, in accordance with a directive from the Prime Minister, been engaged in making "a careful survey of the whole field of legislation (including Defence Regulations and other subordinate legislation) to determine which war-time powers must be retained and which can be dispensed with in the transitional period".[2] Accordingly, the end of hostilities with Germany in May, 1945, found the Coalition Government with a blueprint for the handling of emergency powers. On 8th May, 1945 (VE Day) there were 342 Defence (General Regulations) and 345 other emergency regulations in existence.[3] The following day, Mr. Morrison announced that 179 of these regulations—eighty-four of the general regulations and ninety-five of the others—had been revoked. Among those revoked were regulations 1AA, 2C, 2D, 18B, and 39BA—regulations, according to Mr. Morrison, "to which Parliament [had] rightly given especially vigilant attention because of their effect on the general field of civil liberties".[4] Thus, the war-time regulations which had infringed most heavily on British personal liberties disappeared in one swoop on the day after the German surrender.

On 10th May, 1945, the Coalition Government introduced the Supplies and Services (Transitional Powers) Bill to enable certain defence regulations to be continued for a period of two years for the general purposes of maintaining supplies and services, facilitating demobilization and resettlement, facilitating the readjustment of industry, and assisting in the rehabilitation of other countries. Before the bill was considered by the House, however, the Coalition Government came to an end (on 28th May), and a "caretaker" Government, headed by Mr. Churchill and composed of Conservatives and a few National Liberals, decided not to proceed with it, claiming that the time was not opportune for giving Parliament the opportunity of reviewing the

---

[1] 401 H.C. Deb. 5s., 2015-2089.

[2] Winston S. Churchill, *Closing the Ring* (Boston: Houghton Mifflin Co., 1951), 170-171; 671-672.

[3] 414 H.C. Deb. 5s., 112.

[4] 410 H.C. Deb. 5s., 1908.

entire question of emergency powers. Instead, the new Government decided to extend the remaining regulations under the Emergency Powers (Defence) Act for six months beyond their previously-appointed expiration date, i.e., until 24th February, 1946. Mr. Morrison, from the Opposition front bench, warned that the bill gave the Government "complete and unchecked power, within a doubtful realm of law, to make orders and directions of a legislative character, without the slightest possibility of Parliamentary check",[1] but the bill was assented to by Parliament without prolonged discussion.

On 15th June, 1945, the Parliament which had been elected in 1935 was dissolved, and in the balloting in the General Election on 5th July, the Labour Party won an overwhelming victory. By the end of the summer, the war with Japan was brought to a successful close, and the new Government was ready to address itself to the question of emergency powers in the light of the problems of transition and reconstruction.

[1] 411 H.C. Deb. 5s., 432.

CHAPTER VI
EMERGENCY POWERS SINCE 1945

WHILE few members of the war-time Parliament doubted that it would be necessary to continue some emergency economic controls for a time after the war in order to deal with the inevitable problems of transition and reconstruction, it may be doubted whether many anticipated that, at the date of this writing, more than seven years after the end of the hostilities, the British executive would continue to possess and exercise broad discretionary powers over many aspects of the life of the community. Such, however, has been the case. In 1945 Parliament authorized the Government to continue to exercise economic controls over industry, commerce, labour, and prices in order to bridge, as expeditiously and as painlessly as possible, the transition from a war-time to a peace-time society. The strain of war, however, had taken its toll on the economy, and with the passing of time in the post-war period, Britain's economic condition worsened. The necessity of increasing production and of balancing its international payments led the Government, in 1947, to ask Parliament to extend greatly the scope of its emergency powers so that it might direct all of the resources of the community to serve the interests of the community. While the Government was exercising its emergency powers for these purposes, Parliament was asked, in 1950 and 1951, to further extend them in order that Britain might embark upon a programme of rearmament as part of her defence effort. In sum, by virtue of successive grants of emergency powers in the post-war period, the Government continued to exercise broad powers over the economy. The powers were not contemplated to be used, nor have they been used, to interfere with such basic liberties as *habeas corpus*, speech, or press. Nevertheless, the ramifications of the term "economy" have become so great (including, among other things, direction of labour and control of production, consumption, and possession) that, during the post-war period, as in the years 1939-1945, the executive was empowered to legislate on important matters closely affecting the life of the individual.

All of the post-war activity with regard to emergency powers took place on a stage on which the scenery was significantly different from that which adorned the setting of war-time emergency powers. The most obvious distinction, of course, is that since 1945 emergency powers were used for peace-time purposes. The peace-time atmosphere in which the powers were granted and exercised was responsible for a development of great importance to a study of parliamentary control—a return to the normal operation of British political life. The post-war Parliament which conferred emergency powers and served as watchdog over their administration was one which had returned to its normal organizational pattern in which a formal, organized partisan Opposition faced an executive which was not of the Coalition variety. A brief discussion of how the return to normal political life occurred will serve to set the stage for an analysis of parliamentary control in the post-war period.

While all parties in the war-time Coalition Government had appreciated the necessity of continuing some controls into the post-war period in order that the Government might deal with the problems of reconstruction and transition, it became increasingly evident, towards the end of 1944, that the various members of the Coalition approached the post-war problems with differing remedies. As the war-time Government began to devote more attention to a consideration of post-war domestic problems, it became difficult for its members to agree on anything except the prosecution of the war. Pressure for a new General Election at the earliest possible moment was heavy, and on 7th October, 1944, the National Executive of the Labour Party stated that "Labour's participation in the Government should continue just so long as, in the opinion of a party conference, it is necessary in the national interest and for fulfilling the purpose for which the Government was called into being".[1] Mr. Churchill, however, was not anxious to see the war-time Coalition break up. He had espoused, in 1943, a Four Year Plan to deal with social and economic reconstruction after the war, and he desired a continuation of the Coalition Government in order to carry out the plan.

[1] R. B. McCallum and Alison Readman, *The British General Election of 1945* (London: Oxford University Press, 1947), 4.

To the leaders of the Labour and Liberal Parties, however, Mr. Churchill's plan was unacceptable, and Mr. Arthur Greenwood, a leader of the Labour Party, thought that the Prime Minister's suggestion that the plan should be administered by a Coalition Government was "flabbergasting".[1] By the spring of 1945, Labour and Conservative ministers of the Coalition were attacking each other openly over reconstruction policy, and there appeared to be little likelihood that the General Election would not be fought on party lines. Churchill continued, nevertheless, to hope that post-war emergency powers might be exercised by a Coalition, and he told the Conservative Party Conference in March, 1945, that if the Conservative Party should be successful in the General Election, he would attempt once more to form a Coalition Government.[2] The cleavages among the three major parties on post-war policy, however, were too great, and, with victory over Germany in sight, the Coalition had become extremely restless. Mr. Churchill proposed to the Labour and Liberal leaders that they should either agree to remain in the Coalition until the defeat of Japan or that they should withdraw immediately following the defeat of Germany. The Labour and Liberal leaders feared that their agreement to remain in the Coalition until the defeat of Japan would either preclude the holding of a General Election in the near future or would make a coupon election out of a General Election, if one were held. They rejected Mr. Churchill's suggestion that a referendum might be held on whether or not there should be a General Election. Accordingly, they chose to break the Coalition as soon as Germany was defeated, and, on 28th May, 1945, the Coalition Government came to an end.

The termination of the Coalition Government meant a return to the normal play of politics in Britain, and the General Election of 5th July was fought on party lines. The issue of post-war controls played an important part in the campaign. While the Conservatives recognized the necessity of retaining controls for as long as the emergency should last, they made known their determination to prevent the use of emergency controls for other purposes. Conservatives accused Labour of being doctrinaire in its attitude towards controls, while Labour campaigners charged

[1] *Ibid.*, 10.   [2] *Ibid.*

the Conservatives with wanting to end controls immediately so that, in the words of the Labour Party manifesto, *Let Us Face the Future*, "the profiteering interests and the privileged rich" would have "an entirely free hand to plunder the rest of the nation as shamelessly as they did in the nineteen-twenties".[1]

While it was not made explicit at the time, the underlying issue in the difference of opinion which developed between Churchill and the Labour and Liberal leaders with regard to the continuation of the Coalition during the transition period was, to a large extent, the question of whether or not emergency powers should be exercised by a party government. The issue had been articulated somewhat more explicitly during the campaign by some Conservatives who expressed the fear that a Labour Government might use emergency controls to carry out Socialist planning policies. The question is an interesting one, and one which has a bearing on the study of emergency powers in post-war Britain, since those powers were exercised by a Labour Government from 1945 to 1951, and by a Conservative Government after 1951. It has been contended by a recent student of emergency powers in Britain that "one of the essential prerequisites" of the constitutional exercise of emergency powers, the neglect of which would constitute "a disregard of the theory of constitutional emergency powers and the fundamental principles of democracy", is that the government which exercises such powers "should be representative of every part of the community interested in the conquest of the crisis and in the maintenance of the constitutional order".[2]

The *caveat* that party governments should not exercise emergency powers appears to be based upon the belief that "such authority must never be exercised to the advantage of one part of the population".[3] The assumption is that unless there exists a

---

[1] *Ibid.*, 54.

[2] Clinton L. Rossiter, *Constitutional Dictatorship* (Princeton: Princeton University Press, 1948), 170, 298, 304. The formation of Coalition Governments in 1915 and 1940 to exercise the emergency powers which had been granted to party governments in 1914 and 1939, respectively, is cited as proof of the contention, and it is further alleged that as a result of MacDonald's forming a "National Government" in 1931, after he had been informed that his government would not be granted emergency powers unless Opposition leaders were assured of sharing in their exercise, Coalition Government was "more firmly established" as an instrument of crisis government in England (*ibid.*, 181-183).

[3] *Ibid.*, 304. In France, the sentiment expressed by *Le Temps* in December, 1936, that "the power to legislate by decree should in no case and under no pretext be given to a party government" was reflected in the failure of several governments during the inter-war period

[Continued on opposite page.

Coalition Government in which the various parties are able to restrain and balance each other and thus insure that the conferred powers are used only in the interests of all, the powers are likely to be used to enhance the interests of certain segments of the community at the expense of the community as a whole. More explicitly, the assumption would appear to deny the possibility of effective legislative control of the exercise of emergency by a party government.

The statement of the assumption in this way, however, suggests the existence of a different approach to the problem of insuring that emergency powers should not be abused. After the formation of the Coalition Government in May, 1940, members of Parliament had not infrequently complained that the absence of a formal Opposition in the House of Commons made parliamentary supervision of the executive extremely difficult, if not impossible. "In the normal course of peace-time politics there is the clash of opinion"; one of the back-benchers proclaimed in 1944, "that is the best safeguard that this House of Commons can have, and the sooner we can return to the normal clash in this House and the normal duel in the country, the better".[1] Thus, a return to the normal partisan organization of Parliament seemed to many to constitute the most effective safeguard which could be achieved against executive action. Sir Ivor Jennings had found a reasonably effective substitute for a formal opposition in the war-time activities of individual back-benchers, but he looked upon the transfer of the critical and informative functions of Parliament to unorganized private members as only a temporary expedient which demonstrated the flexibility and viability of the British constitutional system. However, "were this situation to continue for long," Jennings believed, "the bases of the British Constitution would be overthrown," for "the British system is a system of party government and . . . the maintenance of the rule of law . . . depends primarily on the vigilance of the Opposition in the House of Commons and on the pressure which public opinion exerts upon that House".[2]

---

to receive *pleins pouvoirs* from the French Parliament because of objections to the politics and policies of the seekers of emergency powers. See Lindsay Rogers, "Personal Power and Popular Government," *The Southern Review*, III (Autumn, 1937), 225-242.

[1] Mr. Buchanan, 402 H.C. Deb. 5s., 1244.

[2] Sir Ivor Jennings, *The Law and the Constitution* (3rd edition; London: University of London Press, 1943), xxiv, xxi.

An analysis of parliamentary and executive activity in the area of emergency powers from 1945 to 1951 may help to provide an answer to the problem which has been raised. The extent and application of the powers conferred, the methods used by Parliament to supervise the exercise of the powers, and Parliament's reactions to the prolonged peace-time possession by the executive of emergency powers are subjects worthy of careful consideration in the attempt to assess the ability of Parliament to play the role of watchdog over the executive.

One of the opportunities which Parliament has to exercise control over emergency powers and delegated legislation arises on the passage of the enabling statute. On this occasion Parliament may prescribe the extent of the powers, the purposes for which they are to be used, the length of time they are to be valid, and the opportunities for subsequent legislative and judicial surveillance of the subordinate instruments. That this occasion can be used by the legislature to enforce its will upon the executive has been demonstrated by the notable success which Parliament enjoyed in 1940 in forcing the Government to define clearly the powers for which it was asking in connection with the establishment of war-zone courts.[1]

Post-war emergency powers have been based on several statutes, the first of which was the Supplies and Services (Transitional Powers) Act, 1945.[2] With the emergency powers continued by the Caretaker Government due to expire in February, 1946, the Labour Government which had been returned in the General Election of July, 1945, decided to ask Parliament to continue a large part of the economic powers for a further period of five years and to grant limited new powers to provide for more effective price control. The Labour Government's Bill was substantially similar to the Coalition-sponsored Supplies and Services Bill which had been discarded by the Caretaker Government. It empowered the King in Council, by Order in Council, to extend any existing defence regulation contained in parts III and IV (which pertained to ships and aircraft and essential supplies and work, respectively) of the Defence (General) Regulations if it appeared necessary or expedient to His Majesty to do so for any of the following purposes:

[1] See pp. 83-87.   [2] 9 & 10 Geo. 6, c. 10

(*a*) to secure a sufficiency of those supplies and services which are essential to the well-being of the community or their equitable distribution or their availability at fair prices, or

(*b*) to facilitate the demobilization and resettlement of persons and to secure the orderly disposal of surplus material, or

(*c*) to facilitate the readjustment of industry and commerce to the requirements of the community in time of peace, or

(*d*) to assist the relief of suffering and the restoration and distribution of essential supplies and services in any part of His Majesty's dominions or in foreign countries that are in grave distress as the result of war.

Section 2 of the Act authorized the Crown to make new defence regulations for controlling prices to be charged for goods and services of any kind.

The most important difference between the Labour Government's Bill and that which had been sponsored by the Coalition Government was that the powers were to be granted for five years instead of two. While no opportunity for parliamentary supervision in the form of annual renewal was granted, it was provided that, since the Bill was only an enabling measure, the Government would, by Order in Council, have to decide which defence regulations were to be continued for transitional purposes, and both Houses of Parliament would have forty days (as compared with twenty-eight days under the Emergency Powers Act) in which to move prayers for the annulment of the Orders in Council.

An important extension of parliamentary control was provided in that Parliament was authorized to pray not only against the Orders in Council but also against subordinate instruments made under the defence regulations. It would thus be possible to pray against both the defence regulations (the children of the enabling statute) and the statutory rules and orders made under them (the grandchildren of the enabling statute). It had not been possible for Parliament to pray against the grandchildren of the Emergency Powers (Defence) Act.

The Government explained the need for the Bill on legal and economic grounds. The legal case was that the defence regulations were to be used for other than war purposes, and therefore new legislation was needed to insure that governmental action would be *intra vires*. This contention was not challenged by the Opposition. Since the Government's economic case for the Bill was based largely on the arguments made in the Coalition Government's White Paper on Employment Policy,[1] the Opposition offered no resistance to the economic necessity of the measure. Conservatives and Liberals, however, demonstrated strong opposition to the powers being granted for five years, with the Conservatives wanting to reduce the time limit to two years, and the Liberals to one year. The Government contended that it could not embark upon a long-term plan if its powers were to be conferred for only two years. After a debate of almost two hours on Mr. Anthony Eden's motion to reduce the time limit, the five-year period was sustained by a vote of 306 to 183. Mr. Eric Fletcher, a Labour member of the Scrutinizing Committee, cautioned the House that, in the face of the conferral of such wide powers upon the executive, decisions would be made by statutory rules and orders which would "impinge closely on the public life of the community," and that, accordingly, it was "increasingly necessary that Parliamentary control over subordinate legislation should be strengthened and upheld".[2] Another Labour member of the Scrutinizing Committee, Mr. Sydney Silverman, urged the House to watch carefully the exercise of the powers and "to bring to the notice of the House each abuse as and when it occurs".[3] At the end of the debate on the Third Reading, Mr. Eden again appealed to the Government to assent to the two-year limitation in order "to get the whole nation behind them when they are taking powers over the life of every citizen".[4] The Government did not accede to the request.

While the defence regulations which were continued in force by virtue of the Supplies and Services (Transitional Powers) Act were concerned with giving the executive wide powers over the economy, the continuance of certain other regulations which were due to expire in February, 1946, was also deemed desirable by the Government. Accordingly, in November, 1945, the

---

[1] Cmd. 6527 (London: His Majesty's Stationery Office, 1944). See, especially, paragraphs 17 and 19.

[2] 414 H.C. Deb. 5s., 147-148.

[3] *Ibid.*, 803.   [4] *Ibid.*, 1637.

Emergency Laws (Transitional Powers) Bill was introduced to extend, in whole or in part, until 31st December, 1947, some fifty-one Defence (General) Regulations and the provisions of Codes of twenty-eight other Defence Regulations. These regulations covered a wide variety of subjects, such as control of explosives (2BA), control of highways over or near defence works and protected places (16), billeting (22), power to require nurses to continue in employment in mental institutions (32AB), compulsory treatment of venereal disease (33B), seducing persons from duty and causing disaffection (39A), opening on Sundays of cinemas in areas of England and Wales where forces were quartered (42B), unlawful gaming parties (42CA), power of Post Office officers to require production of identity cards (60CC), and entry upon and inspection of land (85). The Government spokesman indicated that some of the regulations had proved so useful that Parliament would probably soon be asked to sanction their being permanently placed on the Statute Book, but that no regulations were being made permanent under the Bill, and that the Bill gave no power to make new regulations. Members of the Opposition criticised the Bill for being a conglomeration of regulations designed for war-time, lacking classification and clarity, which unnecessarily interfered with individual liberty in peace-time. After a five-and-a-half hour debate, during which it was contended that the measure was "a stealthy encroachment upon the standard of . . . pre-war liberties"[1] and a "product of totalitarian minds",[2] the Bill was passed by a vote of 290-128.

The most significant outburst of parliamentary activity with regard to emergency powers in the post-war period was occasioned by the Government's introduction of the Supplies and Services (Extended Purposes) Bill in August, 1947. The year 1947, introduced by a winter characterized by the breakdown of fuel and electricity supplies, was one of almost continuous austerity. An adverse balance of trade had resulted in the virtual exhaustion of Britain's dollar resources, and supplies to consumers had been reduced to a minimum. The purpose of the new legislation was to extend the purposes for which the powers granted by the 1945 statute could be used in order that the Government

---

[1] Mr. W. S. Morrison, 416 H.C. Deb. 5s., 260.

[2] Major Boyd-Carpenter, *ibid.*, 296.

might increase production and stimulate exports. The Government's case for the new Bill was that there was some doubt in its mind whether the existing purposes under the 1945 statute would sanction the uses to which the executive wished to put its powers, and so Parliament was being asked to authorize the new purposes in order to forestall the possibility that the courts might declare Government actions in the existing emergency *ultra vires*. The Attorney-General said that the main purpose of the bill was to "remove doubts", and the Lord President of the Council, Mr. Herbert Morrison, told the House that it was "profoundly important" that Ministers should "be able to put their hands on their hearts and conscientiously assert that they are acting within the law".[1] The additional purposes listed in the bill for which the regulations, which were in force by virtue of the Supplies and Services (Transitional Powers) Act, 1945, could be used were:

(*a*) for promoting the productivity of industry, commerce, and agriculture;

(*b*) for fostering and directing exports and reducing imports, or imports of any classes, from all or any countries and for redressing the balance of trade; and

(*c*) generally for ensuring that the whole resources of the community are available for use, and are used, in a manner best calculated to serve the interests of the community.

The Opposition waged an all-out fight against the measure. The Government had originally wanted to take all stages of the Bill on the same day, but, having received protests from the Opposition against such a procedure, decided not to do so. The principal bone of contention was the wide grant of powers contained in purpose (*c*) above. To Opposition demands that the Government tell the House what it intended to do with its power under the Bill, Mr. Morrison replied:

We have no preconceived notions as to precisely how we propose to utilize it. What we need is the power to utilize it. [HON. MEMBERS: "Oh."] Certainly, if the House expects the Government to act with vigour in this situation, as the Opposition have demanded and the Conservative press have demanded, then the Government should have adequate powers with which to do it, and we are not going to be cross-examined in advance on what exactly we are going to do with the powers when we get them. There is no legitimate case for doing so, none whatever. We shall use them as we go along for the purposes set out in the Bill, and we shall be accountable to Parliament for the action which we take.[1]

Mr. Morrison told the House that he did not want members to think that the Bill was a "deep dark plot . . . to conduct a social revolution by Defence Regulations,"[2] but his failure to be specific on how the powers were to be used evoked an attitude of strong scepticism on the part of the Opposition. Mr. Churchill thought it was a "far-fetched argument that the courts would deny the Government the powers they already have on the grounds that the state of transition from war to peace is over", and cautioned that "when a false motive, a false pretext, is put forward . . . one feels it is all the more necessary to find out what is the true motive of the Government in bringing forward the Bill".[3] Opposition fears that the Government had an ulterior motive in seeking the new powers were reinforced by a Labour back-bencher's statement that the Bill symbolized that "this is not going to be another 1931", and that it marked "the end of all those delusions that have been growing up on the other side that, finally, the time would come when this Government would turn back from their Socialist path". "In this crisis," he averred, "we either go forward to full Socialist planning or back to a pool of unemployed—one way or the other".[4]

Churchill believed the Bill was "a blank cheque for totalitarian government," and that the only guarantee that the House could have against the powers being abused resided in the character of the Ministers and in the confidence which the House had in them. "We are told," Mr. Churchill stated, "that these powers are no greater than those which were granted to the Government of which I was the head in May, 1940. But that was a moment when invasion, death, and the physical destruction of our whole race and state seemed to be at hand or threatening. Moreover, there is a great difference between entrusting powers

[1] *Ibid.*, 1798.   [2] *Ibid.*, 1799.   [3] *Ibid.*, 1803-1804.
[4] Mr. Crossman, *ibid.*, 1819-1820.

to a Government representing all parties in the nation, joined together in a common cause, and entrusting the same powers to men who barely held a majority in the country even in 1945, who have shown themselves again and again in the past two years always to be ready to put party before country, always ready to scorn the feelings and harry the interests of their political opponents. . . ."[1]

A member of the Scrutinizing Committee contended that parliamentary safeguards meant "remarkably little when it comes to this kind of legislation."[2]   Reference was made to views expressed in former times by such important members of the Government as the Minister of Fuel and Power (Mr. John Strachey) and the President of the Board of Trade (Sir Stafford Cripps),[3] and the crux of the matter for Mr. Churchill was the confidence which the House could repose in the wielders of the power:

> We see the right hon. Gentleman the Lord President and others there who have shown themselves to possess many qualities of self-restraint, and who have had experience, but they are no longer free agents. We are giving these great powers, but will they be free to use them? At any moment the convulsion may take place in the privileged, protected conclaves of the party, and the present Prime Minister may be discarded as lacking in colour, or for some other reason—although I thought his colour was pretty red anyhow—and in his place one may have the Minister of Health [Mr. Aneurin Bevan], or some one like that, to exercise these powers.
>
> These are not powers which we are giving only to a particular set of men; they take their place on the Statute Book, and there they are to be used, and can be used, with any amount of political spite.[4]

---

[1] *Ibid.*, 1805-1806.   [2] Mr. Maclay, *ibid.*, 1851.

[3] Sir Stafford Cripps had written, in 1933, in connection with the possible future advent to power of a Socialist Government: "The Government's first step will be to call Parliament together at the earliest moment and place before it an Emergency Powers Bill to be passed through all its stages on the first day. This Bill will be wide enough in its terms to allow all that will be immediately necessary to be done by ministerial orders. These orders must be incapable of challenge in the Courts or in any way except in the House of Commons. . . . It is probable that the passage of this Bill will raise in its most acute form the constitutional crisis." (Sir Stafford Cripps, "Can Socialism Come by Constitutional Methods?" in Christopher Addison *et al.*, *Problems of a Socialist Government* [London: Victor Gollancz Ltd., 1933], 43.)

[4] *Ibid.*, 1970-1971.

The Opposition contested the Bill stage by stage. The general position of those who opposed it was that no further surrender of the powers of Parliament and the liberty of the individual should be made even in the face of a difficult economic situation, while those who supported the measure insisted that the executive should be fortified with all the powers it considered necessary to lead Great Britain through the great economic crisis. The debate was often impassioned, but the Government whips drove the measure through. At the end of a five-hour second reading debate, Mr. Churchill's motion to postpone consideration of the Bill for three months was defeated, 251-148. In a long, all-night session which started at 3.30 on the afternoon of 11th August, 1947, and continued until after eight o'clock the following morning, the Bill went through its committee stage and third reading in the House of Commons. The Conservatives felt "bound to take [their] stand . . . on the rights of private property"[1] and indicated their intention to "resist to the end" the powers sought under the bill.[2] Mr. Morrison assured the House that the Government would not use its powers under the Bill to nationalize the steel industry, and the Government accepted the amendment of the leader of the Liberal party (Mr. Clement Davies) that nothing in the Act should be held to authorize the suppression or suspension of any newspaper, periodical, book, or other publication. But it successfully resisted all other amendments.

The House of Commons debate on the Supplies and Services (Extended Purposes) Bill was a long one, and an important one. There were many members of both the Government and the Opposition who, as one observer has noted, "realized that the House was debating more than an important Bill; it was face to face with the great dilemma of the modern democratic state; the curtailment of liberties in order to cure economic illness".[3] The powers demanded were great, and the failure to indicate with any precision the uses to which they were to be put was disturbing. Thus, the Bill was a potentially dictatorial instrument, entrusted to a party government. Yet, with its passage, the Opposition did

[1] Mr. Churchill, *ibid.*, 1971.

[2] Brigadier Head, *ibid.*, 1977.

[3] Lindsay Rogers, "Variations on Democratic Themes," *Political Science Quarterly*, LXIII (December, 1948), 495.

not anticipate an overturning of traditional British Constitutionalism. The Government had not abused its powers under the
1945 statute and the Lord Chancellor "made a point of some
substance when he showed how far the former measure could have
been stretched but had not been".[1]   Probably more important,
however, was the fact that Churchill and other prominent
members of the Opposition had worked closely during the war
with Government leaders such as Mr. Attlee and Mr. Morrison,
and had come to know them. "I do not think right hon. Gentlemen opposite are likely to be second Hitlers," said Mr. Churchill
during the debate; "they may use his words, but they have not
got his guts, nor, I am glad to say, his criminality".[2]   Less
belligerently, Mr. Harold Macmillan confided he did not think
that the Ministers who then exercised "some fleeting control over
the Government [were] likely to prove great tyrants," since they
held "reasonable views," "had wide experience," and were "too
sensible to misuse these powers".[3]

The various non-economic control defence regulations which
had been continued under the Emergency Laws (Transitional
Provisions) Act, 1946, were scheduled to expire at the end of
1947.   The Government announced, in November, 1947, that
about half of these regulations, including the controversial 33B
(venereal diseases) and 39A (seducing from duty and causing
disaffection), would be allowed to lapse at that time.   In order
to extend the life of the remainder of the regulations (about
twelve of them until the end of 1948, and the rest until 10th
December, 1950), Parliament passed in December, 1947, the
Emergency Laws (Miscellaneous Provisions) Act.   The Bill was
well received, and passed its second and third readings without
division in the House of Commons.

Under the provisions of the Supplies and Services Acts of 1945
and 1947 and of the Emergency Laws Acts of 1946 and 1947, all
authority to make use of defence regulations was to end on
10th December, 1950.   Contending that Britain's continuing
economic difficulties and her embarkation upon a programme of
rearmament necessitated the extension of emergency powers, the

---

[1] *Spectator*, CLXXIX (15th August, 1947), 196.

[2] 441 H.C. Deb. 5s., 1971.

[3] *Ibid.*, 2218.

Labour Government, which had narrowly been returned to office in the General Election of February, 1950, asked Parliament to continue for another year the Supplies and Services Act and most of the defence regulations which had been carried on by virtue of the Emergency Laws (Miscellaneous Provisions) Act, 1948. The Lord President of the Council, Mr. Herbert Morrison, reviewed the status of the defence regulations which had been continued by post-war statutes, and informed the House that out of 152 Defence (General) Regulations which had been in force at the beginning of 1946, seventy-eight had been allowed to lapse. He assured the House that there existed inter-departmental machinery which constantly kept under review the necessity for continuing the defence regulations, and that, especially in the area of economic controls, the President of the Board of Trade and other Ministers had maintained strong vigilance to insure that no unnecessary controls were retained. Nevertheless, Mr. Morrison believed that, given the economic circumstances in which the country found itself, there was "an overwhelming case for the continuance of emergency powers," and that the re-armament programme "put the need for the continuance of various temporary powers beyond all question".[1] Parliament would be asked, however, at an appropriate time, to decide which emergency powers should be enacted into permanent legislation. The Lord President indicated that some emergency powers had already been transformed into permanent legislation, as, for example, in the case of the Exchange Control Act, 1947, which had provided permanent powers of exchange control comparable to those previously contained in the Defence (Finance) Regulations, 1939. The main groups of emergency powers still needed were those which gave the Government: (1) power to control shipping and civil aircraft in order that they might be available to meet any emergency; (2) general requisitioning powers needed for housing and education, and by the armed services; (3) economic controls required in connection with balance of payments, use of natural resources, equitable distribution, and price control; (4) power to control employment; and (5) the powers needed by the Ministry of Supply to control buying and manufacture. Mr. Morrison told the House that the Govern-

[1] 478 H.C. Deb. 5s., 2500.

ment was asking reluctantly for a renewal of the power to control employment, and, that, while such power was not currently being exercised, the executive believed that any responsible Government should keep the power in reserve. If the emergency powers were not renewed, Mr. Morrison stated, "the gravest consequences would follow to the economic and social well-being of our people as well as to the rearmament drive".[1]

In a debate which lasted more than four-and-a-half hours, the Opposition indicated that it did not intend to vote against the continuance of emergency powers for another year because it did not want to hinder the rearmament programme. For the most part, Opposition sentiment reflected apprehension of the effect on the sovereignty of Parliament of the long continuance of emergency powers. The leading Opposition speaker warned that the Conservatives expected the Government to undertake a careful and serious review of all its emergency powers so that at the end of 1951 it could come before the House with a concrete blueprint, indicating which powers should be made permanent by statute, and which should be abolished.[2] The leader of the Liberal Party, alarmed that "very little interest [was] being taken in this subject by members of all parties in the House", warned:

> The sovereignty of Parliament is certainly involved in this. All the time we have been called upon to surrender our rights and privileges more and more to the Government of the day. This continuous erosion, done bit by bit, is far and away more dangerous to liberty than any attack from outside. We are all awake to that and we are ready to defend our liberties, but this "drip, drip, drip" of erosion is gradually destroying the House more than anything else.[3]

As in the debate on the Supplies and Services (Extended Purposes) Act in August, 1947, it was again contended by the Opposition that the Government was retaining emergency powers for the purpose of applying Socialist planning. "Those required to rivet Socialism are retained and strengthened; those required for the safety of the State are allowed to go," exclaimed

[1] 478 H.C. Deb. 5s., 2509.

[2] Captain Crookshank, *ibid.*, 2517-2518.

[3] Mr. Clement Davies, *ibid.*, 2521-2524.

one Opposition back-bencher. The Government, he continued, was "using Defence Regulations to apply the so-called planned economy," but neither Parliament nor the people would tolerate "a cloaking of long-term political objectives behind the machinery of emergency powers."[1] Emergency powers, another back-bencher stated, were "a convenient cover for the Socialist Party to do things which otherwise they would have great difficulty in selling to the country," and the Government could not be trusted "to use the powers in the long-term interest of the nation and not of their own political party".[2] Labour back-benchers responded that "very little . . . had been done under the regulations which was abnormal or against the interests of the country,"[3] and that "a high degree . . . of Parliamentary control over the Executive had been maintained".[4]

The Bill passed its second reading without a division. On the committee stage, objection was taken by Opposition members, occasionally joined by a Government back-bencher,[5] to the continuation of several specific defence regulations. In many cases, Government spokesmen indicated that they were working on permanent legislation to supplant the particular regulation under discussion. Towards the end of the debate, the leading Opposition speaker declared that he believed that the Opposition attack on the prolonged continuance of defence regulations had been successful "because more than one Minister has said he will look at it again."[6] The Home Secretary concluded the debate by assuring the House that the Government was engaged in "a most careful survey" of the entire field of emergency powers in order to determine which powers should become permanent and which should be discontinued.[7]

The soothing effect of the Home Secretary's assurances upon the Opposition's apprehensions was short-lived. A few days later, the King's Speech, opening the new session of Parliament,

[1] Mr. Derek Walker-Smith, *ibid.*, 2545, 2550.

[2] Mr. Maclay, *ibid.*, 2550, 2553.

[3] Mr. John McKay, *ibid.*, 2541.

[4] Mr. Eric Fletcher, *ibid.*, 2562.

[5] For example, Mr. Sydney Silverman, a Labour member of the scrutinizing committee, thought that Regulation 42CA (unlawful gaming parties) was "one of the worst examples of delegated legislation that there has been." *Ibid.*, 2609.

[6] Captain Crookshank, *ibid.*, 2633.

[7] Mr. J. Chuter Ede, *ibid.*, 2636.

referred to plans of his Ministers, "in order to defend full employment, to ensure that the resources of the community are used to best advantage and to avoid inflation," to introduce legislation making available to the Government "on a permanent basis but subject to appropriate Parliamentary safeguards, powers to regulate production, distribution and consumption and to control prices."[1] Mr. Churchill immediately protested:

> I thought we had reached a working arrangement about this last week. I thought we had the answer that the Government would have an annual review. The Lord President of the Council said that the Supplies and Services Act would be permanent.* We asked that it should be annual and he then said that it would be annual. Yet within a few days he has turned round with a rapidity which would excite the envy of the nimblest squirrel and comes here and says, "We must have a Bill to make these war-time regulations permanent." . . . It seems that without any doubt whatever this measure will give the Executive powers utterly beyond anything which is compatible with a decent and reasonable Parliamentary system.[2]

The Prime Minister, Mr. Attlee, defended the proposed legislation as "a step that any Government would have to take" in the existing condition of the world if it wanted to maintain full employment and avoid inflation.[3] Opposition front-benchers, however, took sharp exception to the Government's proposal. Mr. R. A. Butler warned that if the Government persisted in its plans "they will be in for the biggest fight of their lives in this Parliament; and we shall be inspired by that spirit which inspired our ancestors, namely, the retention of individual liberty and the power of Parliament over the Executives".[4] The leader of the Liberal party stated that "if the Government intend to introduce legislation of a war character it must be met with the most fierce opposition",[5] and Mr. Harold Macmillan counselled:

---

[1] 480 H.C. Deb. 5s., 7.

[2] Ibid., 22-23. The reference (*) is probably to Mr. Morrison's speech on 8th June, 1949, at the Labour Party Conference at Blackpool, in which he said: "The Executive and the Government have no intention that the Supplies and Services Act shall come to an end. It is an essential basis for the organization of economic planning and control, and therefore we shall place a revised and permanent version of that Act on the Statute Book if we are returned to power" (*The Times* [London], 9th June, 1949, 2).

[3] Ibid., 38.   [4] Ibid., 172.   [5] Ibid., 319.

Just because certain powers are necessary, just for this very reason, any Executive which has a due regard for democracy and freedom should itself be only the more anxious to be charged with those powers with the full support and under effective control—and by that I mean really effective control—and by periodic review by a free Parliament ... If I might describe the difference between the periodic and the permanent, I would say that the Lord President of the Council would like Parliament to put the bottle permanently on the mantelpiece, so that, like Mrs. Gamp, he could put his lips to it when he was so "dispoged". For my part, I think it is better to keep it under lock and key and for Parliament to have the key.[1]

While Parliament was awaiting further word from the Government with regard to the incorporation of economic controls into permanent legislation, the movement of events occasioned a new extension of the scope of emergency powers. In the light of Britain's rearmament programme and her participation in the United Nations action against North Korea, the Government introduced, on 21st February, 1951, the Supplies and Services (Defence Purposes) Bill to enable the Government to use existing defence regulations for the following new purposes:

(a) providing or securing supplies and services required for the defence of any part of His Majesty's dominions or any territory under His Majesty's protection or in which he has jurisdiction, or for the maintenance or restoration of peace and security in any part of the world, or for any measure arising out of a breach or apprehended breach of peace in any part of the world; and

(b) preventing supplies or services being disposed of in a manner prejudicial to the defence of any of His Majesty's dominions or any such territory as aforesaid or to peace and security in any part of the world or to any such measures as aforesaid.[2]

The Bill, Mr. Morrison told the House, was not concerned with long-term economic control, gave no new powers to make defence regulations, and contained a guarantee that it would not be used to authorize the suppression or suspension of newspapers or other publications. Since defence and rearmament were not

[1] *Ibid.*, 882-883.   [2] 14 & 15 Geo. 6, C. 25.

among the main purposes contemplated by Parliament when the 1945 and 1947 statutes were passed, he explained, the Government believed that Parliament should expressly sanction the use of the powers for those purposes. "We do that," Morrison continued, "because, as the House well knows, we are a very, very constitutional Government." He admitted that, while the language of the 1947 Act was broad, it became somewhat strained when it came to "the use of requisitioning powers for a specific military operation on the other side of the world", or to the use of economic controls for preventing vital supplies from reaching Communist countries. Mr. Morrison concluded by stressing that the present "short and modest bill" was intended primarily to remove doubts, and by saying that the fact that the Government did not need to ask for any sweeping powers showed "how wise we were to keep the Supplies and Services Act going for five years and to make it renewable".[1]

While Opposition members indicated that they would not vote against the measure since they agreed that it was necessary for defence purposes, they utilized the four hour debate which ensued to reaffirm their hostility to any permanent extension of emergency economic controls and to call attention to the "chaotic state" of emergency powers which had arisen "from the simultaneous exercise of powers for the purposes of rearmament and of disarmament [and] of mobilization and demobilization".[2] Sir David Maxwell Fyfe pointed out that one hundred defence regulations and sixteen subsidiary codes were being used for three contradictory purposes, and cautioned:

> It is no easy job to work a Parliamentary democracy. It is far easier to govern with a heterogeneous bag of powers supported by heterogeneous Acts which can be used for any purpose that is desired. But that is not the way we shall achieve respect for what we all want.[3]

To one Opposition member it was "an illuminating illustration of the events of the last five-and-a-half years that it apparently requires an Act of Parliament to enable the Government to use

[1] 484 H.C. Deb. 5s., 1301, 1304, 1307.

[2] Mr. McCorquodale, *ibid.*, 1309; Mr. Boyd-Carpenter, *ibid.*, 1319.

[3] *Ibid.*, 1365.

defence regulations for the purpose of national defence".[1] Some criticism of the Bill itself came from Government back-benchers, one of whom thought it "a very tall order indeed to give a Government power by delegated legislation to do anything they like with supplies and with services 'for the maintenance or restoration of peace and security in any part of the world'. "[2] The Government gave an assurance that Regulation 58A (Control of Employment) would not be used to direct people to perform specified services or to remain in specified employment unless and until an immediate attack on the country was expected, and the Solicitor-General promised to consider Sir David Maxwell Fyfe's proposal that temporary orders under Regulation 16 for stopping up highways should be made by statutory instrument. The Bill passed its second and third readings without division, and became law on 26th April, 1951.

The Labour Government was not able to carry out its proposal to put its emergency economic control powers into permanent statutory form. In addition to being influenced by the strong hostility which the Opposition had displayed towards the proposal, the Government was dissuaded by the serious rift within the Labour Party which came to a head in the spring of 1951 and which further threatened the Government's already precariously small majority in the House of Commons. By the time the main occasion for parliamentary consideration of the fate of emergency powers again arose, in November, 1951, another General Election had been held and the Conservatives, having won a small majority in the House of Commons, had organized the Government.

There had been an aggravation of Britain's economic position during 1951. The gap in sterling as well as dollar payments continued to grow, and by autumn a serious deterioration of the balance of payments situation had developed. The new Conservative Government, therefore, on 14th November, 1951, asked Parliament to continue in force for another year (until 10th December, 1952) virtually all of the defence regulations then in force. The new Home Secretary, Sir David Maxwell Fyfe, indicated that the powers were required to cope with defence, economic difficulties, and other post-war problems. One of the

[1] Mr. Boyd-Carpenter, *ibid.*, 1323.
[2] Mr. Sydney Silverman, *ibid.*, 1358. See also similar criticism by Mr. William Wells, *ibid.*, 1315.

leaders of the Labour Opposition, while indicating that his party would not oppose the continuance of the emergency powers, could not resist reminding members of the Government of certain aspects of recent parliamentary history:

> I have always understood—though I may be wrong about this—that the Tory Party have previously attacked this measure which we are now invited to renew for a year on the ground that it was one which interfered with individual liberty. The Financial Secretary called it an intolerable system, his colleagues attacked it on the ground that it was one which imposed a kind of economic dictatorship. In the course of the debates in this House we have had all sorts of other high sounding and equally vacuous but derogatory expressions used in regard to the system which the Government are now asking us to renew.[1]

Many observers have commented that the root of the problem of emergency powers and delegated legislation lies in the passing of broad enabling acts. "If the power to legislate by delegation could be more strictly and more amply defined, as indeed it used to be in Victorian days," Professor E. C. S. Wade has advised, "then a good deal of the criticism would disappear."[2] Similarly, Sir Cecil Carr has urged that much of the difficulty of subsequent attempts to control executive action would be obviated if Parliament were given "the chance to lock the stable doors before the horses are stolen".[3] Yet, from the preceding survey of parliamentary activity attending the successive grants of emergency powers to the executive after 1945, it must be concluded that Parliament did not prove itself an effective locker of stable doors. A party government with a majority in the House of Commons received the crisis powers which it requested. The powers asked for were broad because the Government believed it needed flexibility and discretion if it was to deal with the emergency effectively. Occasionally, a limiting amendment was accepted, and sometimes an assurance was given as to how the powers would or would not be used. The Opposition could, and did,

---

[1] Sir Hartley Shawcross, 493 H.C. Deb. 5s., 1066-1067.

[2] *Third Report from the Select Committee on Procedure* (1946), 287.

[3] Sir Cecil T. Carr, "Delegated Legislation," in Lord Campion *et al.*, *Parliament* (London: George Allen & Unwin Ltd., 1952), 251.

accuse the custodians of having designs upon the horses, or call attention to the fact that not only the horses, but elephants as well, might walk through the stable doors. But Government supporters in the House of Commons could be counted on to give the executive the enabling statute it believed it needed.

There were two reasons why Parliament could not circumscribe the grants of emergency powers which it made to the executive in the post-war period. The first was to a large extent inherent in the concept of emergency powers. Crises must be dealt with with speed, discretion, and flexibility of approach, and these attributes do not stem from precisely-drawn enabling statutes. The second reason arose from the British party system. Party discipline was strong enough to insure that a Government with a majority in the House of Commons could get the powers it asked for.

This is but part of the story, however. M. Léon Blum once told the Chamber of Deputies that the question of *pleins pouvoirs* was "without a doubt a question of constitutional law, but it [was] above all a question of confidence".[1] So, also, in post-war Britain, the question of emergency powers was ultimately a question of confidence. In the narrow sense of the term, the Labour Government enjoyed the "confidence" of a majority in the House of Commons, and it could, therefore, in theory and in law, have used its crisis powers to do almost anything it chose, for the powers were so broad as to preclude challenge by the courts. More than the confidence of the majority in the House was involved, however, for what made the conferral and exercise of the powers constitutional in the broad sense was the necessity of the Government's retaining, to quote Blum again, "the double confidence of Parliament and the country".[2] It could retain such "double confidence" only if it did not abuse its powers. The powers were broad, and liable to abuse. The Opposition drew many general indictments, but had difficulty in proving the charge.[3]

[1] Cited by Lindsay Rogers, "Personal Power and Popular Government," *The Southern Review*, III (Autumn, 1937), 239.

[2] *Ibid.*, 241.

[3] A Conservative leader, Mr. Harold Macmillan, said on 7th November, 1950: "I fully admit that the Government have had many powers which they have not used. It is arguable that under Regulation 55 they might have seized the coal industry, gas, electricity and steel without all the trouble of Parliamentary Bills and long and wearisome debates. I think that those powers are there but they have not done that." 480 H.C. Deb. 5s., 882.

K

It is worthwhile now to determine how much the machinery of parliamentary control over subordinate legislation contributed to the "question of confidence". Accordingly, the attempts of Parliament to utilize its formal instrumentalities of control for the purpose of ferreting abuses and holding the executive accountable for its exercise of emergency powers in the post-war period will next be considered.

CHAPTER VII

THE SCRUTINIZING COMMITTEE

THE Select Committee on Statutory Rules and Orders (known since December, 1947 as the Select Committee on Statutory Instruments) was established in June, 1944, in response to prolonged parliamentary insistence that formal machinery was needed to lessen the onerous task of individual members in scrutinizing subordinate legislation—a task which had become especially burdensome in the face of the great number of regulations, orders, etc. which were being made under the war-time Emergency Powers (Defence) Acts. The scrutinizing committee was intended to be the watchdog for the parliamentary watchdog, the more keenly-sensed puppy which would emit warning barks to arouse the mastiff to the fact that an intrusion had taken place. Its job was to scrutinize all subordinate legislation on which Parliament might take action, and, under its original terms of reference, to draw the attention of the House to statutory instruments which imposed charges, were excluded from challenge in the courts, made some unusual or unexpected use of statutory powers, were unjustifiably delayed in being published, or were in need of elucidation. As will be noted later, the committee's terms of reference have since been somewhat enlarged, and suggestions have been made for still further enlargements.

The committee consists of eleven members, chosen on the basis of party strength in the House of Commons. During the 1948-49 session, for example, it consisted of one Liberal, three Conservatives, and seven Labour members. The committee has, however, attempted, and attempted successfully, to work on a non-partisan basis so that it might function in the semi-judicial capacity contemplated by both the House and the Government at the time of its inception. Formal votes on whether or not to report a particular instrument are rarely taken, but on the few occasions when there have been differences of opinion necessitating a formal vote, the vote has not followed party lines. The committee has scrupulously attempted to avoid becoming involved with questions of merit or policy in order to preserve its impartial outlook. To add further to the committee's non-partisan stature, a convention has developed that the chairman of the group should be a member of the Opposition. Sir Charles MacAndrew and Mr. Godfrey Nicholson, both Conservatives, were, successively, chairmen under the Labour Government, while Mr. Eric Fletcher, Labour, became chairman when the Conservatives took office in October, 1951.

It has been possible for a few back-bench members of Parliament to remain on the committee for five years or more, and thus to develop a strong awareness and appreciation of the problem of parliamentary control over subordinate legislation. The present chairman, for example, has been a member of the committee since 1945. Others who served for five years or more include Sir Charles MacAndrew, Mr. E. P. Smith, Mr. Hector Hughes, Mr. Frederick Willey, and Mr. Sydney Silverman.

During the summer of 1944, the committee met weekly, but since that time it has met fairly regularly at fortnightly intervals while Parliament is in session. Sir Cecil Carr, K.C.B., Q.C., LL.D., was in attendance at all meetings. Sir Cecil, Counsel to the Speaker, was editor of *Statutory Rules and Orders* for several years and is widely acknowledged as the leading authority on the subject of British delegated legislation. Each week Sir Cecil examined all the statutory instruments laid before the House upon which parliamentary proceedings could be taken. He drew up a memorandum, commenting on those instruments which he thought the committee would want to consider. Members of the committee examined the instruments and the memorandum, and the group met to discuss. If the committee believed that an instrument arose under one of its orders of reference it ordered the clerk either to secure a memorandum from the Government department involved or to summon a departmental witness to its next meeting. After considering the oral or written testimony from the department, the committee then determined whether or not to call the attention of the House to the instrument.

From its establishment through the 1950-51 session, the committee looked at about six thousand statutory instruments, or an average of about 860 a year. The largest number examined by the committee in any one session (1948-49 session) was 1,300. About 40 per cent of the instruments examined arose under emergency legislation.[1] Less than half of the total number of statutory instruments made fell within the purview of the committee, since it was limited by its order of reference to look only at those pieces of subordinate legislation upon which parliamentary proceedings may be taken.[2]

The task of the committee in examining such a large number of statutory instruments was extremely burdensome. Sir Charles MacAndrew has stated that "looking through all these things is really a life's work",[3] and another member of the committee, Mr. Sydney Silverman, testified in 1946 that "every member of the scrutinizing committee feels that he is not doing his job properly, and that it is a physical impossibility for the committee, as at present constituted, to do its job properly".[4] The addition, by the Supplies and Services (Transitional Powers) Act, 1945, of the orders made under the defence regulations (the grandchildren of the enabling act) to the instruments requiring scrutiny by the committee increased the group's work tremendously. In January, 1946, for example, the committee was faced with the task of examining 118 pieces of subordinate legislation (forty-seven of them being orders made under defence regulations), as compared with twenty-one regulations which required consideration in January, 1945. Sir Charles McAndrew told the Lord President of the Council that he did not believe it was possible for the committee to continue to function under such an overwhelming burden, and he announced later that, in his opinion, the committee could not have continued to operate without the benefit of Sir Cecil Carr's experience and hard work.[5] The Speaker revealed that Sir Cecil was working about twelve hours a day at the task.[6]

Out of the more than six thousand regulations, rules, and orders which the committee had examined up to the middle of

---

[1] This is an over-all figure for the period 1944-1951. In 1946-47, 71 per cent of the instruments examined by the committee arose under emergency legislation; in 1947-48, 52 per cent; in 1948-49, 50 per cent; in 1950, 48 per cent; in 1950-51, 40 per cent.

[2] It is difficult to arrive at an exact percentage figure because the number of statutory instruments registered is computed on a calendar year basis, while the number of statutory instruments examined by the committee is computed on a sessional basis.

[3] Third Report from the Select Committee on Procedure (1946), 248.

[4] Ibid., 151.   [5] Ibid., 252.   [6] Ibid., 95

1951, the special attention of the House was drawn to eighty-two. Thus, only slightly more than 1 per cent of all the subordinate legislation examined has been reported as falling within the committee's terms of reference. The term of reference which enables the committee to draw the House's attention to unjustifiable delays in publication or in laying before Parliament was responsible for the reporting of thirty-seven instruments, the largest number in any category. The committee made it a practice to require the rule-making authority to give an explanation in every instance where the instrument had not been published or laid before Parliament within seven days of signature. Twenty-seven instruments were reported for unjustifiable delay during the 1945-46 session, but by the end of October, 1946, the committee was able to report "a notable improvement in punctuality".[1] Two instruments were reported under this heading in 1946-47, one in 1947-48, none in 1948-49, and one in 1950. Although five instruments were called to the attention of the House during the 1950-51 session because of unjustifiable delay, the committee reported in July, 1951, that "instances of delay in publication and presentation are exceptional".[2] All of the five cases of unjustifiable delay reported during the 1950-51 session were due to slowness in printing the related schedules accompanying the instruments, and, according to the committee, steps had been 1950-51 session that such delays would not occur in the future. The existence of the scrutinizing committee appears, therefore, to have remedied one parliamentary grievance which had caused considerable concern prior to the setting up of the committee.

The committee drew the attention of the House to twenty-five instruments which appeared to make some unusual or unexpected use of the powers conferred by the statute under which they were made. This is perhaps the most important category from a constitutional point of view, and it is the term of reference which borders most closely on authorizing a consideration of policy or merits. The committee has, however, worked hard to make the line between policy and "unusual or unexpected use" a clear one. "The line taken from the beginning has been,"

[1] First to Twenty-First Reports and First to Third Special Reports from the Select Committee on Statutory Rules and Orders ,etc. . . . . H.C.R. 187, Session 1945-46 (London: His Majesty's Stationery Office, 1946), xxiv.
[2] Special Report from the Select Committee on Statutory Instruments, H.C.R. 239, Session 1950-51 (London: His Majesty's Stationery Office, 1951), 3.

according to Sir Cecil Carr, "if you have a price-fixing order for potatoes or whatever you like, and the price goes up 2d., or down 2d., that is policy and merits, but if you found it went up suddenly by 10s., that was something you might regard as an unusual or unexpected use of the power."[1] Parliament's aim, under this term of reference, was, in the words of the member of Parliament who successfully moved the establishment of the committee, to prevent a Minister from being able "to use his powers in a way not contemplated by Parliament when it invested him with those powers".[2] That the committee considered an instrument very carefully before reporting it under this heading can be seen from its treatment of the Somerset Bulls Order. The order, which stipulated that all bulls in the county of Somerset must be tethered, was made under Defence Regulation 55, which provides for the general control of industry. The committee at first thought that this was a case of unusual and unexpected use of statutory powers, but it was explained to committee members that the order was necessary to carry out the policy of milk supply. Discovering also that a similar order had been made in 1943 for the county of Cheshire, the committee decided not to call the order to the special attention of the House.[3]

Since the committee does not report frivolously on unusual and unexpected use, and strives also to avoid questions of policy and merits, its reportings of instruments under this heading often involved matters of considerable constitutional importance. In December, 1945, for example, the committee drew the House's attention to an Order in Council amending Defence Regulation 42CA which purported to give to any constable the right to arrest anywhere at any time, without warrant, any person whom the constable reasonably suspected of having taken part in an unlawful gaming party. A prayer was brought on in the House by Mr. Boyd-Carpenter who protested that the House had not

---

[1] *Third Report from the Select Committee on Procedure* (1946), 250. The committee reported an order in May, 1947, that was very similar to Carr's hypothetical case. The Raw Cocoa (Control and Maximum Prices) (Amendment) Order, 1947, purported to increase the price of cocoa from 51 shillings to 119 shillings per cwt. Mr. Erroll prayed against the order on 14th May, 1947, and the Ministry of Food responded that the world shortage of cocoa and the removal of controls in the United States had skyrocketed the price. The Ministry's explanation was not entirely satisfactory, and the prayer went to a division, where it was defeated, 140-43 (437 H.C. Deb. 5s., 1634-1670).

[2] Hugh Molson, *Delegated Legislation* (London: Hansard Society, 1946), 8.

[3] *Third Report from the Select Committee on Procedure* (1946), 251.

intended the defence regulation to be used to authorize arrest without warrant in peace-time. Without further debate, the Home Secretary announced that he would immediately revoke the order and advised the House to accept the prayer.[1]

Another order reported by the committee under this heading which involved an important constitutional issue was the Registration for Employment Order of 1947. The object of the order, which was made under Defence Regulation 58A, was to compile a list of various categories of persons, known picturesquely as "spivs," "drones," "eels," and "butterflies," and to compel them to engage in essential work. One of the aspects of the order which the committee did not like was the admission of the Ministry of Labour that "spivs," "drones," etc. were not easily definable and that, therefore, the Ministry would have to proceed on a trial and error basis. More disturbing to the committee, however, was the fact that people were to be forced to register for employment not by an order which Parliament might scrutinize, but by public notices and posters to be placed in employment exchanges and post offices. On 3rd December, 1947, Mr. Frank Byers put down a prayer in the House against the order, claiming that Parliament's constitutional position was being seriously weakened since public notices did not come before the House at all. The Minister of Labour said he would insure that, in every case, a copy of the public notice would be placed in the library of the House. Not satisfied with the concession, the supporters of the prayer pushed it to a division, which was won by the Government, 223-178.[2]

The Knacker's Yard Order of 1948, reported by the committee on the ground of unusual and unexpected use, also created much interest from a constitutional point of view. Made under Defence Regulation 55 (general control of industry), it required all knackers in England and Wales to secure an operating licence from the Ministry of Food.[3] Sir John Mellor prayed against the order of 3rd December, 1948, and was joined in his prayer by Mr. Eric Fletcher, a Labour member of the scrutinizing

[1] 417 H.C. Deb. 5s., 1245-1249.

[2] 445 H.C. Deb. 5s., 483-534.

[3] Since some members of Parliament expressed ignorance of what a "knacker" was, it may be advisable to cite Webster: "One who buys and slaughters worn-out or useless horses and sells their flesh for dog's meat, etc."

committee. Stating that the order raised "a matter of considerable constitutional importance," Mr. Fletcher asked members not to approach the issue in a partisan manner. "In future," he added, "no one will be able to run a knacker's yard unless he has a licence from the Minister of Food; that is to say, a new direct interference with the freedom of the subject to run that particular kind of business is being introduced by a statutory instrument." According to the Minister of Food, the order was a legitimate exercise of the Government's powers under Regulation 55, since that regulation authorized orders to be made for the control of the food industry, and since knackers' yards were being used as a source of food for human consumption.[1]

The foregoing examples indicate that the committee enjoyed considerable latitude under its directive to report on unusual or unexpected use of statutory powers. While avoiding involvement in the political stickiness of merits, it was able, nevertheless, impartially to direct the attention of the House to several significant instances of what appeared to be doubtful constitutional propriety.

The committee brought to the House's attention twenty instruments whose form or purport was considered to need elucidation. It would appear that lack of clarity in subordinate legislation has been on the increase, since the committee reported six instruments under this heading in both the 1950 and 1950-51 sessions, as compared with one each in the 1947-48 and 1948-49 sessions, and two each in the 1944-45, 1945-46, and 1946-47 sessions. Instruments were sometimes reported under this heading because of carelessness of departmental officials with regard to references in the setting up of an order.[2] More often, however, the order so reported was vague or confusing as to intent, sometimes reflecting the vagueness or the confusion of the issuing department with regard to the order. The Road Haulage and Hire (Charges) (Amendment) Order, 1946, for example, was intended to authorize some change in prices for the services concerned, but Mr. Boyd-Carpenter, in moving the annulment of the order in the House, stated that he could not tell from reading

---

[1] 458 H.C. Deb. 5s., 2351-2378.

[2] See, for example, Mr. David Renton's prayer against the Cheese (General License and Amendment No. 4) Order, 1950 (475 H.C. Deb. 5s., 319-331).

it whether the effect of the order was to raise or lower prices. The Minister said that, while the order was intended to effectuate a price increase, he could not tell precisely what the effect would be.[1]

The committee had no occasion to report any instrument under the first two of its original terms of reference, i.e., on the ground either of its imposing a charge on the public revenues or of its being made in pursuance of an enactment containing specific provision excluding it from challenge in the courts. Since the establishment of the committee, two new terms of reference have been added.[2] In November, 1946, the committee was able to persuade Parliament to add a new order of reference which enabled it to report an instrument purporting to have retrospective effect where the parent statute confers no such express authority. Only one instrument was reported under this heading. A further order of reference, added in December, 1947, enabled the committee to report an instrument if there appeared to have been unjustifiable delay in sending a notification to the Speaker under section 4(1) of the Statutory Instruments Act, 1946, where an instrument has come into operation before it has been laid before Parliament. Only one instrument was reported on this ground.[3]

By means of its special reports, the committee was able to make several recommendations on various aspects of parliamentary control of delegated legislation. It launched a broad offensive against unintelligibility in subordinate legislation. In 1946, while the Speaker was confessing to the House that he had "always hoped that these orders would be framed in language which an ordinary person like [himself] could understand,"[4] the committee expressed its belief that "the most successfully framed

[1] One sentence of the order read in part: "What the last mentioned figure would have been cannot be exactly stated as no calculation has been made on that basis, but broadly speaking it would probably have been approximately. . ." Mr. E. P. Smith called this "one of the most picturesque and dithyrambic sentences which it has ever been my lot to encounter." It reminded him, he said, "of a lovely, cloudy landscape by Constable" (432 H.C. Deb. 5s., 289-300).

[2] Actually, three changes have been made in the terms of reference. In December, 1945, the committee recommended that the term of reference which permitted it to call the House's attention to unjustifiable delay in publication should be amended to permit it to report also upon unjustifiable delay in laying an instrument before Parliament. The recommendation was accepted by the Government.

[3] While the total number of instruments reported by the committee from its establishment through the end of the 1950-51 session was eighty-two, when a breakdown of categories is made, the total number of instruments reported appears to be eighty-four. This apparent discrepancy is due to the fact that two instruments were reported under two headings.

[4] 423 H.C. Deb. 5s., 998.

document is one which is self-explanatory" and urged the framers of statutory instruments to "allow themselves a more generous range of expository expression".[1]

In 1948, the committee observed that instruments were some-times so clearly drafted as to need no explanatory memorandum,[2] but in 1950 it again reminded the departments of "the continuing need to make statutory instruments simple and easily understood by the general public".[3] The campaign against unintelligibility apparently met with considerable success, since, in 1951, the committee commented on the "care, skill and indeed on occasion candour" displayed by the departments in their attempt to make orders helpful and concise.[4]

The committee also pressed for the more extensive use of short titles for statutory instruments. "Not every instrument, naturally, can have so compendious a name as 'The Cucumbers Order' or 'The Spoilt Beer Regulations,' " it reported in 1946, "but ingenuity might usefully be employed to cut down such cumbrous labels as 'The Artificial Insemination (Importation and Exportation of Semen and Artificial Semen) Regulations,' 'The Control of Fuel (No. 3) Order, 1942, General Direction (Control of Heating and Hot Water Plants) No. 6,' or 'The Compensation of Displaced Officers (War Service) (Forms for Teachers) Regulations.' " Short titles, the committee said, should be short, and descriptive rather than technical.[5] By 1949, the committee reported that short titles were almost always conferred, and that some of the longer titles had been shortened.[6]

Occasional failure of departments to cite the precise statutory

---

[1] The committee cited the following as an illustration of an order which it thought conveyed "little meaning" to the ordinary citizen: "The Laundry (Control) (No. 2) order, 1942, shall have effect as if subparagraph (3) of paragraph 2 were omitted, and the Laundry (Control) (No. 2) order, 1942, is hereby revoked." The effect of the order, according to the explanatory note, was to relieve launderers of the necessity of notifying the Board of Trade if they wished to close down their businesses (*First to Twenty-First Reports and First to Third Special Reports from the Select Committee on Statutory Rules and Orders, etc.*. . . . H.C.R. 187, Session 1945-46, xxv.)

[2] *Reports from the Select Committee on Statutory Instruments.* . . . H.C.R. 324, Session 1948-49 (London: His Majesty's Stationery Office, 1949), 11.

[3] *Reports from the Select Committee on Statutory Instruments.* . . . H.C.R. 178, Session 1950 (London: His Majesty's Stationery Office, 1950), 12.

[4] *Special Report from the Select Committee on Statutory Instruments.*. . . H.C.R. 239, Session 1950-51, 4.

[5] *First to Twenty-First Reports and First to Third Special Reports from the Select Committee on Statutory Rules and Orders, etc.*. . . . H.C.R. 187, Session 1945-46, xxvi.

[6] *Reports from the Select Committee on Statutory Instruments.* . . . H.C.R. 324, Session 1948-49, 11.

authority under which they proceed when making subordinate legislation caused the committee continuing concern. In its special report for the 1946-47 session, the committee pointed out that a recital of the statutory power under which an instrument was made would be helpful to anyone who might want to challenge the *vires* of the instrument in court and also to the scrutinizing committee which, since it was directed to call attention to unusual and unexpected use, had to know the exact source of the department's authority. Some departments objected to identifying the specific powers invoked on the ground that it was sometimes difficult to isolate one or two sections of an enabling statute (or of several enabling statutes) and that, moreover, even if it were possible to do so, such action might create difficulties if the instrument should be challenged in court as *ultra vires*. The committee was unwilling to accept the departmental objections,[1] and Mr. Morrison told the Chairman of the scrutinizing committee that he would take up the matter with the departments.[2] By 1951 the committee was able to report that "valuable work [had] been done by the departments in meeting this point," although it still required emphasis.[3]

A special grievance arising out of emergency powers was reported by the committee. It noted in October, 1946 that, under the Emergency Powers (Defence) Act, 1939, it had sometimes to consider five generations of law-making, i.e., (a) the statute, (b) the defence regulations made under the statute, (c) the orders made under the defence regulations, (d) directions made under the orders, and (e) licences issued under the directions. It was, the committee thought, "by no means clear that Parliament contemplated these cumulative delegations," since "they tend to postpone the formulation of an exact and definite law and . . . encourage the taking of powers meanwhile in wider terms than may ultimately be required". It was hoped that, with hostilities over, the departments might content themselves with the grandchildren of the statute.[4] By July, 1948, the

---

[1] *Reports from the Select Committee on Statutory Rules and Orders, etc.* . . . H.C.R. 141, Session 1946-47 (London: His Majesty's Stationery Office, 1947), x.

[2] 443 H.C. Deb. 5s., 2011.

[3] *Special Report from the Select Committee on Statutory Instruments.* . . . H.C.R. 239, Session 1950-51, 4.

[4] *First to Twenty-First Reports and First to Third Special Reports from the Select Committee on Statutory Rules and Orders, etc.* . . . H.C.R. 187, Session 1945-46, xxvii.

committee was able to report that at least one department had curtailed the pedigree by replacing directions with orders, but it reiterated that it remained "unconvinced that, when Parliament by statute delegates to a Minister a power to legislate by statutory instrument, the delegation can or should be interpreted (in the absence of specific provision to that effect in the statute) as authorizing him to empower himself or other Ministers to make other ranges of instruments". The administrative convenience of sub-delegation was appreciated, but it was feared that important actions might be taken thereby which would escape the scrutiny of Parliament.[1]

The Statutory Instruments Act, 1946,[2] is a monument to the effectiveness of one of the committee's reports. In its first special report, issued in October, 1944, the committee called attention to certain anomalies which it had observed in the machinery of parliamentary control and of the rules of publication. The first irregularity with which the committee was impressed was the diversity of the periods prescribed by various statutes for the laying of regulations, rules, orders, etc. before Parliament. While some statutes prescribed twenty sitting days, others authorized twenty-one, twenty-eight, thirty, or forty sitting days, or forty days excluding prorogation or adjournment in excess of four days, or simply one month. The Donoughmore Committee, too, had been impressed with the "extraordinary and quite illogical differences in the number of days specified in different statutes",[3] and Sir William Graham Harrison, First Parliamentary Counsel, had testified before that committee that the number of days prescribed was "a mere matter of chance" depending upon the time limit he happened to have in mind while drafting the statute.[4] The scrutinizing committee suggested that the period should not only be uniform, but also long enough so that it could not elapse while the House was adjourned or in recess.

The second difficulty in the machinery of parliamentary control to which the report alluded was the effect of the vague

---

[1] Reports from the Select Committee on Statutory Instruments, etc. . . . . H.C.R. 201, Session 1947-48 (London: His Majesty's Stationery Office, 1948), xiv-xv.

[2] 9 & 10 Geo. 6, c. 36.

[3] Report of the Committee on Ministers' Powers, Cmd. 4060 (London: His Majesty's Stationery Office, 1932), 42.

[4] Minutes of Evidence Taken Before the Committee on Ministers' Powers (London: His Majesty's Stationery Office, 1932), 19.

directive in statutes that subordinate legislation be laid before Parliament "as soon as may be". This venerable formula— "almost a sacramental phrase", according to C. K. Allen[1]—and its Victorian predecessor, "forthwith", had achieved through longevity an impregnable position in the inkwell of parliamentary draftsmen without acquiring any corresponding position of legal force or meaning. The debate in the House of Commons in August, 1944, on the failure to lay the National Fire Service Regulations[2] had not succeeded in clearing up doubts as to the purpose or legal effect of the phrase beyond bringing about a general agreement, shared by both Parliament and Government, that a lapse of three years did not constitute compliance with the "as soon as may be" directive. With the National Fire Service Regulations experience still fresh in mind, the scrutinizing committee recommended that the "as soon as may be" formula should be replaced by a requirement that instruments be laid before Parliament within a specified number of days. "Arrangements for laying regulations," the committee advised, "should be as automatic as the arrangements for printing."

It was further noted that there appeared to be no principle governing the choice of whether an affirmative or a negative resolution procedure should be applied to regulations, etc. made under a particular statute. The Donoughmore Committee had also drawn attention to the existence of at least five different laying procedures and had concluded that it was "impossible to discover any rational justification for the existence of so many different forms of laying or on what principle Parliament acts in deciding which should be adopted in any particular enactment".[3] The scrutinizing committee recommended that subordinate legislation which imposed taxes or modified the terms of a statute should require an affirmative resolution, but could see no reason why such orders as those authorizing the opening of cinemas on Sunday in certain localities should require the same procedure.

Finally, the committee's report drew attention to certain seemingly unnecessary technicalities which arose from the operation of the Rules Publication Act, 1893, and concluded that the time might be propitious for a complete review of that statute.

[1] Allen, *Law and Orders*, 113.
[2] See pp. 110-111.
[3] *Report of the Committee on Ministers' Powers*, 42.

The committee especially criticised the antecedent publicity requirement of that act which provided that the Minister must publish a draft of his order in the *London Gazette* and allow a forty-day period before its coming into operation to permit interested parties to make representations. In the committee's opinion, the safeguard did not have enough value to warrant its retention.[1]

In introducing the Statutory Instruments Bill on 6th November, 1945, the Solicitor-General stated that the Coalition Government had devoted much time and thought to the anomalies concerning delegated legislation which had been reported by the scrutinizing committee, and had appointed Sir David Maxwell Fyfe to make a detailed study of the problems. The Statutory Instruments Bill, which substantially embodied the conclusions reached by the Coalition Government, was intended to remove most of the irregularities cited by the committee. First, the Bill introduced the term "statutory instrument" to apply to all subordinate legislation. Secondly, a uniform laying period of forty days, to be computed in terms of actual sitting days, was to be ordained for all statutory instruments. Thirdly, the vagueness surrounding the phrase "as soon as may be" with regard to the presentation of instruments to Parliament was to be remedied by requiring that the printed copy of each instrument show the date on which it came into operation. The Treasury was to be charged with making periodic reports to Parliament, in which it would draw attention to any instrument which had been printed but not laid. Fourthly, the Bill would repeal the Rules Publication Act, 1893, while reproducing those parts of it which still retained value. The most important section of the Rules Publication Act to be dispensed with was the antecedent publicity requirement. The Government spokesman noted that prior consultation by the Minister with the interests affected before the making of an order had become standard procedure and that, moreover, experience had indicated that in only a very few instances had publication in the *London Gazette* caused any one to come forward during the forty-day period to advance any point of view which had not been considered by the Minister in his informal consultations with the interested parties.

[1] *Special Report from the Select Committee on Statutory Rules and Orders, etc.* .... H.C.R. 113, Session 1943-44 (London: His Majesty's Stationery Office, 1944), 3-4.

Members of the House welcomed the introduction of a standardized forty-day laying period, and expressed little concern over the repeal of the Rules Publication Act. A great deal of opposition, however, was evinced to the fact that the Bill still permitted subordinate legislation to become law before it was published. The Conservatives, stressing that justice should take precedence over administrative convenience, announced that they would vote against the Bill unless it embodied the general rule that no order should be law until published. This had been one of the recommendations of the Donoughmore Committee.[1] Mr. Eric Fletcher and Mr. Sydney Silverman, Labour members of the scrutinizing committee, joined the Conservatives in this demand, stressing the injustice of making individuals answerable in criminal courts for offences which they could not know they had committed.

A straight party division did, in fact, take place upon the second reading, but, taking note of the House's criticism, the Solicitor-General introduced an amendment during committee stage which provided that statutory instruments would have to be laid before Parliament before they became operative. If, however, great urgency dictated that an instrument become effective as soon as made, the Minister would be required to send a notification of this fact to the Speaker and the Lord Chancellor. Once again, however, the legal effect of failure to lay was not settled definitely. The Solicitor-General indicated that failure to comply with the new requirement would not invalidate the instrument, although the Minister concerned would be liable to Parliament for his failure to conform with the parliamentary directive.[2]

The Statutory Instruments Act did not deal with the question

---

[1] *Report of the Committee on Ministers' Powers*, 66.

[2] Sir Frank Soskice, 417 H.C. Deb. 5s., 1176. Another case of failure to lay came to light in 1951. In April, 1951, the Speaker ruled that two orders, one made by the Ministry of Supply under Defence Regulations 55 and 55AB, and the other by the Board of Trade under the Goods and Services (Price Control) Act, 1941, had been improperly laid because certain documents called Related Schedules (or Deposited Schedules) whose legislative legitimacy was questionable but which constituted an important part of the orders, had not been physically laid with the orders. The Government undertook an investigation and found that, under the Speaker's ruling, about 250 orders, going as far back as 1942, had been improperly laid. The Government insisted that the legality of all the orders was beyond dispute, but introduced an indemnity bill to atone for its failure to obey the parliamentary mandate. The indemnity bill was passed, but several Conservative members decried its necessity and used the occasion to deprecate the unsettled state of parliamentary procedure with regard to delegated legislation. (491 H.C. Deb. 5s., 331-370, 24th July, 1951.)

of devising a rule for the use of the affirmative and negative resolution procedures. The Government stated that it had not attempted to suggest a standard procedure on this point because of its belief that "Parliament must, in its choice of affirmative or negative procedure, depend on the actual type of regulation which is in question, and the actual type of the enactment under which the regulation is made."[1] To date, no action has been taken by Parliament to establish a clear rule in this area.[2]

In addition to the recommendations which the scrutinizing committee made, there have been other attempts to improve the machinery of parliamentary control. In February, 1951, Sir Herbert Williams asked leave to bring in a Bill which would authorize Parliament to debate those instruments which are merely laid before Parliament without being subject to either the affirmative or the negative resolution procedure, but his request was denied by a vote of 248-192.[3] On several occasions some members of Parliament (including Messrs. Eric Fletcher and Sydney Silverman, both members of the scrutinizing committee) asked that Parliament be given the power to amend statutory instruments.[4] Members often complained, when praying against a piece of subordinate legislation, that their intent was not to annul the instrument, but merely to obtain some specific modification of it. The Labour Government resisted the proposed change on the ground that it would create serious administrative difficulties, especially since both Houses would have to concur in any amendment.

The most significant of the attempts to improve the machinery of parliamentary control, and the one which related most closely to the work of the scrutinizing committee, resulted from the appointment of a Select Committee on Procedure in August, 1945. In moving the setting up of the committee, Mr. Morrison expressed the hope that it would direct its attention towards devising

[1] *Reports from the Select Committee on Statutory Rules and Orders, etc.* . . . H.C.R. 141, Session 1946-47, xi.

[2] On 28th January, 1949, Sir Wavell Wakefield introduced a Private Member's Bill to provide that all statutory instruments which are required to be laid before Parliament should be subject to the negative resolution procedure and to extend the praying period from forty to fifty days. A total of six minutes' discussion was devoted to the Bill over a period of four consecutive Fridays, and the Bill appears to have withered from lack of parliamentary nourishment.

[3] 484 H.C. Deb. 5s., 1291-1300.

[4] 493 H.C. Deb. 5s., 1009; 478 H.C. Deb. 5s., 2525. Sir C. K. Allen has made the same suggestion (*Report from the Select Committee on Procedure* [1946], 265-266).

additional means of parliamentary control over the executive,
and he elaborated his sentiments in the following words:

> I am getting rather bored by these monotonous, stereo-
> typed speeches about delegated legislation, particularly when
> they come from rather backward-looking politicians.   It
> really is nonsense. We have had delegated legislation right
> through this century, if not before. Every Government has
> engaged in it—Tory, Liberal, Labour, Coalition.   The
> tendency is for it to increase and it is bound to be so. What
> is the good of boggling at something which is bound to increase
> if the whole legislative process is to survive at all? . . . We can
> debate until we are blue in the face, but for this Government
> or any other Government delegated legislation has increased,
> will increase, and, in my judgment, ought to increase. . . . The
> real aim should not be to resist the principle of delegated
> legislation, but rather—and this is the really important thing
> —as was done by [Mr. Molson] in the last Parliament and
> Sir Herbert Williams . . . to devise a Parliamentary check
> whereby the Government is not able to take liberties, at any
> rate without the House knowing about them.[1]

The principal plan to improve parliamentary machinery for
controlling executive action in the realm of delegated legislation
which was put before the committee was the suggestion of the
then Clerk of the House, Sir Gilbert Campion (now Lord
Campion), that the powers of the scrutinizing committee should
be extended. Pointing out that, in his opinion, parliamentary
control of delegated legislation was deficient largely because the
House did not have adequate time to deal with it, and seeing no
prospect of increasing the amount of time available for consideration of subordinate legislation, Sir Gilbert made two specific
proposals. His first recommendation was that the scrutinizing
committee be empowered to consider and report on the merits,
as an exercise of the powers delegated, of all statutory instruments
which were subject to prayer. The committee should take into
account the various practical considerations which a department
was thinking of when making a particular instrument, and should
then determine whether the instrument was well designed for its

[1] 413 H. C. Deb. 5s., 1050-1051.

purpose. Sir Gilbert stressed the fact that the committee should not consider the merits of the parent act, but admitted that it might be difficult to maintain the distinction. Sir Gilbert's second suggestion was that the scrutinizing committee might examine and report on grievances arising out of statutory instruments which were in operation. This, he believed, would enable the committee to inquire into specific cases of administrative action, and would enable the House to wield systematic control over the effects of delegated legislation.

A distinguished array of witnesses, including Mr. Speaker (Colonel Clifton Brown), Mr. Herbert Morrison, Sir Charles MacAndrew, Sir Cecil Carr, and Professors C. K. Allen and E. C. S. Wade, all expressed serious doubts as to the value of Sir Gilbert Campion's suggestions. The two leading objections to a consideration of the merits of subordinate legislation were expressed by Sir Charles MacAndrew when he stated that "if the merits of statutory instruments are to be reported upon by the Select Committee its work would not only be very greatly increased, but its deliberations would be changed from being semi-judicial to wrangles on party lines". Supporters of the Government, he added, constituted a majority of the committee, and, if matters of policy arose, it would be doubtful whether the committee would ever be able to report on any instruments.[1] The Government's objection to the proposal was that, since the committee would be considering policy, the attendance of Ministers before it would be required in order that they might defend the subordinate legislation.[2]

Sir Gilbert Campion's second suggestion—that the committee be empowered to investigate grievances arising from operating statutory instruments—also encountered considerable opposition from those called upon to testify. Mr. Speaker believed that the consideration of grievances would lead the committee into the field of merits,[3] and Professor Allen thought that if the suggestion were adopted the committee would find itself completely overwhelmed, "since grievances are a very common affliction of mankind, and many persons suffer from them chronically".[4] The

---

[1] *Third Report from the Select Committee on Procedure* (1946), 243.
[2] *Ibid.*, 100.   [3] *Ibid.*, 96.
[4] *Ibid.*, 262.

practical difficulties of operating under such a term of reference were stated perhaps most graphically by Sir Cecil Carr:

> Cases of hardship may arise by hundreds, if not thousands. How are they to be sifted? Will every discontented motorist be allowed to complain of the application of the Control of Motor Fuel Order? Will every householder be allowed to raise his troubles over the restriction on repairs or the delay in de-requisitioning of premises? A single petitioner appearing in person might well occupy more than a day's sitting; organizations representing trades and industries might occupy several days with objections to a regulation or order (for example, the Motor Vehicles [Construction and Use] Regulations). It will be difficult to deal with particular cases without study of official correspondence and perhaps departmental files; will these be made available?[1]

The Government found itself also unable to recommend this suggestion of Sir Gilbert Campion because it "would have the effect of enabling the Select Committee to enquire into all phases of Government administration within the very wide field now covered by delegated legislation".[2]

In its report, the Select Committee on Procedure stated that Sir Gilbert Campion's suggestion "would go some way to supplement the inadequate and unsatisfactory opportunities which the House at present possesses for exercising its control over one aspect of administration". The committee believed, however, that the question of parliamentary control of delegated legislation deserved more intensive consideration and recommended that the House of Lords be invited during the next session to participate with the House of Commons in establishing a joint committee to inquire into "the delegation of legislative power and the procedure of the Houses in relation thereto".[3] The Government announced later that it considered the proposed enquiry "premature, so long as the scope and form of subordinate legislation is influenced by war-time powers, and until experience has been gained of the working of the Statutory Instruments Act, 1946".[4]

[1] *Ibid.*, 244.   [2] *Ibid.*, 100.   [3] *Ibid.*, xii.
[4] 435 H.C. Deb. 5s., 31-32, 17th March, 1947.

Some discontent with the operation of the scrutinizing committee continues. It has been contended, for example, that the value of the committee is restricted since the narrowness of its terms of reference limits the number of instruments which it can call to the special attention of the House. Moreover, it is argued, if the function of the committee is, as Sir Charles MacAndrew has said,[1] to save members the time of looking through all of the instruments to find out which interest them, then the committee must be adjudged only partly successful, since it has been the merits of instruments (which the committee is precluded from considering) which have, for the most part, attracted the House's attention. The analysis of prayers after 1945, which is made in the next chapter, confirms the impression that policy and merits have been the aspects of statutory instruments that have stimulated the greatest parliamentary interest. In the pursuit of delegated legislation from this point of view, however, members have received no assistance from the committee. Sir Cecil Carr has concluded that the work of the committee "is imperfectly geared in with the machinery of parliamentary control" since "members of the House usually table their motions for annulment long before the committee has reported on, or perhaps even seen, the challenged instrument; and the reasons for their challenge will probably be reasons which the committee was debarred from considering".[2]

Thus, on the surface at least, there would appear to be some appeal in Lord Campion's suggestion that the orbit of the committee be extended to allow it to report on the merits of statutory instruments, as an exercise of the powers delegated. Upon closer consideration, however, the reasons which led the Government and most of the witnesses before the Select Committee on Procedure to oppose the suggestion seem convincing. The constitutional difficulties involved in such an enlargement of the scrutinizing committee's scope would appear to be great. It is difficult to see how the committee could avoid becoming involved in matters of partisan politics. A decision, for example, as to whether a reduction of two ounces a week in the meat ration was

---

[1] *Third Report from the Select Committee on Procedure* (1946), 254.

[2] Sir Cecil Carr, "Delegated Legislation," in Lord Campion *et al.*, *Parliament* (London: George Allen & Unwin Ltd., 1952), 251.

necessary to insure the equitable distribution of goods at fair prices could seemingly lead the committee into a consideration of the overall food purchasing policy of the Government, which might, in turn, lead to the necessity of considering the merits of the Government's balance of payments policy. If such questions, going to the heart of Government policy, were discussed by the committee, it can hardly be imagined that Government supporters would not defend that policy, and, it must be remembered, Government supporters constitute a majority of the membership of the committee. Even in the most unlikely event that a report should be forthcoming, reporting adversely on the merits of an instrument, a serious threat to the principle of ministerial responsibility would be involved. One observer has pointed to the existence of the Estimates Committee to show that a parliamentary committee can concern itself with questions of merit without impairing the principle of ministerial responsibility,[1] but it is interesting to note that, in 1931, Sir Malcolm Ramsay, Comptroller and Auditor-General, stated that he did not believe that any substantial economies had resulted from the work of the committee, and he attributed this fact to the difficulties "which are inherent in any attempt to institute detailed examination and control by the House of Commons without offence to the cardinal doctrine of Cabinet and Ministerial responsibility".[2]

Moreover, as one observer has noted, the scrutinizing committee stems originally from the recommendations of the Donoughmore Committee, and "the criticisms of delegated legislation voiced to the Donoughmore Committee were above all 'procedural' ". The Donoughmore Committee did not consider "the territory which lies between *vires* and policy . . . to be narrow".[3]

In addition to the constitutional difficulties which would attend any enlargement of the committee's scope to permit it to consider merits, there are certain important practical difficulties. As has been noted previously, the committee is already overworked, and its successful operation, even under its present terms

[1] A. H. Hanson, "The Select Committee on Statutory Instruments, 1944-49," *Public Administration*, XXVII (Winter, 1949), 284.

[2] W. Ivor Jennings, *Parliament* (Cambridge: Cambridge University Press, 1940), 309, quoting from H.C.R. 161 (1931), 366.

[3] F. A. Stacey, "The Select Committee on Statutory Instruments," *Public Administration*, XXVIII (Winter, 1950), 333-335.

of reference, appears to depend in large part upon the assistance which it receives from the long personal experience of the Counsel to the Speaker with statutory instruments. To a suggestion that another scrutinizing committee might be set up to relieve the existing one of some of its burden, Mr. Morrison responded that "the trouble is to find another Sir Cecil Carr (that might be difficult) who is of great value to the committee".[1]

In the light of these considerations, it seems unfair to say, as one observer does,[2] that the Labour Government ignored Campion's suggestions because it was complacent about the value of existing machinery of control and also because it was afraid that to so extend the scope of the committee's work would foster obstruction and thus delay the Government's policy of social and economic reforms. It is true that, during the war-time debates on the establishment of the committee, one Labour back-bencher had charged that the sentiment for the establishment of the committee was "the thin end of the wedge for the obstruction of necessary post-war legislation," and that "examination [was] only an excuse to cover obstruction and delay".[3] Nevertheless, the Labour Government looked sympathetically upon all recommendations of the committee and permitted it three additions to its terms of reference. Speaking for the Government, in May, 1946, Mr. Arthur Greenwood stated that "we are evolving a new Parliamentary technique", and he paid homage to the scrutinizing committee "to whom this House is very deeply indebted for the heavy work they have done".[4]

The great value of the scrutinizing committee resides in the fact that it has been able to operate as a non-partisan, semi-judicial body. Because the terminology of enabling statutes has been so broad as virtually to exclude judicial consideration of questions of *vires*, the committee, under its directive to report on unusual and unexpected use, has been able to do much to check abuses of the powers conferred. It is unlikely that more than a very few constitutional improprieties in statutory instruments escape the attention of the committee. When an instance of

[1] *Third Report from the Select Committee on Procedure* (1946), 151.

[2] Hanson, *op. cit.*, 285.

[3] Mr. Moelwyn Hughes, 400 H.C. Deb. 5s., 278–280. Mr. Hughes later served as a member of the scrutinizing committee.

[4] 422 H.C. Deb. 5s., 1882.

constitutional impropriety is detected and reported, the committee's report carries considerable prestige with the House and the Government.

The knowledge by departments that the committee is looking at many of their orders undoubtedly has had a salutary effect. Many procedural improvements have been made as a result of the committee's vigilance and reports. Untidy corners have been cleaned up in anticipation of the committee's searchlight being flashed into them.

In itself, the scrutinizing committee constitutes a valuable safeguard against the executive. Its work, however, is virtually the only aspect of parliamentary activity concerning delegated legislation which is not marked by political partisanship. To inject partisanship into the operations of the committee would undermine its effectiveness. One need not be concerned that political partisanship with regard to delegated legislation has been frustrated. The second technique of parliamentary control, the prayer, which will next be considered, offers adequate assurance of its continued vitality.

CHAPTER VIII

PRAYERS AS A TECHNIQUE OF PARLIAMENTARY CONTROL: 1945-1951

IT MAY be well to summarize the procedure which has been devised for parliamentary control of delegated legislation. Briefly stated, all statutory instruments whose parent statutes make provision for parliamentary action upon them (by way of either affirmative resolution or prayer for annulment) are examined by the scrutinizing committee to see if they fall within its terms of reference. If the committee believes that any particular instrument is one to which the special attention of the House should be drawn, it reports that instrument to the House, together with the evidence which the department has submitted to the committee. Normally the work of the committee ends at that point, for its members have generally maintained a policy of neither moving prayers nor participating in debates on them, although there have been a few exceptions to this practice.[1] The task of securing discussion of statutory instruments, whether reported by the committee or not, therefore rests ultimately upon individual members of Parliament.

A member who seeks information about an instrument may put a Question to the Minister concerned and may try to raise a debate on the matter on the Adjournment. Both of these methods of securing information and debate on statutory instruments are sometimes used, but both suffer, from the member of Parliament's point of view, from limitation of time. Because it is exempted business and furnishes the opportunity for relatively prolonged discussion, the prayer is much preferred by members in dealing with subordinate legislation, and is, accordingly, widely used. Formally, a prayer is a motion to annul a statutory instrument, which, if successful, results in the revocation of the

---

[1] Mr. E. P. Smith (Conservative), for example, while a member of the committee, moved a prayer in July, 1948, against the Poisons (Amendment No. 2) Order, which had been reported by the committee; and in June, 1946, he prayed against the Penicillin Control Order. Mr. Eric Fletcher (Labour) took part in the debate on the motion to annul the Knacker's Yard Order.

instrument against which it was directed. Informally, however, the prayer, like so many other formal aspects of British constitutional procedure, is often used for other purposes.

While seemingly about the business of urging the annulment of a statutory instrument, members often are merely using the prayer procedure to elicit information or to express a grievance with regard to some procedural or substantive aspect of delegated legislation. The prayer has also been used as a weapon by the Opposition to exhaust the Government, as was done in the 1950-51 session. The varied uses to which the prayer may be put make it an extremely valuable parliamentary technique, but serves also to make it somewhat difficult to assess its role among the procedures of parliamentary control of delegated legislation. The frequency of its use can be measured; the motivations behind its employment are more difficult to appraise. Certain conclusions, however, may be made. When a prayer is put forward for the purpose of eliciting information, and the information is supplied by the Minister, the prayer is usually withdrawn. Similarly, when a member wishes to express a minor grievance he is often content, having expressed it, to withdraw his motion. Withdrawals are also normal procedure when concessions are made by the Minister, although if sentiments are strong and the concession is thought to be inadequate, the prayer may be pressed to a division. Those prayers which are pressed to a division would appear to reflect the issues upon which the Opposition feels strongly. The application of closure by the Government may be taken as a further measure of the intensity of parliamentary sentiment. In the post-war period it became, in fact, standard practice for the Government to attempt to avoid very late or even all-night sittings by imposing closure, usually after a debate of an hour-and-a-half or two hours, on those prayers on which the Opposition demonstrated great vitality. Approached with these considerations in mind, an analysis of prayers from 1945 to 1951 reveals a great deal about parliamentary concern with delegated legislation.

It is interesting, first, to determine what action the House took on the instruments called to its special attention by the scrutinizing committee. Of the eighty-two instruments reported by the committee throughout the 1950-51 session, prayers were moved to secure discussion on just over half of them. Prayers against twenty-six instruments reported by the committee were withdrawn, ten were negatived, four were divided against unsuccessfully, and two were successful. It is difficult to escape the impression that most of these prayers did not excite much interest in the House. While four of them gave rise to debates lasting for more than an hour-and-a-half,[1] the average time devoted to each instrument prayed against was about forty minutes. That twenty-six prayers were withdrawn is indicative of the fact that in a large percentage of these cases the member moving the prayer was seeking an explanation or mildly censuring the Minister concerned. Having received a satisfactory reply or having administered the reprimand, the mover was content to withdraw his prayer. It cannot be assumed that there was more than a handful of members present during most of these debates. On 26th July, 1948, for example, Mr. E. P. Smith prayed against an instrument which the committee had reported on the ground of unusual and unexpected use.[2] He stressed the importance of the prayer by calling attention to the fact that only his intense feeling about the impropriety of administrative action in this instance had caused him, as a member of the scrutinizing committee, to move the prayer. Unfortunately, Mr. Smith was unable to elaborate his sentiments, for the House was counted out for lack of forty members seven minutes later, at 11.46 p.m. Undaunted, he brought on his prayer again on 29th July, but a Labour member pointed out that only five persons, including Mr. Smith, were occupying the Opposition benches, and it is clear in this case that the discussion on the prayer was allowed to proceed only by leave of Government back-benchers.

On at least four occasions, however, the movers of prayers which had been reported by the committee were able to keep a good house. On the four prayers which were pressed to the division lobbies, the Opposition vote was, respectively, 178,[3]

---

[1] Registration for Employment, 3rd December, 1947, two hours and thirty-eight minutes; Raw Cocoa, 14th May, 1947, one hour and fifty minutes; Regulation 68D, 25th January, 1945, one hour and thirty-six minutes; Knacker's Yard, 3rd December, 1948, one hour and thirty-one minutes.

[2] Poison (Amendment No. 2) Rules.

[3] Registration for Employment, 3rd December, 1947.

ninety-six,[1] fifty-one,[2] and forty-three.[3] It is interesting to notice that while both the Registration for Employment Order and the Raw Cocoa Order raised significant constitutional issues,[4] the former prayer was also used as a peg upon which to hand a full-dress policy debate, and the difference in the size of the Opposition vote is notable.

It is perhaps significant, too, that the Government did not move closure on any of the prayers directed at instruments reported by the scrutinizing committee. While it is possible to interpret this as solicitude for the parliamentary machinery of control, the facts would appear to indicate that, except for the few prayers which also raised questions of policy, there was no need to impose closure because there was no danger of an undue amount of parliamentary time being consumed by the prayers.

The two prayers against instruments reported by the committee which were successful and resulted in the annulment of the instruments deserve mention. Mr. Boyd-Carpenter's prayer against the Order in Council amending Regulation 42CA (which gave to constables the power to arrest without warrant) is one of the shortest prayers on record, having occupied only twenty minutes of parliamentary time. The Home Secretary stated that he had decided, even before seeing the report of the scrutinizing committee, to rescind the regulation, and he advised the House to accept the prayer.[5] The success of Sir John Mellor's prayer on 25th July, 1950, against the Housing (Rate of Interest) Regulations may be described as accidental. The mover of the prayer stated that he did not wish to annul the regulations since he did not object to their substance. Two Government supporters, however, apparently wearied by the late hour and prolonged discussion, and desirous of activity, volunteered to act as tellers for the ayes. The Government whips, caught unprepared, did not appoint tellers for the noes, and the Speaker declared the prayer successful.[6] Almost immediately, however, even before the regulations were revoked, the Government made a new order

[1] Air Navigation, 19th February, 1946.
[2] Coal Industry, 30th January, 1947.
[3] Raw Cocoa, 14th May, 1947.
[4] See p. 151.
[5] 417 H.C. Deb. 5s., 1245-1250.
[6] 478 H.C. Deb. 5s., 395-417.

reproducing identically the title and substance of the regulations which had been successfully prayed against. No opposition to the new order was demonstrated.

Of the remaining forty instruments reported by the committee against which prayers were not moved, three which were subject to the affirmative resolution procedure were discussed on motions to approve.[1] Therefore, thirty-seven of the eighty-two instruments drawn to the attention of the House by the scrutinizing committee were not subjected to parliamentary discussion. Seventeen of these were reported for unjustifiable delay in publication or laying, eleven for unusual and unexpected use, eight for need of elucidation, and one for unjustifiable delay in notifying the Speaker. For the most part, the failure of the House to follow up on these instruments does not reflect disregard for the committee's work. It would appear, for example, that four-teen instruments to which the House's attention was directed during the 1945-46 session because of unjustifiable delay in laying before Parliament were not prayed against because of the fact that motions of annulment had already been moved in that session against thirteen instruments reported on the same ground. With regard to several of the other instruments, it would appear that the House was satisfied with the explanations given by the departments to the scrutinizing committee. Since the "unusual and unexpected use" category, however, is likely to include those instruments most constitutionally questionable, and, since, as has been noted previously, the committee has exercised great care in dealing with subordinate legislation under this term of reference, it is somewhat surprising that eleven instruments called to the House's attention on this ground should not have been followed up.

Members of the House of Commons did not direct their prayers only at instruments called to their attention by the scrutinizing committee. From 1st August, 1945, to 4th October, 1951, about 150 prayers were moved to annul statutory instruments not reported by the committee.[2] On these prayers, members

---

[1] Workmen's Compensation (Supplementation) Scheme, 1951, 489 H.C. Deb. 5s., 1129-1140, 25th June, 1951; Herring Industry Scheme, 1951, 31st July, 1951, 491 H.C. Deb. 5s., 1382-1400; The Leather (Charges) (No. 1) Order, 1947, was debated on the Adjournment, 13th February, 1948 (447 H.C. Deb. 5s., 757-768).

[2] Since one prayer was sometimes directed at more than one instrument, the number of instruments in this category prayed against was in excess of 200.

were on their own; it was necessary for them, without any formal machinery, to examine the statutory instruments laid before Parliament and to do the necessary research and preparation upon which to base prayers. It will reveal a great deal of the House's interests to see what subjects sufficiently concerned its members to cause them to expend the time and energy necessary for the presentation of a prayer without the guidance of the scrutinizing committee.

While a few of these prayers were concerned with procedural or constitutional matters,[1] the great majority of them raised questions of merits and policy. Occasionally one of these prayers was used as a peg upon which to hand a major policy debate. Sir David Maxwell Fyfe's prayer against certain railway regulations on 10th May, 1950, gave the impetus to a great seven-hour debate on railroad policy and administration,[2] a six hour discussion of Government policy with regard to the direction of labour developed on the prayer to amend the Control of Engagement Order on 3rd November, 1947,[3] and on 18th July, 1946, a five hour debate ensued on Mr. Churchill's motion to annul the bread rationing order.[4] Usually, however, the merits or policy criticized by prayer covered narrower ground and occupied less time. For example, members protested at the lack of variety in available cheese,[5] questioned the effectiveness of the Government's decision to conserve fuel by restricting advertising lighting,[6] or challenged the necessity of limiting the freedom of design of button-makers.[7]

While some of these prayers were put down against regulations dealing with a wide variety of subjects, such as National Insurance, National Health, Education, and Town and Country Planning, the subordinate legislation which received the greatest parliamentary interest was that arising under emergency powers.

---

[1] For example, Sir John Mellor prayed against the Regulation of Payments Order (15th April, 1947) in order to protest against the use in the order of the phrase "all the powers enabling;" Sir Herbert Williams did not find the Stopping up of Highways (Various) (Revocation) (No. 3) Order in the Vote Office and put down a prayer against it in order to find out why it had not been laid (7th March, 1951).

[2] Railways (Additional Charges) Regulations, 475 H.C. Deb. 5s., 397-534.

[3] Control of Engagement Order, 1947, 443 H.C. Deb. 5s., 1343-1462.

[4] Bread (Rationing) Order, 1946, 425 H.C. Deb. 5s., 1448-1542.

[5] Cheese (Control and Maximum Prices) Order, 1946, 423 H.C. Deb. 5s., 2008-2028.

[6] Advertising and Lighting (Prohibition) Order, 483 H.C. Deb. 5s., 1872-1895.

[7] Casein Goods Order, 1st July, 1947, 439 H.C. Deb. 5s., 1271-1286.

Something close to two-thirds of all the prayers put forward without the benefit of the scrutinizing committee's spadework from the 1945-46 session through the 1950-51 session were directed at instruments made under the Supplies and Services (Transitional Powers) Act, 1945, or the Goods and Services (Price Control) Act, 1941. These were the instruments which imposed controls, and it was the merits of these controls that elicited the greatest parliamentary interest in the area of delegated legislation. This impression is substantiated not only by the fact that prayers laid down expressly to debate various aspects of the Government's economic policy constituted the largest single category of all prayers in the post-war period, but also from a perusal of the parliamentary action taken on these prayers. Of the sixty-seven prayers which ended up in the division lobbies, thirty were concerned with rationing and price control, twenty with other forms of economic control, and the remainder with various subjects not arising under emergency powers. The size of the Opposition vote on the fifty-eight prayers which went to the lobbies from the beginning of August, 1945, to the General Election of February 1950, also reflects the House's disposition to discuss aspects of economic control policy in preference to other matters arising under delegated legislation. The six largest Opposition votes, for instance, were polled on prayers dealing with economic controls.[1]

In addition, prayers concerned with policy and merits generally enjoyed greater support in the division lobbies than those which raised procedural and constitutional points. While 178 members divided against the Registration for Employment Order, and ninety-six against the Air Navigation Order, both of which had been reported by the scrutinizing committee on the ground of unusual and unexpected use, the size of these votes is open to two interpretations since important policy matters were also discussed on both these prayers. The Raw Cocoa Order, which was reported by the committee on the same ground and which also raised certain policy questions, attracted only forty-three members into the Opposition lobby, and was considerably outshone by several purely "housewives'" prayers which raised

---

[1] Bread Rationing, 182; Registration for Employment, 178; Petrol Rationing, 160; Control of Engagement, 144; Fuel Rationing, 141; and Soap Rationing, 105.

no constitutional questions. A prayer against an order reducing the tea ration, for example, enticed eighty-five members into the Opposition lobby, two others protesting the shortage of imported green vegetables and imported cherries in parts of Scotland won the support of sixty-three and sixty members, respectively, while another two which objected to the rationing of oatmeal polled fifty-nine and fifty-three Opposition votes, respectively, with the division on the latter taking place at four o'clock in the morning. On four other prayers involving rather important constitutional questions, the size of the Opposition vote was seventy-seven, fifty, thirty-seven, and sixteen,[1] while prayers against the rationing of gas and electricity, animal feed, coal, pears, and cucumbers resulted in Opposition votes of seventy-nine, seventy-four, fifty-three, thirty-nine and thirty-seven, respectively. It should be noted that the smallest vote in support of any prayer which went to a division during this period was recorded on a prayer protesting an increase in meat prices. The absence of support for this particular prayer, however, would appear to reflect the House's lack of enthusiasm for the politics of its mover and seconder, Messrs. Piratin and Gallacher, at that time the House's two Communist members.

For the purpose of attempting to determine the intensity of sentiment on prayers, only the period from August, 1945, to December, 1949, has been considered here. One reason for limiting the analysis to this period is that this is the period between the General Elections of 1945 and 1950, and thus comprises one Parliament, in which the strength of the major parties remained virtually unchanged. The more important reason, however, for so limiting the scope of the analysis of discussions on prayers is that, after the General Election of 1950, the prayer technique was put to a new use. In the General Election of February, 1950, the Labour Government was returned with a majority in the House of Commons of only six over all other parties. A majority so small was virtually unworkable, and it was fairly evident that there would have to be another General Election in the near future. In 1946, the parliamentary correspondent of *New Statesman and Nation* had noted that prayers against statutory

[1] Seizure of Food, 26th November, 1946; Food Rationing, 10th November, 1948; Turbo-Alternators, 20th January, 1948; Fire Services (Discipline), 7th April, 1948.

instruments, being exempted business, were "a formidable weapon of the Opposition" and that "by praying every night against a dozen Orders in Council, the Opposition could make all-night sittings a daily routine".[1] While it can hardly be supposed that members of the Conservative Opposition in 1950 and 1951 received their inspiration from this particular source, there is considerable evidence to indicate that they came to regard the prayer principally as a political weapon to hasten the new General Election in which they hoped to be victorious. While the number of prayers moved in the 1950 session was actually greater than the number put down in the 1948-49 session, only two went to the division lobbies in 1950 in comparison with eight in 1948-49, and the division on one of these prayers occurred only because Government supporters acted as tellers for the ayes.[2] During the 1950-51 session, when more than twice as many prayers were moved than had been put down in the two previous sessions combined, only seven prayers were pressed to lobby divisions, and on two of these occasions, again, Government supporters acted as tellers for the Opposition, with a resulting Opposition vote of zero on both occasions. Of the five remaining prayers of this session which were divided against, two were successful,[3] and two came within a few votes of being successful.[4]

The impression that the Opposition used the prayer procedure as a sort of hit and run weapon designed to exhaust the Government is bolstered by the interesting record of events in February and March, 1951. On 20th February and 7th March, prayers kept the House in session until after 12.30 a.m., and on 8th March, in the guise of an educational campaign,[5] members of the Opposition moved seven prayers after 2 a.m., resulting in the House's sitting until almost six o'clock in the morning. On one of these prayers, Sir Herbert Williams was able to resist a motion

---

[1] *New Statesman and Nation*, XXXII (10th August, 1946), 93.

[2] See Housing (Rates of Interest) Regulations, See p. 172.

[3] Cheese Rationing (9th April, 1951) and Plasterboard Prices (5th July, 1951).

[4] Agricultural Lime Scheme (18th April, 1951) and Railways (Additional Charges) (Amendment) Regulations (23rd April, 1951).

[5] Mr. Harmar Nicholls, in moving the annulment of the Sewing Cotton and Threads (Maximum Prices) Order, at 2.13 a.m. said: "One advantage of submitting a Prayer, even at this late hour, is that one can burn some midnight oil with a view to keeping well-informed other hon. Members who may have been taking advantage of the opportunity to sleep on previous nights" (485 H.C. Deb. 5s., 866, 8th March, 1951).

that he "be no longer heard", but his attempt to read the text of several lengthy schedules was called "pure obstruction" by Mr. Speaker.[1]

On 13th March at 1.25 a.m., an Opposition member's announcement that he would not move his prayer because of the lateness of the hour evoked a strong protest from the Home Secretary at the discourtesy of the action to the President of the Board of Trade, who had been waiting to answer the prayer. The lateness of the hour, however, did not deter another Opposition member from moving another prayer which kept the House in session until half-past two. On the following evening, 14th March, after two prayers had been moved and discussed, the Government, over Opposition protests that private members were being deprived of their rights, moved the adjournment of the House, although there was another prayer on the Paper. The same evening, in a speech in Surrey, Mr. Robert Boothby, a Conservative member of Parliament, and a Minister in the war-time Coalition Government, discussed some aspects of parliamentary procedure, and, referring to the Labour Government, said:

> We shall harry the life out of them—and we shall keep them up day and night. The only way to get rid of them very quickly is to wear them out. There is no other way to do it. We have just got to go cracking on. We will make it absolutely intolerable for them. We will make them sit up day and night and grind away until they get absolutely hysterical and say "We cannot stand any more." This is what we are going to do for the next two or three months division after division, and we go at it in squads.[2]

Reactions to the Boothby speech were immediate. On the following evening, two prayers were discussed until 1.30 a.m. The fate of one of them was put to a voice vote, and the Speaker declared that the ayes had it. Upon being questioned by the Home Secretary, the Speaker announced that he had been

---

[1] As the evening grew longer tempers grew shorter. Mr. Nally charged that the prayers were "carefully timed by the Opposition so as to cause the maximum inconvenience to those of us who are without cars," and Mr. Speaker, reminding the House that he had to be on duty again at 11 o'clock, said that "the business of the House comes first, but there are human considerations." Close to dawn, Mr. William Ross cautioned that "the prayers of the wicked will be as nothing." (*Ibid.*, 874, 886, 901.)

[2] *The Times* (London), 15th March, 1951, 4.

mistaken and that, therefore, the prayer had not been successful. Under criticism of his ruling from several members of the Opposition, the Speaker announced:

> I do not want to be indiscreet in what I say, but we understand from the Hon. Member for East Aberdeenshire (Mr. Boothby)—[HON. MEMBERS: 'Oh!'] Yes, I do not mind saying that—and it has not been repudiated in any way. I am quite prepared to give all these Prayers a fair run, but not more . . . I said what I said. All these things were at the back of one's mind . . . for the rest—the speech of the Hon. Member for East Aberdeenshire—one is bound to consider things. One knows he is an ex-Minister and I presume one must bear that in the back of one's mind. I was prepared to be perfectly fair, but in view of what I heard from an ex-Minister, I will not be hard on giving the closure.[1]

The President of the Liberal Party, Mr. Philip Fothergill, described the strategy outlined by Boothby as "thug tactics," and Mr. Frank Byers, Chairman of the Liberal Executive, stated that it was "the duty of the Liberal Party to disassociate itself from such tactics and to refuse support for Conservative motions which form part of this irresponsible harassing campaign".[2] In a retaliatory move, designed to discourage the Opposition in its prayer campaign, about one hundred back-bench Government supporters introduced a motion to provide that no alcoholic beverages of any kind should be sold or consumed within the precincts of the House of Commons after 10.00 p.m. on any day when a prayer was scheduled to be moved.[3] *The Times* commented that "the Conservatives appear . . . to be seeking to exhaust the members of the Government and to drive them from office by depriving them of their sleep".[4]

On 19th March, the Home Secretary, Mr. Chuter Ede, interrupted the first prayer of the evening and moved the adjournment for the purpose "of considering the way in which this House

---

[1] 485 H.C. Deb. 5s., 1931-1932, 15th March, 1951.

[2] *The Times* (London), 19th March, 1951, 4.

[3] *Ibid.*, 16th March, 1951, 4.

[4] *Ibid.*, 21st March, 1951, 5.

is being treated by the continual moving of these Prayers for no other reason than the physical exhaustion of hon. Members and Ministers of the Crown". Mr. Ede, recalling that past indulgences in such tactics had left as their legacy such restrictions on parliamentary freedom of speech as the closure, the kangaroo, and the guillotine, made an overture to the Opposition in the following words:

> It is part of the duty of the House to keep a close check on the Executive. It is one of the fundamental duties not merely of the Opposition but of every member of the House to see that a close check is kept on the Executive. One of the ways of doing this is by the prayer method. We are anxious that there should be no denial to the Opposition of this method of checking the Executive. But it is only reasonable to say that this method should be operated in circumstances which enable the House to perform its duty of checking effectively. That has not been done during the past fortnight or so.
>
> We are exceedingly anxious that this method should be continued effectively and we are willing to enter into conversation with either the right honourable Gentleman who marshals the forces opposite or the platoon-sergeants who are put up each on his appropriate night to conduct a guerilla warfare in order that the House may be kept out of bed. We do not think that is an effective way of the House discharging its duties, but we are willing to consider with those who have this sudden excess of piety the way in which we can pray at a time when they are more likely to be effectively heard both in this House and in the country.[1]

On the following day, Mr. Churchill suggested that he and the Home Secretary should meet to discuss the situation. It was reported that an all-Party conference on the subject of prayers and the efficient supervision of delegated legislation was to be held in April, and *The Times* expressed the hope that the conferees would give impetus to a process of inquiry and recommendation which might lead to an improvement in the entire machinery of

[1] 485 H.C. Deb. 5s., 2248-2249.

examining delegated legislation.[1] While there is no knowledge
of what occurred at the conference, it may be surmised that some
understanding was reached with regard to late prayers, for,
although twenty-four motions to annul were discussed from April
to the end of the session in October, only one of them kept the
House up after midnight.

What conclusions can be reached after describing all of this
activity on prayers in the post-war period? One fact stands out
clearly. In spite of the formal averments frequently made by
Ministers, and some members of Parliament, that prayers are not
only Opposition business but also House of Commons business,
the fact is that they were almost exclusively Opposition business.
They were Opposition business because, for the most part, they
were moved for the purpose of criticizing Government policy.
Out of the more than 170 motions to annul statutory instruments
laid down between 1945 and 1951, only three or four were moved
by Government supporters, and with one exception,[2] these were
concerned with minor policy matters. Occasionally Government
back-benchers spoke in support of a prayer, but they rarely, if
ever, went into the Opposition lobby to express their sentiments.
This will not surprise anyone acquainted with the British parliamentary system. Government supporters are elected to, and
expected to, support the Government and its policy, and serious
constitutional difficulties would occur if they did not. This
cardinal principle of the British constitutional system is reflected
also in the fate of the prayers. On only four occasions were
statutory instruments annulled because of successful prayers.
The success of one of these prayers was quite accidental, and
another was due to the Government's recommendation that the
House accept the prayer. On the other two occasions, the
Government was defeated in the division lobbies, but both of these
defeats occurred during the 1950-51 session when the Government
had such a small majority that the illness or otherwise unavoidable
absence from the House of any of its supporters created serious
constitutional problems. Statutory instruments are not expected
to be annulled by prayer, and considerable embarrassment for all
concerned resulted on at least two of the aforementioned occasions

---

[1] *The Times* (London), 6th April, 1951, 5.
[2] Control of Engagement Order, 3rd November, 1946, moved by Mr. Rhys Davies
(Labour).

when instruments were annulled.[1] Occasionally concessions, sometimes important, were made by the Government on policy prayers, but defeats and concessions were exceptions and, as Professor Wheare has pointed out, should be exceptions since "there is something wrong, in British eyes, with a government that cannot win".[2]

On non-policy prayers, involving procedural and constitutional points, the pattern was much the same. The only distinguishing characteristic of these prayers was that, generally, relatively little interest was shown in them by either members of the Opposition or Government supporters.[3]

If the Government usually holds fast against these entreaties, it may well be asked what value all of this activity has had. One could agree, certainly, with Professor Wheare's observation that, minimally, it is better than apathy.[4] Many of the praying members of the House have claimed credit for improving the draftsmanship and intelligibility of statutory instruments, and for expediting their laying and reducing their volume. Certainly the combined efforts of the scrutinizing committee and the praying members have resulted in procedural improvements. In addition, there is good reason for believing that the Government, knowing that a large part of its subordinate legislation was likely to be examined closely by members of the House, has taken greater care in exercising its delegated powers. The decline in the number of instruments reported by the scrutinizing committee in recent years, and the virtual disappearance of reports on instruments under certain of the terms of the reference, may be attributed in part to the House's praying activities.

Perhaps the most important value of prayers, however, has

---

[1] As noted previously, the mover of the prayer against the Housing (Rate of Interest) Regulations had not desired their annulment, and the regulations were immediately reinstituted by a new order. The initial jubilation of the Opposition over the successful prayer on 9th April, 1951, against the order reducing the individual weekly cheese ration from three ounces to two ounces, changed to placid resignation when the Government made a new order re-establishing the two ounce ration because of the incontrovertible fact that there was not enough cheese available for a three-ounce ration.

[2] K. C. Wheare, "Controlling Delegated Legislation: a British Experiment," *Journal of Politics*, XI (November, 1949), 764.

[3] On all prayers on which divisions occurred, the size of the Government vote generally tended to correlate with the hour and not with the subject matter of the prayer. See Christopher J. Hughes, "Prayers to Annul Delegated Legislation: House of Commons, 1947-48," *Public Administration*, XXVII (Summer, 1949), 111-114.

[4] Wheare, *op.cit.*, 766.

been the fact that they have ventilated grievances arising out of Government policy and administration. Grievances arising out of delegated legislation should be heard, and the prayer has proved to be a most useful technique for serving this purpose. If the grievance is widespread, that fact will be reflected in the House, and the Government will take note of it, and perhaps make a concession. It could not do otherwise, for it must meet the electorate at the next General Election on its record, and a continuous ignoring of widely-felt grievances would very likely be the prelude to defeat. For the most part, however, no concession is made. The Government stands by the order which is the implementation of its policy, and the grievance is resisted. Even so, the member moving the prayer has performed an important service. Minimally, by simply raising the matter in the House, he has largely satisfied his aggrieved constituents or his own conscience, whichever the spur may have been. More importantly, however, he has made it necessary for a Minister to come down to the House, usually at some inconvenience to the Minister because of the lateness of the hour and the pressure of his other duties, and has required the Minister to explain and justify his action. The Minister who will not meet the House fairly on these points soon loses his popularity with the House, and may lose his usefulness to the Government. It seems fair to say, for example, that during the early stages of the war, Sir John Anderson was not a good House of Commons man, and the fact that his handling of critical parliamentary opinion did not satisfy the House may have contributed to his transference from the Home Office in 1940 to the Lord Presidency of the Council. His successor, Mr. Herbert Morrison, on the other hand, while similarly charged with the execution of many regulations which were unpopular in both the House and the country, appeared to possess, from long years of parliamentary service, a sense of knowing what the House would stand for, and what it would not stand for. He has admitted, for example, that he was impressed by the strength of sentiment in the House, and not by the merits of the proposal, that the Government should agree to the setting up of the scrutinizing committee.[1]

The conclusion that prayers have been Opposition business

[1] *Third Report from the Select Committee on Procedure* (1946), 149.

needs to be examined more closely. The reality behind the term "Opposition" was actually, in this area, a small group of Conservative back-benchers who virtually made a profession of praying against statutory instruments. While the few prayers upon which full-dress policy debates were based were generally moved by a Conservative leader of the stature of Mr. Churchill or Sir David Maxwell Fyfe, the largest portion of the more routine prayers were moved by the "inveterate prayers". Almost half of the total number of motions for annulment put forward from 1945 to 1951 were the work of a half-dozen members—Sir John Mellor, Mr. John Boyd-Carpenter, Mr. C. S. Taylor, Sir Herbert Williams, Colonel O. E. Crosthwaite-Eyre, and Mr. Spence. Sir John Mellor would appear to have clear claim to the title of most persistent prayer, having moved or seconded more than forty motions for annulment. However, had Sir Herbert Williams (whom Mr. Morrison once called "a sort of unofficial scrutinizing committee") not been absent from the 1945-1950 Parliament, there is good reason to believe that he might have outshone Sir John, for, having been returned in the General Election of 1950, he proceeded to move or second no less than fourteen prayers in the period from March, 1950, to October, 1951. This hard core of indefatigable prayers was assisted frequently by three other Conservative back-benchers, Mr. Erroll, Mr. Hutchison, and Lord William Scott, and between them it would appear that they worked out a sort of division of labour system. Colonel Crosthwaite-Eyre, for example, concentrated on orders imposing financial and exchange controls, Mr. Hutchison on price controls, Mr. Erroll on industrial and business controls, Mr. Spence and Mr. Taylor on food rationing, while the versatility of Sir John Mellor and Sir Herbert Williams enabled them to initiate, or lend support to, prayers on almost any subject. Whatever their individual or collective motivations may have been, it is abundantly clear that these Conservative private members expended an enormous amount of time and energy in drawing the attention of the House to statutory instruments.

The relative lack of interest in prayers dealing with constitutional issues has been noted, and may to some extent be explained by the fact that the points involved were frequently rather narrow legal ones which had little appeal for the non-lawyers in the

House. However, even when a prayer involving policy considerations was debated before a fuller House, it is clear that usually only a few members had made a sufficiently careful study of the statutory instrument involved to bring informed criticism to the discussion. The possession of the knowledge which is necessary to make one's criticism informed required, generally, a great deal of attention to detail. That most members of Parliament are unable or unwilling to delve into the details of subordinate legislation and administration is easily understandable. They are not, for the most part, specialists and do not desire to become so. They are elected because of their adherence to a general policy. When it is realized that, on the one hand, one of the important factors in the growth of delegated legislation has been the desire of the House to relieve itself of the necessity of concentrating upon details, and that, on the other hand, informed criticism of administration generally requires careful investigation of its fine points, the difficulty of parliamentary control is compounded. "It is a sad commentary on the state that we have got into," said Viscount Hinchingbrooke, "that this great House of Commons of England has been discussing the control and prices of casein buttons."[1] Undoubtedly, the great majority of the noble lord's colleagues, regardless of the benches they occupied, shared his aversion to this pre-occupation with detail.

It must therefore be concluded, from a study of the prayers in the post-war years, that while the practice of delegated legislation and its attendant problems evoked a great deal of parliamentary interest in the abstract, only a handful of members of Parliament, almost all members of the Opposition, were willing to devote their energies to the concentration upon detail necessary for the effective use of the prayer mechanism. Yet in the absence of any settlement of the overall difficulties which the practice of delegated legislation creates, the prayer is perhaps the most potent parliamentary weapon with which to check the executive. But the routine examination of statutory instruments, and the necessity of doing homework on them, would appear to be boring employment to all except the handful of zealous, near-professional watchdogs.

[1] 439 H.C. Deb. 5s., 1282, 1st July, 1947.

CHAPTER IX

CONCLUSIONS

"YOUR business is not to govern the country," Mr. Gladstone told the House of Commons during the Crimean War, "but it is, if you think fit, to call to account those who do govern it".[1] Mr. Gladstone was apparently prescribing a *raison d'être* for a legislature which, due to an exceptional situation, was no longer able to legislate. In our times, such situations are not so exceptional. Indeed, not long after the time of Gladstone's statement, Bagehot was to suggest that, even in normal times, legislation was not one of Parliament's primary functions. In the twentieth century, in response to demands from the executive for powers to deal with economic and social welfare programmes and to meet crises growing out of war and economic difficulties, Parliament has been willing to grant important legislative powers to the Government. Many contemporary observers have shown concern over whether Parliament has been willing or able to exercise effective control over the powers which it has increasingly delegated to the executive.

During the twelve year period from 1939 to 1951 with which this study is concerned, Parliament's legislative powers were in large part surrendered to the executive. From 1939 to 1945, Parliament entrusted the Government with virtually complete power over almost every aspect of the nation's life to insure the successful prosecution of the war. After 1945 the executive had broad powers of control over the nation's economy. With respect to the exercise of these emergency powers, Parliament elected to play the role of watchdog. If it could not govern it could, it hoped, call to account those who did govern and thus prevent discretionary powers from being exercised arbitrarily.

How effectively was Parliament able to perform its chosen role? The war-time Parliament warrants separate consideration,

[1] W. Ivor Jennings, *Cabinet Government* (Cambridge: Cambridge University Press, 1936), 371, quoting from 136 H.C. Deb. 3s., 1202.

and the verdict is that it was able to act as a fairly effective watch-dog. The war-time Parliament appears to have been successful for three reasons. First, although its task of calling the executive to account appeared to be hampered by the absence of a formal Opposition, the British Constitution once more demonstrated its genius for flexibility and adaptability, and the private members came to the fore to carry on the parliamentary function of criticism. This was possible because, in the light of the overwhelming support which the Government enjoyed in the House, private members did not feel compelled to give unwavering and uncritical fealty to it on all occasions. Hence there was a relative freedom from the Government whips for those who cared to avail themselves of it. Second, the war-time Government had no significant legislative programme, and therefore members of Parliament who cared to do so had time to devote much of their attention to the exercise of emergency powers. Third, and more important perhaps, was the fact that war-time emergency powers threatened the basic liberties of the individual and, in their concern to protect these liberties against undue repression, members were not, for the most part, distracted by considerations of political partisanship. Thus the combination of relative freedom of action, availability of time, and singleness of purpose enabled private members to exert strong pressure upon the executive. Using every Parliamentary weapon at their disposal, they attempted to insure that executive action did not exceed the necessities of an admittedly grave situation. The House's concern for the basic liberties was steady and continuous, and the virtually intact survival of those liberties in war-time Britain must be attributed in no small part to the day-to-day interest in their preservation which Members of Parliament manifested.

One other aspect of the war-time Parliament's watchdog activities deserves important mention. Just as experience with DORA and the post-World War I emergency powers statutes had been largely responsible for the outburst of apprehension over delegated legislation which culminated in the appointment of the Donoughmore Committee, so it was the tremendous growth of executive powers pursuant to Parliament's grant of emergency powers in 1939 that brought home to the House of Commons the weakness of its own position in the constitutional balance. The watchdog grew uneasy as it contemplated the paucity of its instruments of control over an executive which had become more legislative than the legislature. The recommendations of the Donoughmore Committee, which had been of little more than academic interest to both Government and Parliament throughout the 1930's, acquired new appeal in the war-time House of Commons. The most significant achievement of Parliament in its quest for a more effective machinery of control was the establishment of the scrutinizing committee in 1944. On balance, then, the war-time Parliament achieved a considerable degree of success in holding the Government accountable for the exercise of its wide powers and in strengthening Parliament's grip on delegated legislation.

In the post-war period there were fewer obvious examples of parliamentary control over the executive. The task of checking the executive reverted to the formal Opposition, and political partisanship once again became an important aspect of parliamentary activity. In addition, the Labour Government had a heavy legislative programme which consumed a great deal of both the time and interest of the House. The Opposition, nevertheless, devoted considerable attention to the problem of emergency powers. While it generally granted their necessity, it showed much uneasiness about entrusting broad discretionary powers to a party government in peace-time, made frequent attacks on the continuance of particular powers, and contended that parliamentary control over their exercise was ineffective. Occasionally, the strength of parliamentary sentiment resulted in the Government's accepting from the House an amendment concerning emergency powers bills. On a few rare occasions, the Government was caught off guard and a prayer against a statutory instrument was successful. Somewhat more frequently, the Government made concessions. In the overwhelming majority of instances, however, in which the executive's requests for, or uses of, emergency powers were challenged by the Opposition, the Government stood firm. It reminded the House that the Government was responsible to Parliament, and did not hesitate to make challenges matters of confidence. Government supporters then faithfully tramped through the division lobbies, and the Government emerged successful.

The general conclusion which emerges from a study of the twelve year period 1939-1951 is that Parliament can play the role of watchdog effectively to the extent that it can bring subordinate legislation under its scrutiny, and, more importantly perhaps, to the extent that it can bring informed criticism to bear upon the executive. Where members of Parliament have shown an interest and an ability to familiarize themselves with the details of the exercise of delegated powers, they have had a strong lever against the Government. It is here that the strength of Parliament as an effective safeguard against abuse of emergency power lies. The Government, no matter how great its majority, cannot afford to ignore legitimate grievances for long, and it must give reasonable and convincing answers to its critics. A Government cannot afford to lose debates continuously even though it may win the divisions. Experience in the twentieth century seems to indicate that a Government with a majority, however small, in the House of Commons can put on the whips and avoid defeat in the House. Therefore, the force of the Opposition lies not in the fact that it may be able to overthrow the Government in the House of Commons but in the fact that it can, if its criticism is sustained and informed, make the Government modify or adjust its actions. So long as a Government knows that it must face the electorate in a free election, it must attempt to retain its popularity. It is for this reason that, at a time when a large part of legislation takes place in the departments, the ability of the Opposition in Parliament to arm itself with a detailed knowledge of the workings of the administration appears to be the key to the successful operation of parliamentary control.

The establishment of the scrutinizing committee, the bringing within the range of parliamentary action of the grandchildren of the enabling statutes since 1945, and the clearing away of certain procedural anomalies as a result of the Statutory Instruments Act, 1946, and as a result of the recommendations of the scrutinizing committee, are, therefore, all steps in the right direction. Each of these actions has had the effect of increasing the potentialities of parliamentary control by bringing the work of the departments more closely under parliamentary surveillance. It cannot be doubted that parliamentary control has been more effective since these developments than it was before them, and the existence of these procedural safeguards probably accounts in part for the fact that there were fewer clear cases of parliamentary victories over the executive on the floor of the House in the post-war period than there were in war-time. The scrutinizing committee should be singled out as a particularly valuable instrument of parliamentary control. It is unlikely that very many serious constitutional irregularities with regard to the use of the powers granted have escaped the notice of the committee. The committee has also done valuable work in eliminating or reducing many administrative practices which had impeded parliamentary control. It can hardly be doubted that the mere fact of the committee's existence, and the attendant knowledge on the part of the departments that the committee was examining with care the products of their legislative incubators, had a salutary effect and made the departments more careful in exercising the powers they possessed.

Existing safeguards against the abuse of delegated powers operate on at least three stages. In the first place, it is now accepted practice for the departments to consult the affected interests before drawing up subordinate legislation.[1] Secondly, the scrutinizing committee has jurisdiction over all statutory instruments which are subject to parliamentary proceedings. It probably catches all instruments of doubtful constitutionality and, in addition, it calls attention to practices which tend to deny Parliament the ability to scrutinize the departmental legislative products. Thirdly, the Opposition in Parliament has the opportunity, through questions and prayers, and on adjournment and supply debates, to raise objections to instances of maladministration and constitutional impropriety and to confront the Government with grievances growing out of the executive's exercise of its powers.

Doubts have been raised as to the adequacy of the existing parliamentary safeguards, however. It has been contended that when powers are granted to a Government in very broad terms as, for example, under the Supplies and Services Act (especially under the purposes established in 1947 and 1951), the term of reference of the scrutinizing committee which permits it to report unusual and unexpected uses is not a closely-knit sieve, for it is

---

[1] Henry Street, "Delegated Legislation and the Public," *Public Administration*, XXVII (Summer, 1949), 108.

not easy for the committee to determine what action is unusual or unexpected when the purposes for which the powers may be used are of such an extensive nature. Moreover, it has been charged that the inability of the scrutinizing committee to consider questions of merits has caused Opposition members to undertake independent inquiries into statutory instruments, and that, accordingly, the burden still rests to a large extent upon the initiative of individual members. This is accompanied by the charge that members of Parliament are overworked and are therefore precluded from devoting much attention to the pursuit of statutory instruments. It is alleged, further, that the House does not have enough time to consider delegated legislation—that, while the range of administrative activity has greatly increased, the amount of parliamentary time available for discussing it has not—and that the average time devoted to discussion of delegated legislation has amounted to only about 1.6 days per session.[1] Finally, it is said, parliamentary opportunities for discussing delegated legislation are unsatisfactory in other ways. Prayers usually come on only at a time (after 10 p.m.) when the praying member has difficulty in keeping a house.

At an earlier time, a study of this sort might perhaps have ended at this point. It might have been concluded that, while parliamentary control of the executive's exercise of emergency powers had certain inadequacies, nevertheless it had been generally satisfactory. The importance of an Opposition (preferably a formal one) might have been stressed and the overall effectiveness of parliamentary activity might have been tested by the fact that no instance of significant abuse of emergency powers was recorded. The writer might have pointed out, as the Donoughmore Committee did, that "emergencies are exceptional; and exceptions cannot be classified in general language,"[2] and that, given an unusual situation, Parliament had shown considerable vitality. Finally, it might have been concluded that Parliament had weathered an exceptional situation and that a return to normal conditions would probably see Parliament again an adequate factor in the constitutional balance.

Nowadays, such a conclusion would be somewhat unsatisfactory.

[1] *Third Report from the Select Committee on Procedure* (1946), xi.
[2] *Report of the Committee on Ministers' Powers*, 52.

A twelve year "emergency" is almost a contradiction in terms. The use of the word "emergency" to characterize the powers and political phenomena discussed in this study is, in many respects, misleading and unreal. Much of what has been associated herein with an emergency interlude must perhaps be accepted as a permanent modification of the British constitutional structure. Given a continuance of an unstable world order, a precarious domestic economic situation, and continued demands for Government action in the realm of social and economic welfare, it is difficult to foresee much of a departure from the "exceptional" type of delegated legislation in which the determination of matters of principle and a generally broad discretion are left to the executive. In such circumstances, the term "subordinate legisla-tion" loses meaning except in a strictly legal sense. The extensive practice of "legislation without a legislature"[1] may be thought to be a good or a bad thing, depending on whether one is to use Sir Cecil Carr's terms, a "Modernist" or a "Methuselah",[2] but it is a tendency too persistent and pervasive to warrant being realistically classed as "exceptional".

It seems unlikely that any British Government, regardless of its political complexion, which is called upon to deal with the great and complicated problems of the modern world will be much tempted to weaken its freedom of action by permitting the courts to exercise any more control over executive action than now exists. Thus, it is difficult to escape the conclusion that Parliament will remain the primary force capable of restraining executive power.

What, then, are the difficulties which stand in the way of Parliament's being able to exercise a more adequate control over a heavily power-laden executive? What are the prospects of Parliament's being able to surmount the difficulties and thus preserve the balance that many regard as essential to the con-tinuance of the rule of law in Great Britain?

If, as has been suggested, the effectiveness of Parliament as a watchdog depends upon the existence of an Opposition which can bring informed criticism to bear upon the Government, the

[1] The term is G. M. Young's, "Future of Parliamentary Government," in Campion, et al., Parliament, 285.
[2] "Delegated Legislation," in Campion et al., Parliament, 248. See the exchange between Dr. (now Sir) C. K. Allen and Mr. Richard Crossman, Labour M.P., on this point (Third Report from the Select Committee on Procedure [1946], 272).

contention that the Opposition lacks time and opportunity for discussing delegated legislation would be a disturbing one. The fact is, however, that the Opposition has adequate opportunity to discuss and criticize the details of administration. It has questions, prayers, adjournment debates, and supply debates. But the latter two opportunities have tended increasingly to be devoted to general policy considerations rather than to questions of administrative detail. The indictment which might be drawn is that the Opposition does not use the opportunities it has with greatest effectiveness. Members are not well informed on the exact uses the executive is making of its powers, and thus they prefer to discuss general policy. "Is that regulation still in existence? I thought that the Minister of Labour in the late Government had actually withdrawn it at the Box," exclaimed the leader of the Liberal Party when the Government, in November, 1952, asked for a continuance of the much-discussed Regulation 58A (control of employment).[1] Mr. Clement Davies' difficulty appears to reflect the inability of members of Parliament generally to maintain a firm grip on the extent and exercise of executive powers. Is this due to over-work or lack of interest? The distaste with which many contemporary members of Parliament contemplate a concentration of their interests on such apparent minutiae as the latitude of design permitted manufacturers of casein buttons has already been noted. It has also been noted that the necessity of doing homework on delegated legislation appears to be boring employment to most members. On the other hand, the activities of the "active back-benchers" in war-time and of the "inveterate prayers" in the post-war period indicate that individual members can become informed, given a desire to become so. Indeed, their activities furnish a key to the possibility of a satisfactory solution of the problem of parliamentary control. They established a division of labour system in which individuals specialized in certain types of orders or concentrated their attention upon the legislative output of particular departments. Whether by design or not, the work of the "inveterate prayers" in the post-war period left other members of the Opposition free to direct their energies towards other aspects of the legislative process.

[1] 507 H.C. Deb. 5s., 2085.

As long as the executive continues to possess wide legislative powers, it would appear desirable that the Opposition should be able to arm itself with sound knowledge as to how they are exercised. A larger number of back-bench members might be delegated to acquaint themselves with the detailed workings of the administration. Since, however, the Government of today is the Opposition of tomorrow, it would appear desirable also to give to a large number of back-benchers of both parties the opportunity of becoming familiar with what transpires in the departments. This would appear to suggest that the establishment of specialist committees in the House of Commons might be an important step towards the realization of a more effective parliamentary control. It will be urged, perhaps, that there are constitutional difficulties involved in such a proposal, and the suggestion would need to be carefully weighed in the light of such objection. The committees might, perhaps, be of an informal character. Certain other proposals might be made which would encounter no constitutional difficulties and yet would be important developments in strengthening the grip of Parliament over the executive. Genocide might be practised on some of the more distant relatives of the enabling statutes without causing undue administrative inconvenience. The membership of the scrutinizing committee might be enlarged, or, what seems even more necessary, the professional staff of the committee might be increased. The ability of Parliament to amend statutory instruments might also be given serious consideration.

Twenty-five years ago, the Donoughmore Committee expressed the doubt "whether Parliament itself has fully realized . . . the extent to which it has surrendered its own functions".[1] Since 1939 it would appear that almost every articulate member of Parliament has, at one time or another, expressed concern over the implications for the House of Commons of the steady growth of executive power pursuant to emergency powers and delegated legislation in general. Parliamentary thought on the subject, however, has become greatly entangled in party politics. Usually a member's concern for the constitutional balance appears to be merely one constituent of an equation whose main factor is policy. Two decades ago, an observer concluded that the concern of

[1] *Report of the Committee on Ministers' Powers*, 24.

members of Parliament over delegated legislation often depended upon the side of the gangway where they chanced to sit.[1] The passing of time has not necessitated a modification of that judgment. At any given time, the majority in the House of Commons (being supporters of the Government of the moment) tend to think that the exercise of broad discretionary powers is in good hands and that, for the time being, there is no cause for alarm. "It is much less dangerous to entrust powers of this sort to a Government whose approach to these problems is as I have indicated than to a Government . . . which had a tendency or a bias towards undue and excessive interference in the affairs of individuals," said Mr. John Boyd-Carpenter, Financial Secretary to the Treasury in 1952,[2] although Mr. John Boyd-Carpenter, Opposition member of Parliament prior to the Conservative victory in 1951, had been among the most vocal critics of the existence of the same emergency powers when such powers were exercised by a Labour Government. Both parties have expressed considerable concern about the inadequacies of parliamentary control. A few years ago a Conservative Home Secretary, in moving the continuation for another year of the Supplies and Services Act (a statute of which his party in opposition had been exceedingly critical), enumerated the various opportunities of parliamentary control and concluded that "according to the side of the House on which one sits, their deficiencies as a form of control become more and more apparent".[3] It is difficult to disagree with Sir Cecil Carr's belief that, for the most part, "these are issues of political partisanship, not of political theory".[4]

Nevertheless, a satisfactory solution to the problem of devising a more effective parliamentary control would appear to depend in large part upon the recognition by all parties—Government and Opposition—that the future effectiveness of the House of Commons is involved. An attitude which both parties have shared—of minimizing the difficulties of parliamentary control when in the Government, and maximizing them when in the

---

[1] Chih-Mai Chen, *Parliamentary Opinion of Delegated Legislation* (New York: Columbia University Press, 1933), 138.

[2] 507 H.C. Deb. 5s., 2169.

[3] Sir David Maxwell Fyfe, 493 H.C. Deb. 5s., 996.

[4] Carr, "Delegated Legislation," in Campion *et al.*, *Parliament*, 248.

Opposition—is not conducive to an impartial inquiry by Parliament into the manner in which the House of Commons can best assert a more effective control over delegated legislation.[1]

To recognize that parliamentary control over the executive might be made more effective is not, however, to detract from Parliament's record during the period surveyed here. That record would appear to indicate that those who mourn the passing of Parliament have perhaps donned their black suits prematurely. The mourners note with uneasiness the decline of the judicial safeguard of *ultra vires*, and they fear that Parliament is in danger of becoming a decree-registering *parlement*. The tack taken is that the resilience of the British Constitution, hitherto its salvation, may soon lead to its undoing. Writers on the British constitutional system, however, must always be wary, for, as Sir Cecil Carr once said, it does not stand still long enough to be photographed. Furnishings are constantly being shifted about on the stage; the decline of one safeguard may find another unobtrusively taking its place; but the stage is cluttered, and it is easy for the observer to be misled.

The centre of the stage, however, belongs to Parliament. During the period under review, the transfer of much of its legislative power to the executive, and the attendant decline of the courts as restraints upon Government action, made Parliament more keenly aware than it normally was of the necessity of maintaining its central position. Parliament maintained its position, and the executive honoured it. The House of Commons remained the highest public forum of the nation. It criticized and it presented grievances, and no Government which had to face a free people in free elections could afford to ignore it.

[1] In November, 1952, the Home Secretary proposed an investigation of the procedure for exercising parliamentary control over delegated legislation, and Mr. Chuter Ede, for the Opposition, agreed that it was "high time we had such an inquiry." (507 H.C. Deb. 5s., 2092.)

BIBLIOGRAPHY

I. PUBLIC DOCUMENTS

House of Commons Debates (H.C. Deb.), 5th series. Vols. 350-507 (1939-52).

House of Lords Debates (H.L. Deb.), 5th series. Vols. 114-177 (1939-52).

Defence Regulations, printed as amended up to and including 24th July, 1940, 5th edition. London: His Majesty's Stationery Office, 1940.

Defence Regulations, Volume I, The Defence (General) Regulations, 1939, printed as amended up to and including 10th August, 1943, 14th edition. London: His Majesty's Stationery Office, 1943.

Defence Regulations, Volume II, Miscellaneous Regulations, printed as amended up to and including 10th August, 1943, 13th edition. London: His Majesty's Stationery Office, 1943.

Defence Regulations, printed as in force on 10th December, 1950, 19th edition. London: His Majesty's Stationery Office, 1951.

Statutory Rules and Orders, other than those of a local, personal, or temporary character for the years 1939-47. London: His Majesty's Stationery Office, 1939-1947.

Statutory Instruments, other than those of a local, personal, or temporary character for the years 1947-51. London: His Majesty's Stationery Office, 1947-51.

Employment Policy. Presented by the Minister of Reconstruction to Parliament by command of His Majesty, May 1944. Cmd. 6527. London: His Majesty's Stationery Office, 1944.

Report of the Committee on Ministers' Powers. Report presented by the Lord High Chancellor to Parliament by command of His Majesty, April, 1932. Cmd. 4060. London: His Majesty's Stationery Office, 1932.

Memoranda Submitted to and Evidence Taken before the Committee on Ministers' Powers. 2 vols. London: His Majesty's Stationery Office, 1932.

Parliamentary Papers. Third Report from the Select Committee on Procedure, together with the Proceedings of the Committee, Minutes of Evidence, Appendix and Index, Session 1945-46, H.C.R. 189-1. London: His Majesty's Stationery Office, 1946.

Special Report from the Select Committee on Statutory Rules and Orders, etc., Session 1943-1944, H.C.R. 113. London: His Majesty's Stationery Office, 1944.

First Special Report from the Select Committee on Statutory Rules and Orders, etc., Session 1944-45, H.C.R. 82. London: His Majesty's Stationery Office, 1945.

Second Special Report from the Select Committee on Statutory Rules and Orders, etc., Session 1944-45, H.C.R. 83. London: His Majesty's Stationery Office, 1945.

Select Committee on Statutory Rules and Orders, etc. Minutes of the Proceedings of the Committee, Session 1944-45, H.C.R. 94. London: His Majesty's Stationery Office, 1945.

First to Twenty-First Reports and First to Third Special Reports from the Select Committee on Statutory Rules and Orders, etc., together with the Proceedings of the Committee and Minutes of Evidence, Session 1945-46, H.C.R. 187. London: His Majesty's Stationery Office, 1946.

Reports from the Select Committee on Statutory Rules and Orders, etc., together with the Proceedings of the Committee and Minutes of Evidence, Session 1946-47, H.C.R. 141.   London: His Majesty's Stationery Office, 1947.

Reports from the Select Committee on Statutory Instruments, etc., together with the Proceedings of the Committee and Minutes of Evidence, Session 1947-48, H.C.R. 201.   London: His Majesty's Stationery Office, 1948.

Reports from the Select Committee on Statutory Instruments, together with the Proceedings of the Committee, Session 1948-49, H.C.R. 324. London: His Majesty's Stationery Office, 1949.

Reports from the Select Committee on Statutory Instruments, together with the Proceedings of the Committee, Session 1950. H.C.R. 178. London: His Majesty's Stationery Office, 1950.

Reports from the Select Committee on Statutory Instruments, together with the Proceedings of the Committee, Session 1950-51, H.C.R. 239. London: His Majesty's Stationery Office, 1951.

II. SECONDARY SOURCES

BOOKS

ADDISON, CHRISTOPHER, et al. Problems of a Socialist Government.   London: Victor Gollancz Ltd., 1933.

ALLEN, C. K., Bureaucracy Triumphant. London: Oxford University Press, 1931.

Law and Orders. London: Stevens & Sons Ltd., 1945.

Law in the Making. 5th ed. Oxford: Clarendon Press, 1951.

AMERY, L. S. Thoughts on the Constitution. London: Oxford University Press, 1947.

ANDERSON, Sir JOHN. The Machinery of Government. Oxford: Clarendon Press, 1946.

ANSON, Sir WILLIAM. The Law and Custom of the Constitution. Vol. I, 5th ed. Edited by Sir Maurice L. Gwyer. Oxford: Clarendon Press, 1922.

BAGEHOT, WALTER.   The English Constitution.   World's Classics edition. London: Oxford University Press, 1941.

CAMPION, Sir GILBERT. An Introduction to the Procedure of the House of Commons. 2nd ed. London: The Macmillan Co., 1947.

CAMPION, Sir GILBERT, et al. British Government Since 1918. New York: The Macmillan Co., 1950.

CAMPION, Sir GILBERT, et al. Parliament: A Survey. London: George Allen & Unwin Ltd., 1952.

CARR, Sir CECIL THOMAS. Concerning English Administrative Law. New York: Columbia University Press, 1941.

Delegated Legislation. Cambridge: Cambridge University Press, 1921.

CHEN, CHIH-MAI. Parliamentary Opinion of Delegated Legislation. New York: Columbia University Press, 1933.

CHURCHILL, WINSTON S. Closing the Ring. Vol. V of The Second World War. Boston: Houghton Mifflin Co., 1951. (London: Cassell & Co.)

The Gathering Storm. Vol. I of The Second World War. Boston: Houghton Mifflin Co., 1948.

The Grand Alliance. Vol. III of The Second World War. Boston: Houghton Mifflin Co., 1950.

The Hinge of Fate. Vol. IV of *The Second World War.* Boston: Houghton Mifflin Co., 1950.

Their Finest Hour. Vol. II of *The Second World War.* Boston: Houghton Mifflin Co., 1949.

CORWIN, EDWARD S. *Total War and the Constitution.* New York: Alfred A. Knopf, 1947.

DICEY, A. V. *Introduction to the Study of the Law of the Constitution.* 9th ed. revised by E. C. S. Wade. London: The Macmillan Co., 1939.

EDELMAN, MAURICE. *Herbert Morrison.* London: Lincolns-Prager, 1948.

FAIRMAN, CHARLES. *American Constitutional Decisions.* Revised edition. New York: Henry Holt & Co., 1950.

FRIEDRICH, CARL J. *Constitutional Government and Democracy.* Revised edition. Boston: Ginn and Co., 1946.

FRIEDMANN, W. *The Planned State and the Rule of Law.* Melbourne: Melbourne University Press, 1948.

GREAVES, H. R. G. *The British Constitution.* 2nd ed. London: George Allen & Unwin Ltd., 1951.

HANKEY, Lord. *Government Control in War.* Cambridge: Cambridge University Press, 1945.

HARRIS, Sir PERCY. *Forty Years in and out of Parliament.* London: A. Melrose, 1947.

HEMINGFORD, Lord. *Back Bencher and Chairman.* London: John Murray, 1946.

HEWART OF BURY, Lord. *The New Despotism.* London: Ernest Benn Ltd. 1929.

ILBERT, Sir COURTENAY. *Legislative Methods and Forms.* Oxford: Clarendon Press, 1901.

The Mechanics of Law-Making. New York: Columbia University Press, 1914.

ILBERT, Sir COURTENAY, and CARR, Sir CECIL T. *Parliament.* 3rd ed. (revised). London: Oxford University Press, 1950.

JENNINGS, Sir W. IVOR. *The British Constitution.* 3rd ed. Cambridge: Cambridge University Press, 1950.

Cabinet Government. Cambridge: Cambridge University Press, 1936.

"Emergency Legislation," *Annual Survey of English Law:* 1939. London: London School of Economics, 1940.

The Law and the Constitution. 3rd ed. London: University of London Press, 1943.

Parliament. Cambridge: Cambridge University Press, 1940.

Parliament Must Be Reformed. London: Paul, Trench, Trubner & Co., 1941.

KAPANI, MÜNCI. *Les pouvoirs extraordinaires de l'executif en temps de guerre et de crise nationale.* Geneva: Imprimerie Genevoise, 1949.

KEETON, G. W. *The Passing of Parliament.* London: Ernest Benn Ltd., 1952.

KEIR, Sir DAVID L. *Constitutional History of Modern Britain.* 4th ed. London: A. & C. Black Ltd., 1950.

KEIR, Sir DAVID L., and LAWSON, F. H. *Cases in Constitutional Law.* Oxford: Clarendon Press, 1928.

KEITH, ARTHUR BERRIEDALE. *The Constitution Under Strain.* London: Stevens & Sons Ltd., 1942.

KIDD, RONALD. *British Liberty in Danger.* London: Lawrence & Wishart, 1941.

LAFITTE, F. *The Internment of Aliens.* London: Penguin Books, 1940.

LASKI, HAROLD J. *Freedom of the Press in Wartime.* London: National Council for Civil Liberties, n.d.

Liberty in the Modern State. Revised ed. New York: The Viking Press, 1946.

Parliamentary Government in England. New York: The Viking Press, 1938.

Reflections on the Constitution. Manchester: Manchester University Press, 1951.

LASSWELL, HAROLD D. *National Security and Individual Freedom*. New York: McGraw Hill Co., 1950.

LEE, JENNIE. *This Great Journey*. New York: Farrar and Rinehart, 1942.

LOWELL, A. LAWRENCE. *The Government of England*. 2 vols. New York: The Macmillan Co., 1912.

MCCALLUM, R. B. and READMAN, ALLISON. *The British General Election of 1945*. London: Oxford University Press, 1947.

MCILWAIN, CHARLES H. *Constitutionalism, Ancient and Modern*. Ithaca: Cornell University Press, 1940.

The High Court of Parliament and its Supremacy. New Haven: Yale University Press, 1910.

MACKENZIE, KENNETH R. *The English Parliament*. London: Penguin Books, 1950.

MAITLAND, F. W. *Constitutional History of England*. Cambridge: Cambridge University Press, 1926.

MARRIOTT, J. A. R. *Mechanism of the Modern State*. 2 vols. Oxford: Clarendon Press, 1927.

MOLSON, HUGH. *Delegated Legislation*. London: Hansard Society, 1946.

MORRISON, HERBERT. *Prospects and Policies*. New York: Alfred A. Knopf, 1944.

NICHOLAS, HERBERT G., *The British General Election of 1950*. London: The Macmillan Co., 1951.

PORT, F. J. *Administrative Law*. London: Longmans, Green & Co., 1929.

ROBSON, W. A. *The British System of Government*. Revised ed. London: Longmans, Green & Co., 1948.

Justice and Administrative Law. London: The Macmillan Co., 1928.

ROGERS, LINDSAY. *Crisis Government*. New York: W. W. Norton & Co., 1934.

ROSSITER, CLINTON L. *Constitutional Dictatorship*. Princeton: Princeton University Press, 1948.

SCHWARTZ, BERNARD. *Law and the Executive in Britain*. New York: New York University Press, 1949.

SIEGHART, MARGUERITE A. *Government by Decree*. London: Stevens & Sons, Ltd., 1950.

TAYLOR, ERIC. *The House of Commons at Work*. London: Penguin Books, 1951.

VISSCHER, PAUL DE. *Les nouvelles tendances de la democratie anglaise: l'experience des pouvoires speciaux et des pleins pouvoirs*. Tournai: Casterman, 1947.

WADE, E. C. S., and PHILLIPS, G. GODFREY. *Constitutional Law*. 4th edition. London: Longmans, Green & Co., 1950.

WATKINS, FREDERICK M. "The Problem of Constitutional Dictatorship," *Public Policy*. Edited by C. J. Friedrich and Edward S. Mason. Cambridge: Harvard University Press, 1940.

WHEARE, K. C. *Parliament and Politics*. London: The Bureau of Current Affairs, 1947.

WILLIAMS, FRANCIS. *Press, Parliament and People*. London: W. Heinemann Ltd., 1946.

WILLIS, JOHN. *The Parliamentary Powers of English Government Departments*. Cambridge: Harvard University Press, 1933.

WILLOUGHBY, W. W., and ROGERS, LINDSAY. *An Introduction to the Problem of Government*. New York: Doubleday, Page & Co., 1921.

ARTICLES

ALLEN, C. K. "Last Words on Regulation 18B," *Law Quarterly Review*, LVIII (October, 1942), 462-466.

"Regulation 18B and Reasonable Cause," *Law Quarterly Review*, LVIII (April, 1942), 232-242.

ARGUS. "Friendly Enemy Aliens," *The Contemporary Review*, CLIX (January, 1941), 53-60.

BENTWICH, NORMAN. "England and the Aliens," *Political Quarterly*, XII (January-March, 1941), 81-93.

CARR, Sir CECIL THOMAS. "A Regulated Liberty," *Columbia Law Review*, XLII (March, 1942), 339-355.

"Crisis Legislation in Great Britain," *Columbia Law Review*, XL (December, 1940), 1309-1325.

"This Freedom," *Law Quarterly Review*, LXII (January, 1946), 58-65.

CHASE, EUGENE PARKER. "War and the English Constitution," *American Political Science Review*, XXXVI (February, 1942), 86-98.

CHORLEY, Lord. "Law-Making in Whitehall," *Modern Law Review*, IX (April, 1946), 26-41.

CHRISTIE, J. "Parliamentary Control of the Delegated Legislation," *Journal of Comparative Legislation and International Law*, XXVI (November, 1944), 62-63.

"Civil Liberties in Great Britain and Canada during War," *Harvard Law Review*, LV (April, 1942), 1006-1018.

CLOKIE, H. McD. "Emergency Powers and Civil Liberties," *Canadian Journal of Economics and Political Science*, XIII (August, 1947), 384-394.

"Parliamentary Government in Wartime," *Canadian Journal of Economics and Political Science*, VI (August, 1940), 359-370.

"The Preservation of Civil Liberties," *Canadian Journal of Economics and Political Science*, XIII (May, 1947), 208-232.

COLE, G. D. H. "Delegated Legislation," *New Statesman and Nation*, XXVII (18th March, 1944), 183.

"Delegated Legislation: the Growth of Regulations," *Round Table*, XXXIV (June, 1944), 204-210.

DE SMITH, S. A. "Delegated Legislation in England," *The Western Political Quarterly*, II (December, 1949), 514-526.

"The Limits of Judicial Review: Statutory Discretion and the Doctrine of Ultra Vires," *Modern Law Review*, XI (July, 1948), 306-325.

"Sub-delegation and Circulars," *Modern Law Review*, XII (January, 1949), 37-43.

DICEY, A. V. "The Development of Administrative Law in England," *Law Quarterly Review*, XXXI (April, 1915), 148-153.

EDE, JAMES CHUTER. "Parliament and the Liberty of the Subject," *Parliamentary Affairs*, I (Winter, 1947), 10-23.

EDEN, CHARLES. "Departmental Despots," *The National Review*, CXXII (February, 1944), 153-157.

EWER, W. N. "The Ministry of Information," *Political Quarterly*, XII (January-March, 1941), 94-101.

FAIRMAN, CHARLES. "The Law of Martial Rule and the National Emergency," *Harvard Law Review*, LV (June, 1942), 1253-1302.

FINER, HERMAN. "The British Cabinet, the House of Commons, and the War," *Political Science Quarterly*, LVI (September, 1941), 321-360.

FOOT, DINGLE. "The Law and the Quislings," *Spectator*, CLXIV (3rd May, 1940), 619-620.

GOODHART, ARTHUR LEHMAN. "Note on Liversidge v. Anderson," *Law Quarterly Review*, LVIII (April, 1942), 232-236.

GREAVES, H. R. G. "Parliament in Wartime," *Political Quarterly*, XII (April-October, 1941), 202-213, 292-304, 419-430.
"Parliament in Wartime," *Political Quarterly*, XIII (January-October, 1942), 78-90, 181-192, 311-322, 437-448.
"Parliament in Wartime," *Political Quarterly*, XIV (April, 1943), 173-184.

GRIFFITH, J. A. G. "The Constitutional Significance of Delegated Legislation in England," *Michigan Law Review*, XLVIII (June, 1950), 1079-1120.
"Delegated Legislation: Some Recent Developments," *Modern Law Review*, XII (July, 1949), 297-318.

HANSON, A. H. "The Select Committee on Statutory Instruments, 1944-1949," *Public Administration*, XXVII (Winter, 1949), 278-288.
"The Select Committee on Statutory Instruments: a Further Note," *Public Administration*, XXIX (Autumn, 1951).

HARRIS, WILSON. "The British Press in Wartime," *Britain Today*, No. 44 (10th January, 1941), 4-8.

HARRISSON, TOM. "The House of Commonsense," *New Statesman and Nation*, XXI (12th April, 1941), 380-381.

HOLDSWORTH, W. S. "Note in re Liversidge v. Anderson," *Law Quarterly Review*, LVIII (January, 1942), 1-3.

HOLLIS, CHRISTOPHER. "The British Constitution in 1952," *Parliamentary Affairs*, VI (Spring, 1953), 165-172.

"House of Commons: National Expenditures," *Journal of the Society of Clerks-at-the-Table in Empire Parliaments*, IX (1940), 80-88.

HUGHES, CHRISTOPHER J. "Prayers to Annul Delegated Legislation: House of Commons, 1947-1948," *Public Administration*, XXVII (Summer, 1949), 111-114.

JENNINGS, Sir W. IVOR. "The Formation of Great Britain's 'Truly National' Government," *American Political Science Review*, XXXIV (August, 1940), 728-736.
"Parliament in Wartime. I," *Political Quarterly*, XI (April-June, 1940), 183-195.
"Parliament in Wartime. II," *Political Quarterly*, XI (July-September, 1940), 232-247.
"Parliament in Wartime. III," *Political Quarterly*, XI (October-December, 1940), 351-367.
"Parliament in Wartime. IV," *Political Quarterly*, XII (January-March, 1941), 53-65.
"The Rule of Law in Total War," *Yale Law Journal*, L (January, 1941), 365-386.

KEETON, G. W. "Delegated Legislation and its Control in England," *South African Law Journal*, LXIX (February, 1952), 33-52.
"Twilight of the Common Law," *Nineteenth Century and After*, CXLV (April, 1949), 230-238.

KOESSLER, MAXIMILIAN. "Enemy Alien Internment," *Political Science Quarterly*, LVII (March, 1942), 98-127.

LASKI, HAROLD J. "Civil Liberties in Great Britain in Wartime," *Bill of Rights Review*, II (Summer, 1942), 243-251.
"Some Reflections on Government in Wartime," *Political Quarterly*, XIII (January, 1942), 57-65.

LINDSAY, KENNETH. "Parliament in War," *Spectator*, CLXV (30th August, 1940), 215.

LOGAN, D. W. "Post-War Machinery of Government: Delegated Legislation," *Political Quarterly*, XV (July-September, 1944), 185-195.

MEGARRY, R. E. "Administrative Quasi-legislation," *Law Quarterly Review*, LX (April, 1944), 125-129.

MORRISON, HERBERT. "British Parliamentary Democracy," *Parliamentary Affairs*, II (Autumn, 1949), 349-360.

N. P. S. "Laying Regulations Before Parliament," *The Law Journal*, XCV (15th September, 1945), 297-298.

ONLOOKER. "Parliamentary Control of Delegated Legislation," *Journal of the Society of Clerks-at-the-Table in Empire Parliaments*, X (1941), 83-91.

"The Ramsay Case," *Journal of the Society of Clerks-at-the-Table in Empire Parliaments*, IX (1940), 64-79.

RAVA, PAUL B. "Emergency Powers in Great Britain," *Boston University Law Review*, XXI (June, 1941), 403-451.

ROBSON, WILLIAM A. "Controls during the Transition Period," *Modern Law Review*, IX (1946), 172-178.

"The Judiciary and the Executive," *Political Quarterly*, XXI (October-December, 1950), 411-418.

"The Machinery of Government, 1939-1947," *Political Quarterly*, XIX (January, 1948), 1-14.

ROGERS, LINDSAY. "Legislative and Executive in Wartime," *Foreign Affairs*, XIX (July, 1941), 715-726.

"Personal Power and Popular Government," *The Southern Review*, III (Autumn, 1937), 225-242.

"Variations on Democratic Themes," *Political Science Quarterly*, LXIII (December, 1948), 481-500.

STACEY, F. A. "The Select Committee on Statutory Instruments," *Public Administration*, XXVIII (Winter, 1950), 333-335.

STREET, HENRY. "Delegated Legislation and the Public," *Public Administration*, XXVII (Summer, 1949), 108-110.

"Subordinate Legislation," *Public Administration*, XXX (Autumn, 1952), 227-261.

WADE, E. C. S. "The British Constitution in 1950," *Parliamentary Affairs*, IV (Spring, 1951), 206-215.

"The Courts and the Administrative Process," *Law Quarterly Review* (April, 1947), 164-173.

WHEARE, K. C. "The British Constitution in 1947," *Parliamentary Affairs*, I (Summer, 1948), 8-19.

"Controlling Delegated Legislation: a British Experiment," *Journal of Politics*, XI (November, 1949), 748-768.

"The Machinery of Government," *Public Administration*, XXIV (Summer, 1946), 75-85.

WILLIAMS, Sir HERBERT. "The A.B.B.s," *Journal of the Society of Clerks-at-the Table in Empire Parliaments*, XIV (1945), 180-183.

NEWSPAPERS AND PERIODICALS

Economist

New Statesman and Nation

New York Times

Round Table

Spectator

The Times (London)

INDEX